Matthew Bush

Pragmatic Passions

Melodrama and Latin American Social Narrative

Ediciones de Iberoamericana

Historia y crítica de la literatura, 74

Matthew Bush

Pragmatic Passions

Melodrama and Latin American Social Narrative

Iberoamericana – Vervuert – 2014

Library of Congress Cataloging-in-Publication Data

Bush, Matthew, 1976-
Pragmatic passions : melodrama and Latin American social narrative / Matthew Bush.
pages cm. -- (Ediciones de Iberoamericana ; 74)
Includes bibliographical references and index.
ISBN 978-8484898351 -- ISBN 978-3-9548738-0-7 1. Latin American literature--History and criticism. 2. Melodrama. I. Title.
PQ7081.B87 2015
860.9'98--dc23

2014042564

Amor de Dios, 1 – E-28014 Madrid
Tel.: +34 91 429 35 22
Fax: +34 91 429 53 97

Elisabethenstr. 3-9 – D-60594 Frankfurt am Main
Tel.: +49 69 597 46 17
Fax: +49 69 597 87 43

info@iberoamericanalibros.com
www.ibero-americana.net

ISBN 978-84-8489-835-1 (Iberoamericana)
ISBN 978-3-95487-380-7 (Vervuert)

Depósito Legal: M-27866-2014

Diseño de cubierta: a.f. diseño y comunicación

Este libro está impreso íntegramente en papel ecológico sin cloro.

For my father

TABLE OF CONTENTS

A NOTE ON TRANSLATIONS

Throughout this study I provide translated passages from the texts under analysis. When reliable translations have been available, I have employed them, unless otherwise indicated. In the case of Roberto Arlt's *El amor brujo*, for which no translation exists, the renditions of the text are entirely mine. Any mistakes here, or anywhere in the arguments presented in this study are solely my responsibility.

M. B.

ACKNOWLEDGEMENTS

Though I was not conscious of it at the time, this book began many years ago when I was a student at the University of Nebraska, Lincoln. It was there that I met my friend and mentor Agustín Pastén who inspired me to pursue an academic career, and to whom I am forever grateful. The study at hand is the culmination of a process of investigation initiated in my doctoral dissertation, which I wrote at the University of Colorado, Boulder. There I had the privilege to study with both Juan Pablo Dabove and Peter Elmore whose examples continue to influence the ways in which I read; even when they cannot be directly quoted, I believe that their intellectual imprint is evident on every page of this book. At the University of Colorado, I also had the opportunity to learn from Leila Gómez, Julio Baena, and Emilio Bejel who selflessly offered their time and guidance, and for that I offer my heartfelt thanks. My thanks also go out to all of my friends and colleagues with whom I shared time in Boulder both in and outside of our seminars.

I thank Lehigh University and the College of Arts and Sciences for a series of writing grants that allowed me to complete this project. I also thank Pat Ward and the Lehigh Libraries staff. In the Department of Modern Languages and Literatures at Lehigh, I have been welcomed into a warm and professionally rewarding academic environment. I thank all of my department colleagues, starting with Marie-Hélène Chabut who was the department chairperson for my first formative years at Lehigh. I am also deeply grateful to my Spanish colleagues Antonio Prieto and Edurne Portela. Both have provided me excellent mentorship and support over the years, including reading early drafts of this study, and for that I owe them my most sincere gratitude.

I would also like to thank several friends who have made helped me to continue to grow both personally and professionally since my arrival in Bethlehem, especially Sara Castro-Klarén and the participants in the Washington Consortium Latin American Theory Seminar. In Peru I thank Alfredo Robles, Irma Moreno, Jeremías Gamboa, Rosario Fraga, Luis Landa, and Malgorzata

Siejka, and so many other friends and family who always have graciously received me in my many travels. I also thank my friends from Nebraska for their companionship and support throughout the years.

I thank María Pizarro for her dedication to this project, as well as the series editors for their consideration of my study. I am also grateful to Laura Kremmel for her thorough revisions of this text. I thank *Modern Language Notes* for permission to reproduce in chapter two of this study a revised version of the article "Sufrimiento y retribución: La teatralidad política de *El tungsteno*," which appeared in volume 125.2 (2010) of that journal.

My most heartfelt thanks go out to my family. To my mother, Dori, for her unwavering support and love. To my brother, Tyler, for his steadfast friendship. To my father, David, who passed after a long illness when this book was nearing completion. My dad was my first model reader, and as a boy, I was always amazed when he knew exactly what would happen next in the television police dramas that he loved. Those lessons have stayed with me forever, and I hope this study lives up to standard that he set for me.

Finally, I thank my wife, Leticia Robles-Moreno, who is always my first interlocutor. Her love, patience, and encouragement over the years have made each new day better than the last, and have enriched each word in this study.

Introduction
Stirring Emotion, Assessing Progress

Melodrama is not so much exaggerated as uninhibited.

Eric Bentley

You cannot define Drama and Melodrama so that they shall be reciprocally exclusive; great drama has something melodramatic in it, and the best melodrama partakes of the greatness of drama.

T. S. Eliot

If emotional and moral registers are sounded, if a work invites us to feel sympathy for the virtues of beset victims, if the narrative trajectory is ultimately concerned with a retrieval and staging of virtue through adversity and suffering, then the operative mode is melodrama.

Linda Williams

We have seen this story a hundred times over: star-crossed lovers pledge faithfulness as they are torn apart by forces greater than themselves as we bravely hold back our sympathetic tears. Or, in another case, a hero escapes peril at the last possible second while the villain swears revenge, and we gasp, then either nervously chuckle or let out an incredulous groan, recognizing that we have fallen for the bait of melodrama. To be sure, the signatures of melodrama are familiar to all of us, even though we often struggle to articulate a clear understanding of what melodrama entails or to recognize its very pervasiveness. Yet, on any given day, we are bombarded from all angles with melodrama in many different forms, each of which applies dichotomic reasoning while striving to affect its public by conjuring emotion.

We perceive the ineffable quality of melodrama in the thrill of cliffhanger action movies. When reading or watching the daily news, we are repulsed by the abject horrors of crime, but equally are absorbed by the sentimental joys of human-interest pieces. We re-live the exuberance of romance and the pangs of rejection when we listen to sappy love songs on the radio. We are intrigued and give ourselves over to the plots of whodunit mystery novels, and, inevitably, we are goaded one way or another by polarizing political discourse aimed to tug directly at our patriotic heartstrings, provoke fear, or conjure up a deep sense of moral indignation. Indeed, the impulses of melodramatic narrative seem to be everywhere we look. Melodrama is located equally in a longing search for some greater meaning beyond the surface of an ever more superficial, technologic hyper-present where historic time is accelerated progressively and desired truths are increasingly ephemeral, as well as in an auto-reflexively ironic form as has become fashionable in the postmodern era.

But as the resort to melodrama as a basic frame of discourse grows in the postmodern epoch where the negative stigma attached to mass media culture is progressively erased, a methodological conundrum surfaces as we are left with a diagnostic category so overly applied that it runs the risk of losing its interpretative strength. If everything may be interpreted through the lens of melodrama, or if everything is somehow inherently melodramatic, how can we then define where the basic narrative of drama (or that of "reality") ends and melodrama begins? If we generally understand melodrama, a hyperbolic form of expression, to be that which exceeds everyday reality and basic narrative conventions, then it would follow that it should be possible to properly isolate melodrama from the quotidian, realist experience. But is it? Is it feasible to interpret both textual and actual events independently of their often-unconscious melodramatic underpinnings, or should we consider the melodramatic as that which fundamentally conditions our conception of the real and, in turn, artistic representations of that reality?

We might begin to answer these questions by noting that the connotations of reality –always multiple, always fragmentary, always partisan– are made clear only when inserted into narrative, and as Peter Brooks has lucidly noted, the narrative mode which fundamentally informs our modern sensibility is none other than that of melodrama (*Imagination* 21). It becomes apparent, then, that melodrama functions not only as a mode for comprehending dramatic action in a given text, but also as a modern means of understanding social and historical processes that are too abstract to grasp in any sort of quantitative manner. Melodrama thus provides a narrative structure that facilitates an understanding of the social. And it is through an active emotional dialogue with the melodramatic text (understood in its broadest sense) that the reader participates in the production of comprehension. Artistic and actual events, perceived through the melodramatic cipher, are grasped as emotionally accentuated episodes to be read as a sequence of interrelated occurrences, engaging the public's understanding of social order and the means by which it may be altered and bettered.

As an inescapable frame of reference for the comprehension of quotidian and larger historical events alike, the ubiquity of melodrama is a basic fact of our contemporary globalized reality, and clearly, Latin American society and its cultural products are not impervious to melodramatic influence. The melodramatic components of the (post)modern Latin American social experience indeed are readily evident to even the most casual observer. For instance, even an audience unfamiliar with Latin American television programming (including sit-coms, conventional dramas, reality shows, news programs, etc.) can easily identify the emotional theatrics of the region's most popular melodramatic export, the *telenovela* (the Latin American equivalent of the United States' soap opera).[1] Yet, when viewed more closely, we may observe that the persistent appeal of melodrama in Latin America goes well beyond that which may be accessed in contemporary television programming. From the era of the wars for independence during the first decades of the nineteenth century onward, melodrama has played an essential role in the process of how Latin America narrates its fictions and how it conceptually organizes and works through conflicts embedded in its very social fabric. Moving fluidly between the spheres of fictional and actual events, melodrama's adaptability is evidenced in the contemporary Latin American context when it is located equally in "serious" or "high" literature grappling with political and social conflicts, as well as in the bombastic rhetoric voiced by the region's most outspoken political figures.

To this end, we may note two distinct examples: Peruvian author Alonso Cueto's novel *La hora azul* (2005), and President Hugo Chávez's use of what *New York Times* reporter Simon Romero has identified as political theater in

---

[1] Certainly the producers of the recent Will Ferrell film *Casa de mi padre* (2012) were counting on the audience's melodramatic recognition and understanding of parodying Mexican films spanning from the so-called "Golden Age" of Mexican cinema up to the blood-soaked narco thrillers of present day. However, the film, which was directed by Matt Piedmont, reportedly grossed just less than 5.9 million dollars, failing to recoup its production costs and evidencing what we might call a melodramatic disencounter.

exhuming the remains of Venezuelan forefather Simón Bolívar. In the first case, Cueto's novel attempts to account for the period of political violence suffered in Peru from 1980 to 2001 through the narrative of family melodrama.[2] To this end, Cueto utilizes an emotionally charged lexicon and repertoire of images to analyze the family as a site of veiled identities and affective bonds, two hallmarks of domestic melodramatic narration. In the latter example, Hugo Chávez employed his melodramatic theatrics –scouring the past for hidden truths, revealing the guilt of a villainous other– in attempts to evidence a Colombian plot to murder the Andean region's founding father, so stirring up the rivalry between Venezuela and its ideologically opposed neighbor during the presidency of Álvaro Uribe. My point is not that these are somehow base or trivial ways of coming to grips with social strife or conceiving political discourse. To the contrary, Cueto's novel is rightly among the most critically recognized works of recent Peruvian fiction, and Chávez's political legacy holds an indisputable position of importance in deciding the course of contemporary Latin American politics. Rather, what these two disparate examples manifest is the wide range of formats that melodrama may assume when informing the Latin American social imaginary.

Melodrama's unique ability to narrate and make sense of the Latin American social experience is fostered by an understanding of social relations in keeping with the historical development of the region. Melodrama thrives in the Latin American context because its ostensibly all-or-nothing categories of narration (good and evil, fidelity and betrayal, suffering and vindication) attempt to impart a hopeful outlook, while simultaneously playing upon what the public remembers and has learned from the polarizing social realities that gave form to the region's history.[3] And the tale that is Latin America's history is indeed rife with melodrama. The traces of what we will later recognize as key elements of melodramatic narration are central to the basic posits of the problematic foundational love story between Spanish conquistador Hernán Cortés and his indigenous mistress Doña Marina, "la Malinche." In this case we may read history as a tale of romance between an imposing adventurer and an ill-fated indigenous woman, which ultimately produces a trail of destruction and an illegitimate child. Accordingly, the means by which this historical event is

---

2 I have written elsewhere on Cueto's novel and its relation to Iván Thays's *Un lugar llamado Oreja de Perro* (2008) through melodrama. See bibliography for complete information.

3 For an engaging discussion of modern history and its relationship with melodrama, see Matthew S. Buckley's "Refugee Theatre: Melodrama and Modernity's Loss."

frequently accessed has all the makings of a successful *telenovela*, which is to say that Latin American history proper indeed begins with the components of stories told time and time again in serialized melodramatic fiction: adventure, passion, and the ramifications of love gone wrong.

Moreover, in recent historical times, boom/bust agricultural cycles together with growth and regression in mineral exploitation –both of which continue to shape contemporary Latin American economies without entirely complying with the promise of sustained import substitution industrialization– gave birth to varying sectors of social and political elite, some conservative and some revolutionary. These cycles also gave rise to a proliferating underclass that dared only to dream of acceding to the domain of social power. The abyss that has separated, and continues to separate, the *haves* from the *have nots* fomented an understanding of social interactions and a form of social imagining that is common to melodrama: an "us" against "them" form of viewing society that may easily adopt different ideological positions, depending on the social milieu in play. But the limitations of such dichotomic comprehension of social interactions –a schematic perception reflected, but challenged, in artistic works of Latin American melodrama– leads to blind spots in understanding the nature of social workings. Things are never quite as simple as they seem, yet, through melodrama, every attempt is made to present a world in stark black and white contrast.

Focusing on melodrama's dual capacity to narrate stories about Latin American society and to provide a means of comprehending social structure, this volume analyzes melodrama's problematic attempts to configure social narratives of the twentieth century in the literary genres of regionalism, *indigenismo*, urban realism, socialist realism, and the novel of the Mexican Revolution. Reading melodrama as a postcolonial aesthetic, this study observes how the melodramatic mode at once represents new forms of identities resulting from the (post) colonial process, while at the same time taking on the precepts of the melodramatic aesthetic itself. Influenced by the historical developments that shaped the region, Latin American melodrama reformulates the most basic characteristics of the aesthetic in order to make it more applicable to the social realities of the Latin American reader/spectator. Latin American melodrama is thus revealed as a malleable structure that is adapted and readapted so as to provide a means of comprehending social change across narrative genres. But in recognizing the wide-ranging applications of melodrama, this study presents neither a condemnation nor a glorification of melodramatic aesthetics. Rather, my aim is to show just how melodrama attempts to demonstrate the possibilities for social justice, but at the same problematizes and often unwittingly betrays the tenets of the melodramatic mode, thus showing the dynamic complexity of Latin American melodrama as a representational paradigm of social narrative.

It is worth noting that the aesthetic mode that so essentially figures into the comprehension of Latin American art and reality should come not from the autochthonous wellspring, but from a foreign context. Such an observation cannot help but highlight the postcolonial character of modern Latin American melodrama, but it also serves as a point of departure to consider the region's adaptations of the melodramatic format. Before it provided the aesthetic foundation for the *telenovela* so widely consumed on a daily basis, melodrama passed through numerous social contexts. It was sometimes praised and just as frequently stigmatized as a "low" narrative mode because of the ostensibly simplistic vision of reality that it presented.

As is generally recognized, melodrama was born in late eighteenth century Europe, specifically during the French Revolution, the historical moment that "marks the final liquidation of the traditional Sacred and its representative institutions (Church and Monarch)" (Brooks, *Imagination* 15). This definitive break is crucial as it creates a social and ethical void in which no dominant moral perspective holds sway as the voice of reason, a chasm that the melodramatic aesthetic will attempt to fill. In the aftermath of the Revolution, popular theater set to music and heavily reliant on pantomime became one of the privileged sites where a new morality, in tune with the social views of the newly ascendant bourgeoisie, shored up what it meant to be a citizen in the new state and what values should be upheld in an age of social instability.[4] This new morally and socially didactic theater would later be recognized as melodrama, and Guilbert de Pixerécourt's play *Coelina ou l'enfant du mystère* (*Coelina or the Child of Mystery* [1800] –an adaptation of a popular novel by Ducray-Duminil) is often credited as being the founding work of classical French melodrama (Marcoux 55). Formulaic works filled with angelic characters born to suf-

[4] On this point, Geoffrey Nowell-Smith's comments on melodrama as a bourgeois aesthetic form are particularly illuminating. Nowell-Smith comments, "In so far as melodrama, like realism, supposes a world of equals, a democracy within the bourgeois strata (alias bourgeois democracy), it also supposes a world without the exercise of social power. The address is to an audience which does not think of itself as possessed of power (but neither as radically dispossessed, disinherited, oppressed) and the world of the subject matter is likewise one in which only middling power relations are present. The characters are neither the rulers nor the ruled, but occupy a middle ground, exercising local power or suffering local powerlessness, within the family or the small town. The locus of power is the family and individual property, the two being connected through inheritance" (269-70).

fer, mustachioed villains bent on swindling the innocent, hidden family ties, and justice exercised in the nick of time quickly found favor beyond France with audiences in the "Minor Houses" of English theater. A host of English playwrights continued to build on the melodramatic repertoire of British theater and, perhaps not surprisingly, melodramatic aesthetics found acceptance in England's North American colonies. Yet the United States' first great work of melodrama would not come in theatrical format (though it was quickly adapted to the stage), but as a novel in Harriet Beecher Stowe's abolitionist classic, *Uncle Tom's Cabin; or, Life Among the Lowly* (1852).

The common critical tendency has been to focus on the French/English/United States' triad when discussing the growth and proliferation of melodramatic aesthetics. This is true in spite of the fact that melodrama had an uncomplicated route to Latin America given Spain and Portugal's continual contact with French culture –particularly in the Napoleonic occupations of the Iberian Peninsula, the historical moment in which the seeds of melodramatic narrative are sown in the "Nuevo Mundo." And though critical inquiry on melodrama has frequently tended to focus on the analysis of theater, and more recently film, it is important to note that concepts of melodrama across all narrative genres, national boundaries, and historical periods aid in the understanding of the melodramatic mode as it is analyzed in this study. Indeed, the early international constellation of both stage and literary melodrama mentioned above shares certain formulaic characteristics that shape our general understanding of melodrama from this initial point in history up to present day.

In the most general sense, melodrama depends fundamentally on the clash of polarized foes, and most importantly, of opposing forces of virtue and vice. The metaphysical forces of good and evil are embodied in characters whose outward appearance is presented as a spectacle of their inner values –the good are physically attractive while the evil's exterior ugliness mirrors their inner corruption. In this same sense, everything about those characters is presented as an extension of their polarized moral values, including their names, their personal histories, and their physical gestures.[5] This dichotomic confrontation is posited in such a way as to draw an emotional response from the audience: in seeing virtue threatened, the public is pushed to fear; in seeing the momentary

5 Peter Brooks has commented at length on this last aspect of characterization noting that the "bodies of victims and villains must unambiguously signify their status" (*Revolution* 18).

triumphs of villainy, the spectator is meant to be enraged; and, in seeing the eventual triumph of good, the audience experiences the satisfaction of justice.

These emotional guideposts reside at the core of the melodramatic project, but it is equally important to note that melodrama is perceived as following a predictable narrative scheme. Melodrama is commonly understood as beginning in a tranquil setting just before serenity is upset by an unethical action perpetrated by the villain. Injustice then reigns as the hero/victim attempts to reestablish order, and discord is finally resolved as good inevitably triumphs over bad, allowing for recognition of the hero's moral virtue and a happy ending. These basic characteristics of melodrama have brought about much critical discussion questioning if melodrama may be defined as a particular genre unto itself, which is inevitably plagued by the proliferation of settings in which melodrama may be detected (mystery, romance, the western, etc.).[6] We may note, however, that although the characteristics mentioned above are recurrent in melodrama, they are not necessarily present in all melodramatic tales. Such is noted by Robert Heilman in *Tragedy and Melodrama: Versions of Experience* (1968) when he observes that melodrama need not end in happiness and may indeed end in disaster, so complicating a static definition of the narrative scheme intrinsic to melodrama (82).

Given the problems inherent to the generic definition of melodrama, it has become the norm to consider the aesthetic following Peter Brooks's criteria of melodrama as a narrative mode, which he first presented in his seminal study *The Melodramatic Imagination: Balzac, Henry James, Melodrama, and the Mode of Excess* (1976). Brooks is explicit on the consideration of genre, and he regards melodrama not as "a theme or set of themes, nor the life of the genre per se, but rather melodrama as a mode of conception and expression, as a certain fictional system for making sense of experience, as a semantic field of force" (XVII). For Brooks, the melodramatic mode works as a "theatrical substratum" (XIII) resid-

---

6 In the discussion of melodrama as a genre, works like Michael Booth's *English Melodrama* (1965), David Grimsted's *Melodrama Unveiled: American Theater & Culture* (1987), Frank Rahill's *The World of Melodrama* (1967), and Michael Hays and Anastasia Nikolopoulou's edited volume *Melodrama: The Cultural Emergence of a Genre* (1996) have played a pivotal role in the debate. This topic has also been highly volatile in the field of film studies and has informed studies like Rick Altman's article "Reusable Packaging: Generic Products and the Recycling Process," Christine Gledhill's "Rethinking Genre" and Ben Singer's *Melodrama and Modernity: Early Sensational Cinema and Its Contexts* (2001), to name just a few of the many important contributions.

ing at the heart of a text. Textual theatrics performed through gesture, heightened registers of recorded speech, and hidden meanings decoded from everyday interactions are the measures by which highly emotional messages are communicated and where the "moral occult" is evidenced. Brooks proposes that this "moral occult is not a metaphysical system; it is rather the repository of the fragmentary and desacralized remnants of sacred myth," summoned up in the text to introduce ethical meaning in a world devoid of any cohesive guiding light (5). Brooks's characterization of the melodramatic mode also evidences that it is deeply invested in the socio-ethical normativity, which melodrama intends to convey under the stresses of post-sacred society. Providing assurance when political and ecclesiastic authorities are unable to present sufficient explanations for the pressures and social paradigms that envelop the common citizen, melodrama, as a narrative mode, recounts tales that propose to illustrate what are believed to be communal truths surpassing material reason: suffering is part of life, hope springs eternal, the just shall prevail.

It is because of its capacity to speak to the basic hopes and needs of the human condition in the face of social strife that melodrama has played such an integral role in the development of Latin American narrative genres. As Nina Gerassi-Navarro has argued in *Pirate Novels: Fictions of Nation Building in Spanish America* (1999), the melodramatic capacity to convey visions of social stability, as well as to define the external forces that threaten concepts of order, is very much present in the nineteenth century Spanish American novel. As is to be expected, those works that Gerassi-Navarro analyzes are far from ideologically neutral, and the critic comments that such texts were primarily utilized by the ruling elite to conceive its relation to popular classes in the nation-building projects of those fledgling states recently liberated from their colonial yoke (149-51). This fact may serve to evidence the underside of melodrama, an exclusive enterprise concerned primarily with its own retention of power, only tangentially interested in any broad acceptance of social democracy.[7] So much is evidenced by Gerassi-Navarro's observations regarding the exclusion of women, indigenous, mulatto, and

---

7 In referring to the "underside of melodrama" I am drawing on Benjamin Arditi's concept of the "underside of populism" as presented in *Politics on the Edges of Liberalism: Difference, Populism, Revolution, Agitation* (2006). Arditi here recognizes the sometimes undemocratic impulse of populism as it seeks to affirm individual power instead of the broad democratic rights that serve as the rallying cry that mobilizes the populist base. I believe that that same undemocratic populist impulse may be located in those foundational national romances that propose to represent a vision for all, but speak only to a few.

mestizo figures from the plots of these melodramatic works (160, 177). Nonetheless, the presence of what may be read through the optic of the melodramatic mode in these early works of Spanish American literature analyzed by Gerassi-Navarro is significant, as it establishes melodrama as an aesthetic of primary importance in the development of Latin American literature.

Melodrama is, in fact, a basic building block in the foundation of Latin American literature as it emerges concurrently to the inception of the Latin American nation states and, therefore, serves as the first narrative mode through which the tales of the new Latin American nations are told. For this reason, it is necessary to begin to consider melodrama, not as the exception, but as the rule of Latin American literature –not as the dramatic oddity, but as an inevitable contributor at the core of Latin American narrative, the "high" and the "low" all at once. To better conceptualize the centrality of melodrama in Latin American narrative, we may draw upon Linda Williams's approach to United States' popular narrative in *Playing the Race Card: Melodramas of Black and White from Uncle Tom to O. J. Simpson* (2001) when she comments, "melodrama can be viewed, then, not as a genre, an excess, or an aberration, but what most often typifies popular American narrative in literature, stage, film, and television when it seeks to engage with moral questions" (17). Following Williams's example, I would propose a parallel thesis: as an aesthetic prevalent during the era of independence in Latin America, when the new modern nations sought to affirm and consolidate their sovereignty, melodrama stands historically at the foundation of the Latin American literary canon. This is not to say, however, that all Latin American literature utilizes melodrama, or that there is some melodramatic exceptionalism inherent to the region on the whole. Rather, I would argue that melodrama is the dominant narrative mode when Latin American literature speaks about politics and social development. Melodrama, then, must be rethought, not as a base or simplistic narrative form of poor taste, but as that which essentially informs the Latin American aesthetic imaginary in the spheres of high and mass media formats alike.[8]

The coexistence of ostensibly separate "high," "low," and popular cultures in Latin America has been outlined clearly in cultural theory.[9] Néstor García

---

8 As an aside, it is interesting to note that, in his approach to melodrama, Peter Brooks utilizes, perhaps paradoxically, highly canonical works of European literature. This fact would once again suggest the pervasive nature of melodrama and the permeability of the high/popular paradigm.

9 Noting the permeability of "high" and "popular" art forms in Latin America, José Ignacio Cabrujas comments that because the high/low dichotomy is lived out with-

Canclini's *Culturas híbridas: Estrategias para entrar y salir de la modernidad* (1990), for one, laid the groundwork for a radical rethinking of the simultaneity of varying historical epochs and cultural formations, bound together by the uneven modernity lived throughout Latin America. This concept of historical and generic heterogeneity is also fundamental to the conception of the postmodern and its literary formulations. Ana María Amar Sánchez's *Juegos de seducción y traición: Literatura y cultura de masas* (2000) takes on this problematic as the critic examines how contemporary literary works make use of elements of mass media culture and thus erode the high/low boundary. The suspension of long held beliefs regarding the hierarchy of genres is particularly relevant to this study, which develops lines of contact between literature, film, and television, and authors whose highly-recognized works have yet to have been classified as melodramatic, perhaps for fear of the stigma that such a connotation might carry.

Yet, within the perspective of this study, to be categorized as melodramatic should not be viewed as an insult to the integrity of a work. Melodrama has bolstered more than two centuries' worth of Latin America's literary production as a common mode of revealing social and political desires, necessities, and shortcomings, a fact evident in a quick glance at the history of foundational Latin American narratives. From José Mármol's *Amalia* (1851) in Argentina to Ignacio Manuel Altamirano's *Clemencia* (1869) in Mexico, from Bernardo Guimarães's *A Escrava Isaura* (1875) in Brazil to Clorinda Matto de Turner's *Aves sin nido* (1889) in Peru, melodrama serves as an essential mode of foundational literatures throughout Latin America. Indeed, formed within the romantic imaginary in which values of individual and artistic liberty were the order of the day, each of these works draws upon stark dichotomies of race, class, and political positioning in an attempt to convey an emotionally charged vision of social justice in keeping with the ideological thrust of the text. And, as Doris Sommer has illustrated in *Foundation Fictions: The National Romances of Latin America* (1991), in order to comply with their particular socio-political aims, works of classic nationalist fiction like those mentioned above make frequent recourse to romance as a means of illustrating harmonious visions of social order. Yet as a consequence of Sommer's readerly approach, melodrama for many readers has become almost synonymous with the idea of romance, which is not entirely the case.

---

in the individual through his or her interactions with narrative and culture, it necessarily leads to contradictions and fusion of the two different spheres as the individual reconciles his or her relationship to cultural events (127).

As is developed throughout this study, Latin American melodrama does indeed return time and time again to the motif of romance to illustrate social conditions. In Sommer's reading, however, romance is the narrative cipher through which everything in the tale must take meaning, and generally does so allegorically. While the strength of this form of reading is evident, it also presents certain limitations to the consideration of melodramatic aesthetics in that romance is not where melodrama necessarily ends. What we discover in melodramatic works of Latin American narrative –and particularly in those works in which social commentary is a primary objective– is that the emotional provocations of romance are projected both within and beyond the romantic anecdote. Melodramatic affectivity is equally distributed among political discourse, ethical composure, and characters' physical posturing and gesticulation. In this sense, love need not allegorically represent the route to justice because those same exalted emotions common to amorous discourse are evenly, and indeed liberally, applied to all textual activity. As such, while romance may be present in the text, it is just one narrative element among many others that embodies the exuberant affective discourse of melodrama.

This distinction of melodramatic narrativity, however, does not dispute the fact that Latin American fiction has often turned to the topic of romance as a means of discussing social unity. As Aníbal González has argued in *Love and Politics in the Contemporary Spanish American Novel* (2010), works of the post-Boom era returned to sentimental narrative as a means of depicting social stability and of enabling communication with the growing public readership following the "new" narrative experiments of the Boom. But, as González shows, in works of contemporary sentimental fiction, disinterested social sacrifice does not operate alone, as self-serving passion inevitably figures into the narration. In González's assessment, sentimental writing in the post-Boom era then oscillates between two forms of amorous expression: that of eros (an unattainable passionate desire destined to produce suffering), and that of agape (a fraternal love, generating communication and understanding) (13-14). González finds a special niche for melodrama in his reading of contemporary sentimentality, noting that "melodrama is, in fact, one of the secrets of the sentimental formula's success," functioning as a form of eros that does not conclude in disaster, or functioning as a simulated eros that nearly complies with the communitarian impulse that he perceives in agape (142). Either way, González's perception of melodrama within contemporary forms of literary narrative is crucial as it stands as one of the few examples of where melodrama has been singled out as a form of "serious" literature, not presented within an ironic or parodic format.

Indeed, it is striking to note the general absence of critical discourse on melodrama in Latin American literature from the early to mid-twentieth century, and particularly in the analysis of social narrative. The neglect of melodrama throughout this period is due in no small part to the rise of *Modernismo*, works of a *Vanguardista* slant, and the writings of celebrated River Plate authors like Jorge Luis Borges, Adolfo Bioy Casares, and Julio Cortázar. Critical discourse on melodrama as a mode of high literature falls by the wayside throughout this epoch, as melodrama itself is understood more commonly as a manifestation of those expressions of mass media culture that have gained increasing importance in the field of Latin American cultural studies. For example, Jesús Martín-Barbero traces the lineage of melodrama in Latin America through exclusively mass media narrative forms: the *folletín*, or serialized periodical fiction of the nineteenth century; *radioteatro* or *radionovelas* (serial radio shows); tangos; Mexican film; the *crónica roja* (sensationalist press); and the *telenovela* (*Laberintos* 449-50). Each of these narrative forms could be classified under the nebulous heading of popular narrative genres as they are intended for a wide but not necessarily formally-critical public, leaving notably absent any reference to supposedly high literature associated with melodrama.

The works left unaddressed by Martín-Barbero's melodramatic mapping and by the analysis of Latin American melodrama at large –precisely those socially-conscious melodramatic texts addressed in this study produced during the early to mid-twentieth century– stand at a critical juncture in Latin American narrative. In re-taking romantic foundational narrative of the nineteenth century influenced by realist and naturalist stylings, and by building toward a crescendo in the innovations of so-called "new" narratives of the Boom, these twentieth century melodramas bridge the gap separating concepts of tradition and innovation. In locating the melodramatic impulses of social realism and the more general "social text" of the early to mid-twentieth century, this study offers a paradigm to comprehend the ubiquity of melodrama, its permutations, and its causes.[10] Such a reading equally balances the aesthetic makeup and social concerns of melodrama, which has not always been the case in contemporary Latin American melodramatic investigation.

In fact, while Latin American melodramatic analysis in general is keenly aware of the social significance and ideological underpinnings of narration, it

---

10 I am here employing Russell Reising's term "social text" as he utilizes it in his study *Loose Ends: Closure and Crisis in the American Social Text* (1996), in which he examines a range of works from Herman Melville's *Israel Potter* to Walt Disney's *Dumbo*.

often fails to account for the very functionality –or lack thereof– of the tale. That is, melodramatic investigation in both Latin America and beyond cogently demonstrates how narrative may present a tale that overtly expounds dominant, bourgeois rhetoric, or, alternatively, how a tale may stage incorporations of popular culture, so contesting "top-down" narrative form and ostensibly vindicating the subaltern. And while these identifications correctly detect opposing ideological presences in the text, they fail to account for the inevitable complications of fictionality. Such analyses implicitly assume that ideology, whichever it may be, can be communicated effectively and plainly without the text deconstructively undoing the very message that it would propose. In other words, melodramatic analysis has commonly assumed that the tale the melodrama was telling did achieve some pure form of communication, capable of producing a demonstrable social impact. This approach, however, does not adequately account for the blind spots and inevitable lacunae of reason covered up in melodrama.[11]

It is, nevertheless, the social trajectory of melodrama that concerns most recent analyses of Latin American *telenovelas* and film. Paramount among those works evidencing the social approach to melodrama is Jesús Martín-Barbero's study *De los medios a las mediaciones: Comunicación, cultura y hegemonía* (1987). For Martín-Barbero, the strength and importance of melodrama as a narrative mode is its capacity to lend legitimacy, via the *telenovela*, to a particular form of narrative specific to those social groups that have been excluded from the hegemonic project of modernity imposed by Latin American nations. For that reason, his analysis primarily focuses not on the devices of melodramatic narrative itself, but rather on the *mediations* carried out by melodrama's public: how melodrama is understood, how it is retold, how it aids in the acknowledgement of peripheral identities, and how, in echoing outmoded narrative techniques, it arbitrates its public's participation in hegemonic national discourse. This final point is crucial as it allows Martín-Barbero to construe melodramatic narration as the voice of familiar time, a time marking personal, family events, differentiated from the historical life of the nation (*Mediaciones* 244). For Martín-Barbero, familiar time has been marginalized by capital-

[11] I offer here a method of reading melodrama similar to that of Annabel Martín in *La gramática de la felicidad: Relecturas franquistas y posmodernas del melodrama* (2005). In her study, Martín reflects upon Spanish melodramas of the era of the Franco's dictatorship, as well as postmodern adaptations of melodrama, probing the crisis of ruling powers hidden within the apparent cohesiveness of melodramatic narrative (80).

ism's influence in the spheres of work and personal relations, making it "anachronistic." The recognizable vestige of that anachronistic family time found in everyday society is embodied in melodrama as a narrative form, as well as in its consumption by the populace, allowing for melodrama to be adopted as a paradigm for understanding and re-narrating social interactions. From this melodramatic perspective, the Latin American popular imagination transforms the totality of social experience into melodrama, so as to secretly avenge the commercialization of daily life and political and cultural exclusion from above (*Mediaciones* 245).

Hermann Herlinghaus's perception of melodrama shares many points of contact with Martín-Barbero's concept of anachronism, and he uses this concept to differentiate between the "narration" of melodrama and the ostensibly legitimate "discourse" of modernity. Herlinghaus underlines the precarious space occupied by melodramatic narration, somewhere between the stages of "emergent" and "residual" cultural developments as they are defined by Raymond Williams (*Rasgos* 48). But this narration is important because of its capacity to communicate knowledge consistent with everyday community practices and justice, inasmuch as those narratives are democratically shared (*Rasgos* 36). In this, what Herlinghaus views as the "intermedial" quality of melodramatic narration is evidenced as it transcends various genres and forms of communication, so manifesting connections among the anthropologic, psychological, and social dimensions of a given tale, a characteristic of the mode that is fundamental to the analyses that follow (*Rasgos* 40-42). Yet in its insistence on the anachronistic quality of melodrama, Herlinghaus's analysis, like Martín-Barbero's, may inadvertently draw a negative connotation to the narrative mode.

Both Martín-Barbero's and Herlinghaus's understandings of melodramatic anachronism implicitly present melodrama as that which, according to their terminology, is outside of time, thus somehow not modern and, therefore, temporally and logically incorrect from the perspective of dominant culture. This reasoning, of course, is framed within a context of melodramatic vindication, possible in the heterogeneous social milieu of Latin American society. But the critics would perhaps involuntarily support the charge that melodrama is that which should not be with regards to modern and high art forms (a problematic affirmation when viewed in light of Peter Brooks's comments regarding the centrality of melodrama in the modern social imaginary). A possible dialogue between high and mass media manifestations of melodrama –one masterfully developed in the works of Manuel Puig and more recently by César Aira, for example– is not reflected upon at length in Martín-Barbero's and Herlinghaus's respective approaches. Their primary objectives lie in their attempts to find evidence of a subaltern perspective in the face of an uneven hegemonic reality. Without question, this reading of melodrama is well-developed and indeed necessary, but it may unintentionally maintain melodrama in a ghetto of "low" art, assuming that its greatest achievement is to represent the underrepresented, and so affirming that it is unworthy of serious narrative critique.[12] In spite of this fact, Martín-Barbero's and Herlinghaus's analyses, concerned as they are with recognition through melodrama –a topic to which I will return throughout this study– have allowed the social structures interpellated through Latin American melodrama to come more clearly into critical focus.

Following Martín-Barbero's line of social inquiry through melodrama, O. Hugo Benavides in *Drugs, Thugs, and Divas: Telenovelas and Narco-Dramas in Latin America* (2008) has demonstrated how *telenovelas* and the narco-dramas of Latin America have aided in the articulation of subaltern identities inhabiting the margins (and sometimes the margins of the margins) of postmodern Latin American society. Benavides argues that melodrama is remarkably effective as a cultural practice because it functions within the hegemonic project of Latin American society at large, while at the same time allowing for the presentation and ongoing reformulation of particular identities through narrative (196-97). For Benavides, melodrama's ambiguous position within hegemonic society lets it function as perhaps being outwardly apolitical, all the while offering "a much more complicated social and political picture than the one embodied in the initial revolutionary postcolonial project, precisely because this was never a concern" (201). Benavides's identification of melodrama as a narrative mode functioning in the Latin American postcolonial social milieu is clearly a strength of his investigation. But what merits closer attention is the manner in which melodramatic aesthetics are transformed in the postcolonial Latin American context.

That aesthetic transformation is a complex and delicate process that, as Neil Larsen notes in *Determinations: Essays on Theory, Narrative, and Nation in the*

---

[12] Martín-Barbero has been nothing short of defiant in his stance exonerating the subaltern perspective encoded in melodrama, proud of analyzing the *telenovela* as it flies in the face of what other critics would perhaps not even consider as fiction because of its bawdy aesthetic (Martín-Barbero and Muñoz 14). But unfortunately, in so closely analyzing the social impact of the *telenovela*, Martín-Barbero falls into the same trap as those who he criticizes by not analyzing the aesthetic, the fictionality of melodrama itself.

Americas (2001), may not offer a panacea against dominant cultural hegemony. Larsen observes that postcolonialist cultural negotiations reflect "the profound transformation of Eurocentrist intellectual culture" (31), while paradoxically reinforcing a hegemonic theoretical approach to the study of the Americas. In spite of this fact, and developing within the context of Latin American cultural "dependency," Carlos Altamirano and Beatriz Sarlo comment in *Literatura/Sociedad* (1983) that the "translations" of cosmopolitan literary tendencies within the Latin American "periphery" are that which constitute the very specificity of the region's literary production (89).[13] For Altamirano and Sarlo, that literary output may participate in this aesthetic modernity in an ambiguous or contradictory manner, but it nevertheless contests a top-down model of dependency in its adaptation of form to the social dynamic of the Latin American "periphery."

Following this latter analysis, melodrama, then, offers a paradigmatic case study of postcolonial Latin American aesthetics. Surpassing many of the guideposts of Eurocentric melodrama as presented above, the recurring feature uncovered in Latin American social melodrama is its refusal to neatly tie up the loose ends of its narratives and present an entirely happy ending, or to present a cohesive representation of glorified suffering.[14] Latin American social melodrama seems to be in a constant battle with its very narrative mode, causing structural fissures that often diverge from standard definitions of melodrama in the United States and Europe. Twentieth century Latin American melodrama in the cases examined here is much more complex in that our heroes are flawed, society is flawed, and the resounding dénouement so necessary to melodrama

13 The notion of cultural dependency is, of course, highly reductive in that it limits the cultural imagination of Latin America to what it might have absorbed from its colonial forefathers. Sara Castro-Klarén's *The Narrow Pass of Our Nerves: Writing, Coloniality and Postcolonial Theory* (2011) vividly demonstrates how such a conception of Latin America enters into immediate conflict when viewed through the writings of El Inca Garcilaso de la Vega and Guamán Poma de Ayala. The project of this investigation differs slightly from Castro-Klarén's insights in that it looks at a no less interesting process of manipulation and adaptation of melodrama to the specificity of the Latin American social experience.

14 Again, my reading of melodrama dialogues with Reising's model for reading the United States social text, when he notes that "no novel, no social text, can resolve in its imaginative work the crises, tensions, and vexations that characterize the social and cultural world of its genesis, that any appearance of having done so is tantamount to political, moral, and rhetorical bad faith" (2-3).

in the Latin American case frequently serves as much to reveal problems and unresolved conflicts as it does to put a positive spin on the tale.

But in presenting its internal conflicts and schisms, Latin American melodrama manages to steer clear of tragedy, no matter how tragic social reality may seem. Differing from the worldview of tragic narrative, Latin American melodrama's characters are constantly in action, rarely paralyzed even when torn asunder by inner monologues or fraught with nagging doubt. Unlike tragedy, which assumes that there is no escape from a catastrophic fate, the protagonists of Latin American melodrama continue to fight the good fight, attempting to change society even when their prospects are grim.[15] That is, unlike Shakespearian tragedy where characters' fates are sealed from the start, Latin American melodrama presents an unflinching belief that change is possible, even when efforts to bring it about end in disaster. Such a problematic social vision is undoubtedly much more in step with reality, but in their uncertain resolutions, the tales of Latin American melodrama draw attention to the very postcolonial conundrums that beset Latin American societies: innovation versus tradition, the local versus the global, revolution versus conservatism. These conflicts that bring about fissures in melodramatic solidity are evidenced in each of the works examined in this study, and may be equally located in contemporary mass media melodrama when it attempts to propose more equitable visions of social justice. This, in turn, serves to illustrate the pervasiveness of melodrama and the way in which the mode problematizes concepts of high and low and of intellectual and mass-mediatized cultures. To this end, the recent *telenovela Victoria* (2008) presents an exemplary case for inspecting some of those same melodramatic impulses present in the works analyzed in this study.

Victoria was adapted for broadcast in the United States by the Telemundo network and was first recorded under the name *Señora Isabel* (1993) in Colombia, and later as *Mirada de mujer* (1997) in Mexico. As the case of *Victoria* illustrates, Telemundo's *telenovelas* offer a vision of a world where national boundaries, regional customs, and spoken accents are blurred to create a multiform, Pan-American society, worthy of critique in its own right. *Victoria* itself tells the tale of a woman, Victoria, who, after twenty-five years of marriage, is betrayed by her husband, Enrique, when he takes a mistress and ultimately decides to abandon his wife and children. Disaster ensues as the separated cou-

---

15 Many critics have reflected on the relationship between melodrama and tragedy. I would mention here the studies of Eric Bentley, Robert Heilman, Geoffrey Nowell-Smith, and William Sharp as influential in the scope of this study.

ple's children are hurried into marriage by an unplanned pregnancy, carry on amorous relationships that challenge social boundaries of age and class, and are the victims of sordid crimes. Victoria is also challenged when Enrique cuts his economic support to the family, but she is able to persevere through all of these familial tribulations because of the romantic relationship she maintains with a younger man, Jerónimo, drawing societal objection for her involvement in a non-traditional relationship.

Victoria and Jerónimo's relationship is the clear focal point of the story, and after suffering innumerable setbacks, the couple eventually is able to live out a happy future together... in Spain. This final point is important because the plot of *Victoria* occurs in an unnamed Latin American country (there are frequent mentions of things that happen "in this country" or "in this city," but a formal name is never given, though the series was filmed in Bogotá, Colombia). Victoria and Jerónimo's happiness, then, is contingent upon their abandonment of their home country, which demonstrates that there has been no greater communal rectification of the injuries that Victoria has suffered for breaking social taboos. Instead of triumphing over social prohibition, Victoria and Jerónimo retreat from it, so complicating the ostensible justice rendered in the *telenovela*'s happy ending. But, as a tale of partial feminine empowerment (lest the viewer forget, Victoria's strength is still heavily dependent upon Jerónimo's capacity to make her feel like a "complete" woman), *Victoria*'s story in some measure undermines the patriarchal standard encouraging female spectators to act for themselves and not to remain trapped in abusive marriages. In this sense, *Victoria* demonstrates that rupture with social protocol is the only way to find that happy ending, opposing the frequently voiced criticisms of the false nostalgia of melodrama and offering new forms of being via the melodramatic mode.

Similarly, the melodramatic social narratives of the early to mid-twentieth century analyzed in this study do not nostalgically attempt to re-live some past order so as to achieve textual resolution, but rather mirror the nineteenth century melodramatic novels of Spanish American piracy analyzed in Nina Gerassi-Navarro's investigation, offering continued breaks from tradition to propose new socio-political models (149). Indeed, these socially oriented works are concerned with finding means of modifying previous social orders to fit with new forms of existence, so highlighting the complex social dialectic of the text. This amalgamation of the old and the new embodied in Latin American social melodrama represents a decidedly heterogeneous social milieu, making melodrama anything but some simplistic lowbrow tale to pass the time.

Yet, because it is plot-driven and often oriented to storytelling instead of ornate aesthetics, melodrama is very much adaptable to mass media formats, as is evidenced in the television and film versions of the works analyzed here. It is perhaps because of this storytelling capacity that the twentieth century social texts' narrative complexity were not always readily evident to critics, a critical problematic evidenced in Françoise Perus's reading of Emir Rodríguez Monegal's approach to works of the Latin American *Vanguardia* and Boom.

In *Historia y crítica literaria: El realismo social y la crisis de la dominación oligárquica* (1982), Perus takes issue with Rodríguez Monegal's affirmations that the works preceding the Latin American avant-garde were simply documentary in nature (65-113). Perus notes that in Rodríguez Monegal's reading of the history of Latin American literature, "true" narrative cannot be observed in the region until the presence of James Joyce, William Faulkner, and Marcel Proust may be felt in the structure of the novel, which Rodríguez Monegal perceives in such authors as Agustín Yáñez, Alejo Carpentier, Juan Carlos Onetti, and João Guimarães Rosa, among others (76-81). From here, Rodríguez Monegal would conclude that the transcendence of Latin American narrative may be located in the ensuing works of the Boom, in which language itself becomes the object of literary focus, thus reflecting deeply philosophical concerns and participating in an international literary sphere no longer concerned with representing the miniscule realities of the quotidian regional experience (Perus, 77-81).

Perus, on the other hand, maintains that Latin American literature embodied complexities comparable to those noted by Rodríguez Monegal long before the Boom. Perus argues that the development of social realism, grounded as it is in the period of transition from an oligarchic society to one governed by bourgeois capitalism (a process first occurring in Latin America during the 1920s and 30s), showcases the complexities of change via the conflicting discourses invoked in social narrative (151-55). The novel becomes a dialogic site where the representations of heterogeneous modes of social existence come into contact, which is reflected in the very narrative forms and voices used to structure the social realist text. Perus observes that social realism rejects foregoing literary styles, particularly those of romantic and *Modernista* impulses, as they supported oligarchic social order (155). Perus thus presents social realism, not as a continuation of the nineteenth century novel, but as the narrative format that represents a definitive break in the literary tradition, an inaugural moment in the aesthetic radicalization of Latin American novel (161).

Perus's approach to reading the innovations of Latin American social realism finds theoretical support in Jacques Rancière's proposal of "regimes of art" in

The Politics of Aesthetics (2004). Rancière separates art into three distinct regimes, the first of which is the ethical regime of images, in which art is subsumed by its functionality and is not perceived autonomously as art per se (in religious iconography, for example). The second category, the poetic or representative regime of arts, breaks from the ethical regime by conceiving of itself as artistic, governing itself through a hierarchy of genre and subject matter in attempts to define the correctness of its speech. A final category is established in the aesthetic regime of arts, in which the guidelines of the representative regime are definitively blurred and the "proper" concept of art gives way to freedom of represented subjects, which embody their own brands of meaning (20-30). For Rancière, the aesthetic regime of the arts is where the revolutionary value of art may be unleashed as it is no longer dependent on categorical definitions to account for its correctness. As the author notes, the inaugural trend in the aesthetic regime of arts is realism:

> [W]hich does not in any way mean the valorization of resemblance but rather the destruction of the structures within which it functioned. Thus, novelistic realism is first of all the reversal of the hierarchies of representation (the primacy of the narrative over the descriptive [...] or the hierarchy of subject matter) and the adoption of a fragmented or proximate mode of focalization, which imposes raw presence to the detriment of the rational sequences of the story. (24)

In Rancière's argument we find echoes of those same affirmations voiced by Perus. Both critics perceive realism, though analyzed in differing contexts, as the watershed aesthetic in the evolution of narrative, allowing for a fragmented perspective that reflects a complex reality no longer governed by "good" or "correct" speech and style. The realist approach then offers a means of expression that liberates subjectivity, cognizant of allowing access to only partial approximations to social reality.

Given its reliance upon a partisan and personalized approach to the social milieu it represents, it is perhaps of little surprise that the melodramatic mode be so basically intertwined with realism. Melodrama is, in fact, so closely bound to realism that critics have encountered difficulty when attempting to somehow draw distinctions between the two. Some, however, have sought to categorically distinguish between melodrama and realism based on reading melodrama as the overdone, bawdy other of restrained, intellectual realist fiction.[16]

---

16 Frank Kelleter and Ruth Mayer, for example, note that, "from the late nineteenth century onwards, literary critics tended to discuss melodrama in sharp counter-distinction to realism, as an outdated and embarrassingly crude approach to the problem

However, in the Latin American case, this distinction appears untenable, as even the earliest works of the region's fiction seem to rely equally on sobering political assessments and emotionally charged theatrics to promote social order. Taking a cue from United States theater critic Thomas Postlewait's historical analysis of realist and melodramatic evolution (54), it is then more productive to consider realism and melodrama in both Latin America and beyond, not as independent modes that evolved in a consecutive order, but as permeable and interdependent means of narration.[17] In the Latin American context, I would contend that melodrama may be understood as a brand of "hyper-realism," an intense, emotionally charged focus on the quotidian "real" event, which invariably dialogues with those same deep philosophical and ideological concerns that are customarily attributed to realism.

The ideological framing of melodrama has not been lost on critics who have noted a range of political positions –from the bourgeois (Gawelti 47, Nowell-Smith 269) to the revolutionary (Gerould 185)– that may be encoded in the melodramatic mode.[18] But, as melodrama works to make complex social situations clear through straightforward language and action, it runs the risk of over-simplifying the intricacy of actual events. In his seminal essay "Tales of Sound and Fury: Observations on the Family Melodrama" (1972), Thomas Elsaesser notes this complication and comments:

> The persistence of melodrama might indicate the ways in which popular culture has not only taken note of social crises and the fact that the losers are not al-

---

of artistic mimesis which the realistic mode of writing supposedly had managed to overcome and leave behind. The very terms *realism* and *melodrama* have thus been used in highly evaluative ways, with *realism* signifying rationality, order, pragmatism, and clear-headedness, while *melodrama* stands for feeling, excess, sentimentality, and grandiose gestures" (10).

17 In the same line of analysis as Postlewait, Ralph J. Poole and Ilka Saal comment that, "while we recognize that melodrama and realism (understood here not simply as certain sets of formal principles, but as dominant modes of cultural production in certain epochs, as *Epochenstil*) evolved at different times (the late 18th/early 19th century, respectively the mid to late 19th century), we also hold that melodrama did not disappear with the emergence of bourgeois realism, but on the contrary, continued to assert its influence *alongside* and *within* the new dominant aesthetic" (7-8).

18 Annabel Martín, commenting upon Spanish melodramas, has also noted the curious fact that melodrama is equally employed by centralists and oppositionists to convey their political messages (39). Additionally, both the studies of James L. Smith in *Melodrama* (1973) and Juliet John in *Dickens's Villains: Melodrama, Character, Popular Culture* (2001) have illustrated melodrama as a means of social protest.

> ways those who deserve it most, but has also resolutely refused to understand social change in other than private contexts and emotional terms. In this, there is obviously a healthy distrust of intellectualisation and abstract social theory – insisting that other structures of experience (those of suffering, for example) are more in keeping with reality. But it has also meant ignorance of the properly social and political dimensions of these changes and their causality, and consequently it has encouraged increasingly escapist forms of mass-entertainment. (47)

Though Elsaesser's commentary refers to film and mass media narrative genres, as presented in this study, the apparent simplification of complex social and political events via melodrama is equally located in what may be considered serious literature. Nevertheless, in both mass media and high formats, for melodramatic socio-political simplification to occur, the narrative depends on a process of textual enactment, rooted in affective performativity, which takes place between the reader and the text.

To discern the performative aspects of the melodramatic text we first look to J. L. Austin's breakthrough study *How to Do Things with Words* (1962). Austin analyzes performative speech acts, which he divides into three categories: the locutionary (an utterance with meaning), the illocutionary (a locution providing force, i.e. informing, ordering, and warning), and perlocutionary (those utterances that generate action, i.e. to get someone to stop talking by saying "stop talking"). The performative capacity of the final two categories is that which most interests Austin as he seeks to demonstrate how language produces action. But in order for that action to be achieved, language is dependent on circumstances surrounding the speech act. For instance, if a judge pronounces, "I find you guilty," the judge must be vested with the authority to adjudicate for that verdict to carry any weight. Those present at the verdict must recognize the judge's authority, and all parties involved must *believe* in the sovereignty of the law enacted and, consequently, carry out the ruling. This laundry list of necessary conditions for performative acts (many of which are difficult, if not impossible, to measure) and the constant slippage between the illocutionary and perlocutionary categories cause a great amount of difficulty –recognized by Austin himself– in determining exactly what a "pure" performative is (148-50). There is one case, however, that is of great importance to the consideration of performative language in melodrama, which Austin decisively excludes from his study: the language of theater, poetry, and soliloquy. For Austin, these artistic applications of language exceed what needs to be considered in the analysis of performative language because, as they do not appear in "ordinary" situations, they are not truly communicative. Austin thus considers such uses of language to be "parasitic" imitations subordinate to the perlocutionary force of effective language (22).

Jacques Derrida counters Austin's parasitic classification in his essay, "Signature Event Context" (1972), showing how both artistic/written and effective/oral languages are reliant upon iteration to produce meaning. In order to be legible visibly or audibly, all language must follow recognized protocols that are continually reproduced. Derrida's gesture is then not to continue to find written language, the basis of artistic performance (the theater, poetry, and soliloquy to which Austin refers), to be supplementary to the "true" presence of the spoken word, but rather to recognize the essential graphemic bedrock of all linguistic communication. That is, oral, like written language, is beholden to, and is an enactment of grammar, an iteration from which it is impossible to produce the singular, "pure" verbal performative that Austin attempts to isolate. Derrida's discovery of this commonality between oral and written language allows us to begin to consider the similar performative nature of the two. Just as the oral and scriptural are linked through their dependence on iterability, so too is the possibility of performatives delineated by the same rules of language within each of these formats. Yet, at the same time, both oral and written contexts offer a space in which discourse is exchanged and where meaning is potentially enacted. This process of enacting meaning is key to the comprehension of melodrama and is elucidated through a phenomenological approach to the text.

In *The Act of Reading: A Theory of Aesthetic Response* (1978), Wolfgang Iser examines this performative potential unlocked in the act of reading. But, for Iser, the performative aspect of literature is not found only in the commonality of language employed across spoken and written contexts, but rather in the play between the reader and the text. Like Derrida, Iser also begins by reading Austin, noting that Austin's parasitic qualification of literature is due to its incapacity to invoke actual conventions and procedures and to be concretely linked to a situational context, so providing solid ground for a measurable performative (a context like that mentioned above in the example of a judge pronouncing a verdict) (60). However, these same shortcomings of literature noted by Austin paradoxically are that which allows Iser to uncover the performative nature of the text.

Iser notes that, in literature, a given text will not obey a vertical hierarchy of social protocol that Austin's approach requires: a normative continuum, a set of procedures in which the "values of the past also apply to the present" (60). Instead, Iser observes that the literary text will selectively include a varied assortment of social conventions, presenting them as interrelated, but organizing them horizontally and so holding them up for critique, which is to strip them of any immanent validity. As such, the social procedures common to everyday life are recognizable in fiction but are presented as estranged from their habitual, coherent context and made the object of textual scrutiny (61). This process has important implications for the reader as "he finds himself obliged to work out why certain conventions should have been selected for his attention." Fictional language is thus revealed as embodying "the quality of 'performance,' in that it makes the reader produce the code governing this selection as the actual meaning of the text" (Iser 61).

For Iser, the performative nature of fictional language, then, is recognizable in the dialogue established between the text and the reader, a dialogue crucial to the composition of melodramatic narrative. It is in fact safe to say that melodrama is only functional inasmuch as there is an active emotional rapport between the reader and the text. Similar to what Iser noted as the performative nature of the reader's responsibility in organizing information, in melodrama, the performative is elicited through the reader's affective response to, and dialogue with the text. In this emotional dialogue, the reader uncovers the gist of the tale and affectively is moved to comprehend the social message encoded in the text.[19] The reader must engage in what Jonathan Flatley terms "affective mapping," which, via a process of self-estrangement, "allows one to see oneself in relation to one's affective environment in its historicity, in relation to the relevant social-political anchors or landmarks in that environment, and to see the others who inhabit this landscape with one" (80). The self-estrangement to which Flatley refers would be a secondary process in the consumption of melodrama, a posterior consideration of how and why we have been affected by the melodramatic tale, which could lead to further socio-political reflection. In this way we come to understand the melodramatic text as a site containing a potentiality of emotional provocation, grounded in particular social and historical concerns, which is only activated when the reader engages the work. By

[19] Melodrama may be analyzed in the terms of Ann Cvetkovich's concept of "an archive of feelings." Cvetkovich offers her entire study as such an archive, presenting "an exploration of cultural texts as repositories of feelings and emotions, which are encoded not only in the content of the texts themselves but in the practices that surround their production and reception" (7). This is slightly different from Sara Ahmed's readerly approach in *The Cultural Politics of Emotion* (2004), in which the author discusses not "emotion as being 'in' texts, but as effects of the very naming of emotions" (13).

relying on the deployment of the emotional "figures" of the text, melodrama affects its public so as to convey its moral and social message.

The emotional figures of melodramatic narrative may be read through those features of what Roland Barthes has defined in *A Lover's Discourse: Fragments* (1977) as the forsaken and unwarranted speech of the lover: speech and narrative gesticulation performed before a mute or perhaps even absent other. Barthes's analysis identifies a series of figures that typify the lover's experience in literary texts: anxiety, waiting, fulfillment, declaration, jealousy, crying, and regret, for example. Importantly, Barthes notes that these figures "take shape insofar as we can recognize, in passing discourse, something that has been read, heard, felt," or in other words, inasmuch as they are communicably shared with the reader, so underlining the relational nature of the lover's discourse (4). Barthes goes on to note that "a figure is established if at least someone can say: *'That is so true! I recognize that scene of language.'* For certain operations of their art, linguists make use of a vague entity which they call linguistic feeling; in order to constitute figures, we require neither more nor less than this guide: amorous feeling" (4).

Barthes's proposition for the formulation of figures through reader response is clear, but we may build upon this proposal in noting that these textual experiences are not necessarily exclusive to the lover's repertoire. Anxiety, fulfillment, regret, and many other figures that Barthes cites may be linked to a variety of non-amorous situations, while their passionate urgency remains intact. Indeed, these figures loom heavily over melodrama without necessarily invoking romance. And, when the figures proposed by Barthes are read from the optic of melodrama, they may be understood as emotionally reaching beyond the confines of amorous speech, also employed to make clear the conflicting elements of complex social situations, so expressing a confluence of thought and emotion.

And this socio-sentimental undercurrent present in melodrama should not be taken lightly as it stands as an indicator of what Raymond Williams has termed in *Marxism and Literature* (1977) as "structures of feeling." In associating melodrama with Williams's concept, it is important to note that melodrama is not in itself a "structure of feeling." Rather, melodrama permits –as we shall see in its varied and even divergent incarnations– the articulation of emotional textual messages with the potential to resonate with, and find acceptance in a greater public. That the social perspectives inscribed in melodrama find reception among the public speaks to the fact that some informally held views are of growing importance to society, but are resistant to being unilaterally codified by historical analysis.[20] These as yet not defined social forms and experiences lived by perhaps large swaths of the public are the evidence of the structures of feeling to which Williams refers, indicating "a social experience which is still *in process*, often indeed not yet recognized as social but taken to be private, idiosyncratic, and even isolating, but which in analysis (though rarely otherwise) has its emergent, connecting and dominant characteristics, indeed its specific hierarchies" (*Marxism* 132). Given the fluidity of these processes, concrete proof of structures of feeling is illusive, but Williams notes that, "the idea of a structure of feeling can be specifically related to the evidence of forms and conventions –semantic figures– which, in art and literature, are often among the very first indications that such a new structure is forming" (*Marxism* 133).

Read through the lens of Williams's interpretation, the various perspectives on social order presented in the melodramatic works of this study may be understood as articulations of emergent structures of feeling, depicted by an author as an unofficial representative voice for a particular historical moment shaped by unique social concerns.[21] That author is responsible for the production of a social text that captures –in both its representation and its allure– the imagination of a given public sector. But for melodrama to achieve its complete social and emotional impact, it must be oriented to a specific public that is sympathetic to its message. This audience may be understood through what Lauren Berlant classifies in *The Female Complaint: The Unfinished Business of Sentimentality in American Culture* (2008) as an "intimate public." Berlant notes:

> An intimate public operates when a market opens up to a bloc of consumers, claiming to circulate texts and things that express those people's particular core interests and desires. When this kind of "culture of circulation" takes hold, participants in the intimate public *feel* as though it expresses what is common among them, a subjective likeness that seems to emanate from their history and their ongoing attachments

---

20 This unfinished aspect of social forms is crucial to Williams's argument. Williams's comments regarding structures of feelings stand as a response to those who attempt to view social forms as clearly defined, calcified elements of the past that may be held up individually for analysis. Williams views the social as a far more fluid site where negotiation is ongoing and meaning cannot be fixed.

21 On this point it is productive to consider the author as an "author function" in light of that which is proposed by Michel Foucault in his seminal essay "What Is an Author?" (1979). Though Foucault refers to this function as an authorization of a brand of discourse or of transdiscursivity, we might consider the perspectives provided by the consecrated authors of melodrama (Henry James or Balzac, for example) to be the authorization of a mode of perception, or a mode of engaging in social relations.

> and actions. Their participation seems to confirm the sense that even before there was a market addressed to them, there existed a world of strangers who would be emotionally literate in each other's experience of power, intimacy, desire, and discontent, with all that entails: varieties of suffering and fantasies of transcendence; longing for reciprocity with other humans and the world; irrational and rational attachments to the way things are; special styles of ferocity and refusal; and a creative will to survive that attends to everyday situations while imagining conditions of flourishing within and beyond them. (5)

By appealing emotionally to these intimate publics, melodrama is able to communicate its particular form of social analysis. This, indeed, should be considered among the primary strengths of melodramatic narrative: to propose a critique of social order by tugging on the heartstrings of its public.[22] And melodrama unabashedly works to choke up the public or goad it into consternation, ostensibly with the hopes of bringing about social change, even if the actual change brought about by any given literary text would be difficult if not impossible to calculate.[23]

Yet, what must be accounted for in any narrative, and what is often hidden in melodrama's emotional appeal, is the actual consistency (or lack thereof) presented within the fictional matrix. Because melodrama is so exceptionally adept in utilizing emotion to convey its vision of social justice, the reader tends to gloss over contradictions in characterization and structuring of the melodramatic tale that would complicate of the story's message. In our sense of relief and happiness at seeing the hero or heroine of melodrama prevail, we tend to

---

22 Though not specifically discussing melodrama, Shirley Samuels notes that didactic emotional staging is the primary characteristic of sentimentality in general, which has often been rebuked for its overt affective intent. Samuels writes, "the reform literature associated with sentimentality works as a set of rules for how to 'feel right,' privileging compassion in calibrating and adjusting the sensations of the reader in finely tuned and predictable responses to what is viewed or read. The discomfort of sentimentality comes from what can be a coerced or artifactual emotional response – being forced to feel what it feels like– a response that raises questions about the moral or political status of the works, or produces an uneasiness regarding what borders on the prurient or salacious aspects of the texts' subjects" (5).

23 On this point, we may recall Jacques Rancière's comment on the impasse of art and politics when he writes that, "aesthetic art promises a political accomplishment that it cannot satisfy, and thrives on that ambiguity. That is why those who want to isolate it from politics are somewhat beside the point. It is also why those who want it to fulfil its political promise are condemned to a certain melancholy" (*Dissensus* 133). Indeed, as much as the works examined here would offer models of social change, their actual impact may be indefinitely frustrated.

forget if justice has come about through the reassertion of an unjust hegemonic order. In our urge to indulge in sympathy for beset victims, we may inadvertently disregard the ideological incoherence and stereotypical representations of minority public sectors. In our desires to see villains punished, we may perhaps ignore that melodrama has incited in us the same bloodlust for which we criticize our textual antagonist. These paradoxes of melodrama have not yet received proper critical attention, but as they reside at the very core of social narrative of the Latin American twentieth century, they must now be given their overdue critical consideration.[24]

This study consists of five chapters charting the proliferation of Latin American social melodrama throughout the early to mid-twentieth century. In this epoch of literary production, I locate melodrama, understood as a "theatrical substratum" (Brooks) inherent to each of these works, in several distinct tendencies that have fundamentally shaped the Latin American literary imagination, including regionalism, *indigenismo*, urban realism, socialist realism, and novel of the Mexican Revolution.[25] This comparative approach thus allows for a broad view of the mechanisms of melodramatic narrative and for an examination of common affective tendencies across a body of texts with distinct concerns, so as to show the very ubiquity of melodrama in framing social critique. The particular works that I analyze in this study were chosen not only because of the authors' prominence as critical voices for expressing dissent with regard to the social situation that they represent, but also because of the way in which these texts, commonly read as socio-political pleas to the broader public, work to personally engage the individual. We find, then, that these ostensibly intellectualized texts function emotionally to communicate their ideological perspectives, thus problematizing dichotomies of affect and intellect, and of facile and serious works of art. In this context, melodrama, understood as a pervasive

---

24 The paradoxes of Latin American melodrama have garnered certain interest in the already mentioned studies of Nina Gerassi-Navarro (with regards to the centrality/exclusion dynamic of women in melodrama) and O. Hugo Benavides (in examining the racial desire/prohibition dialectic of postcolonial society). I would also mention Ana López's "Tears and Desire: Women and Melodrama in the 'Old' Mexican Cinema" as a crucial text on the ambiguous role of women both as objects and spectators of melodrama.

25 In keeping with Derrida's commentary in the essay "The Law of Genre" (1980), I am mindful of the permeability of genre and its impossibility to contain all the meanings of a given selection of works. However, by locating melodrama in so many different Latin American literary tendencies, my intent is to show the ubiquity of the narrative mode.

narrative mode, demonstrates the capacity to function as a "genre-producing machine" and evidences continuity across a broad selection of narrative genres (literature, film, television, and theater) (Gledhill, *Rethinking* 227).[26] The malleability of melodrama allows for the consideration of the transfer of emotion, inherent in melodramatic storytelling, beyond what have been stereotypically considered feminine, sentimental narrative genres, moving into masculine-dominated narrative formats.

This apparent paradox of melodramatic emotionality within masculine-focused narrative is deeply inscribed in this study, as the texts here examined are all written by male authors and in great measure focus on the masculine social experience. This masculine paradigm, however, need not preclude the consideration of melodramatic emotion. As Henry Jenkins comments in his analysis of televised professional wrestling in *The Wow Climax: Tracing the Emotional Impact of Popular Culture* (2007), masculine melodrama maintains a central role in cultural production, even when males are taught to avoid self-reflexion and to disdain theatrical emotionality. As Jenkins notes, stereotypical male avoidance of emotion does not mean that men are without feelings, but that social patriarchy endeavours to find modes to express male emotion while preserving the desired macho archetype. Jenkins notes that, "a first step toward reconsidering the place of male affective experience may be to account for the persistence of melodramatic conventions within those forms of entertainment that 'real men' do embrace –horror films, westerns, country songs, tabloid newspapers, television wrestling, and the like" (77). This is akin to what Jeremy Wallach, Harris M. Berger, and Paul D. Greene term the "affective overdrive" found in the aggressiveness of heavy metal music (13-15). Similarly, the novels examined in this study tell stories of "men being men," never backing down from a fight, fulfilling voracious sexual appetites, and ostensibly shying away from directly expressing how they truly feel. Yet, conforming to a melodramatic norm, these tales are so filled with dramatic adventures that even when men do not *say* what they want or need, their actions do the talking for them.

---

[26] This versatility of melodrama in the twentieth century Latin American social text parallels the adaptability of melodrama in popular film noted by Christine Gledhill, who comments that, "while claims and counterclaims are made about the definition of melodrama as a genre and about its status as a reactionary or progressive, class or gendered form, the question remains, given its various and cross-genre circulation –crime melodrama, romantic melodrama, family melodrama, western melodrama, etc.– as to how melodrama relates to the genre system in the first place" (*Disorder* 64).

An emphasis on narrative action indeed links all of the works in this study, but has not served to define the canonical value of these texts. Some of the works here examined, like Rómulo Gallegos's *Doña Bárbara* (1929) and Carlos Fuentes's *La muerte de Artemio Cruz* (1962), for instance, are consecrated canonical works and are often recognized as the respective authors' greatest contribution to Latin American literature. Others, like César Vallejo's *El tungsteno* (1931) and Roberto Arlt's *El amor brujo* (1932) are considered to be outlying works, anomalies to the authors' highly regarded *oeuvre*. Finally, Jorge Amado's *Gabriela, Cravo e Canela* (1958) is a renowned novel by a celebrated author, but is not necessarily viewed as the crowning work of an illustrious literary career. What these novels demonstrate in their varying degrees of success and centrality to the respective authors' bodies of work is that melodrama serves as a pervasive mode for narrative framing in both the principal texts and black sheep of the Latin American literary canon.

These works grow out of nineteenth century conceptions of literary style and unity but show increasing levels of subtlety and complexity in their melodramatic depictions, and an ongoing and open-ended interrogation of the power of social critique voiced through melodrama. Melodrama in this study expresses both brazen optimism for future economic development and doubt about an increasingly globalized economy and the cultural changes it ushers in. It illustrates a grudging acceptance of the way things have come to be and gives in to outright guilt and depression for having let things get to where they are. The melodrama that courses through these works offers momentary portraits that help to gauge a broader emotional barometer measuring satisfaction with the historical processes that shaped the nations represented in this study, and, in turn, the region on the whole. And while each text examined here does represent a particular national experience, when read together, these works offer broader insight into the dialogue between the melodramatic aesthetic and social narrative in Latin America from the 1920s up until the 1960s, a logical ending point before the self-referential works of melodrama produced in the postmodern era, which would require a different theoretical approach.

The first chapter of this study deals with one of the most renowned works of twentieth century Latin American literature, Rómulo Gallegos's Venezuelan regionalist classic, *Doña Bárbara*. In this chapter I examine several typical elements of melodrama that Gallegos's novel so clearly exemplifies: diametrically opposed heroes and villains, the moralistic clash of virtue and vice, and resolution of conflict in an ostensibly happy ending, all of which are employed in an attempt to discern a route to economic and social modernity. I argue, however, that all of these clear-cut melodramatic elements are at the same time problematized by inconsistencies in characterization and by the novel's resolution, which leaves loose ends –both within and without the structure of the family represented in the text– that exceed the model of melodramatic narration. These elements of the novel serve to question the project of socio-economic progress represented in the text and to expose the complexity of what is generally considered a straightforward classic. Additionally in this chapter, I reflect on the television adaptation of Gallegos's novel, the Telemundo network's recent *telenovela*, *Doña Bárbara* (2008). This latter analysis allows me to problematize some of those social interpretations of melodrama discussed above, calling into question the capacity for recognition of subaltern sectors and the possibilities of any gains accrued through that acknowledgement, while at the same time destabilizing the serious and facile boundary that would distinguish literary and mass media formats.

Chapter two analyzes Peruvian author César Vallejo's novel, *El tungsteno*. In dealing with Vallejo's *indigenista* tale, I demonstrate that it is equal to *Doña Bárbara* in the intensity of its melodramatic flair, but how that melodramatic insistence presents a thoroughly different social and political agenda. Instead of presenting grandiose visions of future economic prosperity through modern capitalism, Vallejo's novel shows the underside of globalization by following an agenda of socialist realism: indigenous peoples enslaved and abused by soulless foreign corporations. I argue that this form of representing indigenous peoples' suffering is used for the exclusive purpose of conjuring melodramatic pity in the reader, thereby convincing him/her of the need for social change presented in the text through the panacea Marxist politics. I read Vallejo's depiction of potential Marxist uprising, however, as a significant imposition of littoral Peruvian social and political views upon the characters that populate this Andean tale. I argue that this heavy-handed political discourse, instead of concretely demonstrating the ideological project of the novel, actually works to complicate its plot. What is presented as a unifying Marxist rhetoric paradoxically underlines the lack of a singular political project that orients the novel, instead calling attention to the heterogeneity of complaints that the text problematically attempts to incorporate. That heterogeneity, thus, becomes the tenuous condition of possibility for the would-be uprising presented in the conclusion of Vallejo's novel.

Chapter three analyzes the critique of melodramatic narration voiced in Argentine author Roberto Arlt's urban sentimental novel, *El amor brujo*. Differing from the works analyzed in chapters one and two, Arlt's novel does not display confidence in melodrama as a means of presenting a call for social order. Instead, Arlt's novel sees urban sentimentality communicated through melodramatic serial fiction as a social ill that creates unrealistic materialist expectations, propping up what the novel's protagonist sees as the evils of bourgeois society. Arlt's novel, however, voices an oblique socio-political critique of bourgeois normativity without directly indicating a clear ideological project. To demonstrate how Arlt launches his circuitous attack on what he perceives as the vacuity of melodramatic sentimentality, I examine *El amor brujo*'s self-conscious play on melodramatic narrative tactics, exemplified in a protagonist who calculates each of his melodramatic actions to draw the most powerful response from his unwitting lover. At the same time, I argue that, while presenting a critique of sentimentality, Arlt's novel is still fundamentally dependent on melodrama as a paradigm for conceiving the individual's role in society –a fact evident in the text's resolution when the novel's anti-hero eventually returns to the middle class norms against which he had so vociferously rebelled. Accordingly, Arlt's novel is shown to strive for a concept of narrative and social order beyond the melodramatic standard, but also as trapped by the threshold of the melodramatic horizon and the ideology that gives it sustenance.

The inescapability of melodrama is equally apparent in chapter four's analysis of Brazilian author Jorge Amado's *Gabriela, Cravo e Canela. Gabriela* is widely understood as marking a transitional period for Amado as he moved gingerly away from the hardline communist politics that had directly influenced his earlier works. In my reading of Amado's novel, however, I argue that these same politics, framed through melodramatic aesthetics, continue to orient the author's work, though perhaps more subtly than before. Historically set in a period of social and economic transformations, *Gabriela* examines local politics and questions what, if any, advances are being made. At the same time, by fusing a tale of uniquely Brazilian regionalist romance with the representation of provincial political intrigue, Amado presents an innovation of socialist realist aesthetics less concerned with overt political messages than with political workings interwoven into the affective functionality of the text. In my analysis of Amado's novel, I demonstrate how melodrama is key to the evolution of this socialist realist aesthetic, but also how this melodramatic modification, perhaps at an unconscious level, illustrates skepticism about the possibility of social change via artistic mediums. Drawing a parallel to chapter one's analysis of the melodramatics of the *telenovela*, this chapter also offers a reading of the cinematographic adaption of Amado's novel in the film *Gabriela* (1983), interpreting the predominance of the film's romantic tale as melodramatic bait that conveys a less evident, but no less vital, political story.

The fifth and final chapter of this study deals with a text frequently read as that which ends the cycle of the novel of the Mexican Revolution, Carlos Fuentes's *La muerte de Artemio Cruz*. Fuentes's novel works through an entire history of the Revolution to take stock of the political transformations undergone, and also of the corruption that was an unanticipated outcome of the revolutionary process. Doubtlessly the least obvious of the melodramatic works included in this study, my reading of Fuentes's novel notes the staying power of melodrama as it inhabits Fuentes's ornate and ostensibly anti-melodramatic Boom-era classic. I argue that underneath the innovative construction of varied and out-of-joint narrative times, in order to present its social critique, Fuentes's novel unexpectedly relies on a series of tried and true melodramatic commonplaces: romance, adventure, hidden identities, and the exercise of poetic justice. In this sense, melodrama provides an ideal means through which Fuentes can voice his historical assessment of the shortcomings of the Mexican Revolution and the characters that gave shape to the event. Running parallel to that historical critique, *La muerte de Artemio Cruz* also shows melodrama as no longer being able to provide hope for a future success (as was the case in Gallegos's *Doña Bárbara*), no matter how problematic this melodramatic enterprise might have been from the start. Fuentes's novel thus evidences a frustration in the grinding wheels of melodramatic narrative resolution, attempting once and for all to destroy melodramatic framing, while still paradoxically relying on melodrama to illustrate the poetic justice of the text.

In each of the texts here examined, the reader observes how melodramatic ends betray the means through which each tale is narrated. That is, in the end, the results to which these stories arrive problematize the ways in which characters have been presented, the coherence of the narratives' respective trajectories, and the supposed social and ethical message of the text. As such, the melodramatic model ceases to work as a flawless mechanism for representing social strife, in spite of the fact that the ideological message that it attempts to present is more often than not clearly understood. This body of texts thus presents a rich field for reflecting upon melodrama's capacity for representing social narrative, a debate enacted in the framing of each of these works and re-enacted in each new reading of the text.

Doña Bárbara or the Complications of Clear-Cut Melodrama

If one were pressed to name a universally recognizable example of Latin American melodrama, *Doña Bárbara* (1929) by Rómulo Gallegos (1884-1969) would almost surely enter into the debate. In this sense, Gallegos's novel retains a particular position in the Latin American social and intellectual imaginary: as an accessible melodrama, it is a work of tremendous universal popularity, but, at the same time, it remains an object of vigorous ongoing critical debate. *Doña Bárbara* is indeed a highly seductive story –as alluring as the Venezuelan plains represented in its tale– that drew in even the man against whom Gallegos wrote his novel. In an often quoted anecdote recording Venezuelan ruler Juan Vicente Gómez's reaction to his first contact with *Doña Bárbara*, the strongman reportedly quipped, "Eso no es contra mí, porque es muy bueno. Eso es lo que deben hacer los escritores en lugar de estarse metiendo en revoluciones pendejas" (qtd. in Liscano 119) ["this cannot be against me because it is quite good. This is what writers should be doing instead of getting involved in damned revolutions" (my translation)]. While Gómez's reaction to the text clearly flies in the face of the logic of Gallegos's novel, it exemplifies the generally positive reaction that *Doña Bárbara* evokes because of the pleasure we attain in reading a good story. And Gallegos's classic work is just that: an enthralling tale, one so appealing that we return to it time and time again in its original written form, its cinematographic adaptations, or its production in the *telenovela* format.

The tale told in *Doña Bárbara* is well-known: Santos Luzardo, a gentleman with a rancher's heart, returns to stake claim to his ancestral homeland, the Altamira ranch, after having received an education in Law in Caracas. But beyond his educational motives, Santos's years of absence from the Arauca River valley are also due to a series of episodes of inter-familial violence that saw Santos's father, José Luzardo, kill Santos's uncle, Sebastián Barquero, and also Santos's brother, Félix Luzardo. Upon Santos's return to Altamira, one seemingly insurmountable obstacle lies in his path to reclamation: the cutthroat "devoradora de hombres" ["man-eater"] Doña Bárbara who, in Santos and his family's absence, has continually encroached on the Luzardos' hacienda, stealing land and cattle. Like Santos Luzardo, Doña Bárbara also suffers the scars of a violent past, embodied specifically in the brutal rape that she suffered in her adolescence. But, where Santos has seemingly recovered from his childhood trauma, Bárbara continues to re-live the aggressions of which she was once a victim, lashing out at any impediments to her rule over the Venezuelan plains. Inevitably, Santos Luzardo and Doña Bárbara become locked in an ongoing, sentimentally-heightened struggle for control, symbolically confronting the concepts of modernity and backwardness, civilization and barbarism, legality and custom, rationality and spiritualism, and, more broadly, good and evil. As in any good tale of moral pragmatism, we are led to believe that justice has prevailed in the end as we see Bárbara ride off into the sunset, having learned her lesson and so permitting a new era of civility under the watchful eye of our hero, Santos Luzardo.

On the surface, then, *Doña Bárbara* looks to be about as cut and dried as can be: a straightforward tale of right and wrong accentuated by harrowing escapades and sexual tension. But below this facade there lie deep-seeded conflicts and contradictions. If, indeed, the solidity of analyses of *Doña Bárbara* once resided in identifying an allegorical conflict between civilization (Santos Luzardo) and barbarism (Doña Bárbara), contemporary critical approaches to the text have evidenced the instability of this ostensibly immutable confrontation. For example, Roberto González Echevarría, in *The Voices of the Masters: Writing and Authority in Modern Latin American Literature* (1985), challenges the univocal allegory of civilization and barbarism, reading *Doña Bárbara* as a confrontation of forms of writing: legitimate or legal script embodied in Santos Luzardo is confronted by Doña Bárbara's erasure of writing's authority. By countering the implicit symbolic conflict of the text, González Echevarría demonstrates that allegory cannot be fixed to the civilization/barbarism dichotomy because it "sets other mechanisms of signification into motion by showing the radical separation between signified and signifier" (47).

Exploring a similar problem inherent in allegory, in *The Spanish American Regional Novel: Modernity and Autochthony* (1990), Carlos Alonso has observed a constant allegorical over-determination in *Doña Bárbara*. For Alonso, allegory thus enters into conflict by producing a ripple effect in the text: one allegorical event references another, which itself offers an unstable symbolic connection between the initial character and a value that he or she embodies. Alonso notes that:

> In the end, this iterative employment of allegory necessarily has the effect of weakening the adequacy and propriety of the original allegorical formulation, since it casts doubt on the finality and immobility of the latent sign whose function is to complement the meaning inscribed in the manifest level; that is, there can be no

> guarantee that the presumed final stopping point of the allegorical chain thus established will not become itself a manifest level to a "deeper," yet more fundamental content. (*Regional Novel* 124)

As Alonso convincingly argues, the discursive technique presumably used to control meaning within the novel may be seen as the same that comes dangerously close to being the text's very undoing, as textual significance is time and time again displaced in the allegorical chain. This provocative approach to the supposedly unambiguous nature of conflict in *Doña Bárbara* unsettles presumptions that Gallegos's work is somehow a facile narrative, made for simple, ideologically-charged consumption.

And, while readings like those offered by González Echevarría and Alonso serve to flesh out the inevitable lacunae of reason that inhabit Gallegos's novel, it is undeniable that *Doña Bárbara* is a work that is meant to be legible, a page-turner where one is induced to keep reading to find out what happens next, how the story ends. In any case, both the complex allegorical dimension of *Doña Bárbara* and the novel's direct and pleasurable reading share a common denominator: they equally rely on the tools of melodramatic narration. It is the melodramatic formulation of *Doña Bárbara* –in its characterization, in its romantic intrigues, in its adventurous episodes, and in its structure and resolution of conflict– that makes it morally, emotionally, and ideologically legible to the reader on the basic plane of what is narrated in the novel.[1] At the same time and on a secondary plane of the text, the complex, proliferating allegory works hand in hand with melodrama, as the symbolic clash between civilization and barbarism is contained within the melodramatic ordering of the novel: characters are

---

1 The plot elements listed here speak to the very essence of melodrama, and, in this sense, it is somewhat surprising that critical analysis has only very lightly explored the melodramatic aspect of Gallegos's classic. To my knowledge, only José Miguel Oviedo and Javier Lasarte Valcárcel have commented specifically on the melodramatics of *Doña Bárbara*, and they have done so mostly in passing. Oviedo notes that, in Gallegos's novel, "la atmósfera es sobrecargada, intensamente emocional, más cerca del melodrama que de la tragedia" (246) ["there is an over-charged, intensely emotional atmosphere, closer to melodrama than to tragedy" (my translation)], which he locates in the overt conflict of good and evil. For his part, Lasarte Valcárcel affirms that the radical changes that Santos Luzardo and Doña Bárbara undergo are symptomatic of melodramatic imagining (178-80). But, beyond these two commentaries, I would be remiss not to acknowledge the deep influence of Peter Elmore in my initial understanding of melodrama in *Doña Bárbara*, particularly in a seminar on the Spanish American regional novel at the University of Colorado.

imbued with specific allegorical characteristics and are then ostensibly positioned in the novel as either melodramatic heroes or villains. Accordingly, in every confrontation in the novel, in every heightened emotional commentary, in every physical gesture, the message of allegory is implicitly, melodramatically communicated.

Indeed, several basic principles of melodramatic narrative are operative in *Doña Bárbara*. From the outset, the reader observes evidence of *Doña Bárbara*'s melodramatic framing in the nominal presentation of characters, even before they are invested with any agency within the text.[2] Naming is quite blatant in *Doña Bárbara*, and while it is obvious that the nominal identification of the characters is intended to mark their symbolic purpose in the text, it is important to note that this is a function of the novel's melodramatic aesthetic. As melodrama strives to explicate the necessary moral order of the represented world, it overtly defines characters' ethical values through their nominal presentation. And, through melodramatic naming, the two principal characters of Gallegos's novel are emblematized and are meant to comply with determined functions and positions within the text: quite clearly, Santos Luzardo is meant to be saintly and enlightened and Bárbara, wild, vicious. Such a titular positioning of characters is indicative of the Manichean worldview that orients *Doña Bárbara*, offering constant confrontations of good and evil, an ethical binary that is central to melodramatic imagining.

Moreover, in assuming a format not entirely unlike that of serialized literature, in which each micro intrigue contributes to a greater narrative displaying the eventual triumph of goodness over the agents of corruption, time after time in Gallegos's novel, the battle between the forces of good and evil is metaphorically enacted.[3] To cite just one example of the good and evil dynamic, the reader observes an early clash of moral ramifications when Santos Luzardo first confronts Altamira's manager, Balbino Paiba. When Santos returns to Al-

---

2 As Emir Rodríguez Monegal once noted, "no es necesario practicar una lectura muy detallada para reconocer en este libro la caracterización arquetípica, que está subrayada hasta por los nombres de los personajes…" (215) ["a detailed reading is not necessary to recognize the archetypical characterization of the novel, which is underlined in the characters' very names…" (my translation)].

3 Marcel Velázquez Castro has noted a similar melodramatic plot format in Peruvian author José María Arguedas's novel *Todas las sangres* (1964). Velázquez notes that, in Arguedas's novel, readerly pleasure is achieved as each micro intrigue offers tension, but consistently fulfills the readers' expectations (9). I have also commented on the melodramatic problematics of Arguedas's novel in the article, "Cohesión y contradicción: Los excesos narrativos de *Todas las sangres*" (See bibliography).

tamira to discover the state of disarray on the ranch, he immediately seeks an explanation, aggressively questioning Paiba, and so asserting his position as the rightful owner of Altamira. Paiba is taken aback by Santos's interrogation and is left virtually speechless, though he is in fact greatly to blame for Altamira's dilapidated state as he illicitly worked side by side with Doña Bárbara to mine the ranch for all its worth in Luzardo's absence. Paiba is only able to muster up a partial renunciation of his post but is only saving face, as it is evident that Santos is firing him.

In this sequence of events, Santos is presented as a leader who is not willing to accept even the slightest affront to his authority, so fomenting his heroic position in the text. But, more importantly, following the melodramatic delineation of conflict in the novel, the reader bears witness to a more crucial ramification of this encounter: the gradual righting of the moral balance of the represented world. Where the dark forces of Doña Bárbara had once intervened to cloud the moral and legal authority of the Luzardos, this dethroning of Balbino Paiba as an authority figure is a perhaps small, but significant, move toward re-establishing ethical order in a world set on its ear; it is a piece of the larger puzzle, a moral reconfiguration of Altamira from which the reader attains melodramatic gratification in seeing justice enacted. Such textual confrontations offer us the emotional thrills of melodramatic narration, as they allow us to position ourselves on the side of the just, fomenting our sense of indignation at those who flout the rules that govern social etiquette. In this way, we become increasingly invested in the story's plot.

This establishment of rapport between reader/spectator and character is indeed a key function of melodrama because a sympathetic view of the protagonist's perils allows us to feel a measure of commiseration for our own experiences, providing for a feeling that we are not alone in the world. As Eric Bentley notes in *The Life of Drama* (1964), melodrama opens avenues for self-pity when "we pity the hero of a melodrama because he is in a fearsome situation; we share his fears; and pitying ourselves, we pretend that we pity him" (200). But even if our feelings of solidarity are self-interested, they, nonetheless, allow for a bond between reader and character to be forged via emotional solidarity, which has the potential to override a distanced and rational approach to the artistic object. In other words, emotion simply overcomes reason, which, in the case of *Doña Bárbara*, communicates affectively (and effectively) the message of civilization. Seemingly minor but emotionally charged episodes similar to that of Santos and Paiba's encounter recur throughout *Doña Bárbara* to indicate the ongoing struggle between good and evil in the text: when

Santos legally outwits Doña Bárbara and the foreign interloper Míster Danger; when Doña Bárbara's henchman, Melquíades "el Brujeador," is eventually vanquished; or when Doña Bárbara's ranch hands become progressively disenchanted and abandon El Miedo.

Yet the consistency of these melodramatic intrigues enters into crisis when we examine how melodrama is utilized to inform the social dimensions of the text. As a *novela de la tierra*, *Doña Bárbara* is deeply invested in providing social commentary. And at the time when Gallegos penned his novel, Juan Vicente Gómez was firmly entrenched in power as Venezuela reaped immense profits from its oil wealth.[4] Given that Gómez's reign marked a period in which Venezuela experienced dynamic economic diversification linked to the petroleum industry, *Doña Bárbara*'s representation of an entirely agricultural economy may be viewed as somewhat peculiar.[5] Doris Sommer has partially resolved this problematic by commenting that the agricultural conflicts of *Doña Bárbara* are likely meant to symbolically represent those problems brought about by the petroleum economy (280). Other critics, however, suggest that Gallegos's novel offers a nuanced vision of the liberal socio-economic agenda countering Gómez's reign. In *Del Lazarillo al Sandinismo: Estudios sobre la función ideológica de la literatura española e hispanoamericana* (1987), John Beverley proposes that Santos Luzardo's efforts to delimit the plains and alter standing ranching practices prove *Doña Bárbara* to be a story detailing the transformation of the Venezuelan agricultural economy into a modern form of capitalist management (*Lazarillo* 110-11). Considering the historical conditions under which Gallegos wrote his novel, these forms of economic transition provide a fundamental backdrop for Gallegos's novel, and the economic restructuring and fluid processes of social transformation depicted in *Doña Bárbara* ultimately demand a transformation of the means of representing narrative conflict. Running parallel to the socio-economic alterations represented

---

4 As Fernando Coronil comments in *The Magical State: Nature, Money, and Modernity in Venezuela* (1997), "as the oil industry expanded in a society whose state had very limited institutional capacities, it promoted the concentration of state powers in the figure of the president" (83). Gómez's virtually unchecked power was wielded against his enemies, forcing intellectuals like Gallegos into exile until the president's death in 1935.

5 Historians, however, have not always noted Gómez's reign as a period of economic diversification and modernization (Coronil 69-75). Rather, Gómez has frequently been perceived as a stumbling block to modernization, and many historians note that it is only with Gómez's death in 1935 that Venezuela entered into contemporary history.

in the text, we see that the protocols of melodramatic narration in Gallegos's novel are manipulated and made more flexible so as to better represent the complexity of the postcolonial social milieu.

Melodrama functions most seamlessly when it works with absolutes and static categories. But, because of the transitional figures and complex social situations represented in *Doña Bárbara*, melodramatic statics become increasingly dynamic, which is evident in the mechanics of characterization in the novel. The heroic Santos Luzardo, for instance, is shown at times to be less than an idyllic, single-tracked melodramatic character, occasionally stepping down from his high moral ground and so placing in doubt the authority of his supposed convictions. Conversely, Doña Bárbara's entirely villainous stature is partially obfuscated when she undergoes a transformation from an arch-evildoer to an incrementally subdued, and even sympathetic, adversary. As Javier Lasarte Valcárcel notes, we witness, then, a "proceso narrativo por medio del cual Santos se 'barbariza' y doña Bárbara se 'ilumina'" (177) ["narrative process in which Santos is 'barbarized' and Bárbara is 'enlightened'" (my translation)]. The polarized conflict of the novel, thus, is eroded to a degree, bending without ever completely breaking the rules of melodramatic engagement –the good are not always good and the bad, not entirely evil.

The complications of Santos Luzardo's melodramatic characterization are palpable in his initial presentation in the text. In the opening chapter of the novel, as Santos's vessel makes its return to Altamira up the Arauca river, the protagonist is described in contradictory terms, as his affective state is visibly exteriorized for the reader. Santos is described as pensive, "como si en su espíritu combatieran dos sentimientos contrarios acerca de las cosas que lo rodean, a ratos la reposada altivez de su rostro se anima con una expresión de entusiasmo y le brilla la mirada vivaz en la contemplación del pasaje; pero, enseguida, frunce el entrecejo, y la boca se le contrae en un gesto de desaliento" (Gallegos 118) ["as though indicating a conflict of emotions concerning his affairs, the quiet pride of his expression would change for moments to a look of enthusiasm, and his eyes would light up joyously as he gazed at the surrounding country; but this would be followed by a frown and a dejected contraction of the corners of his mouth" (Gallegos 4)].[6] As this early passage demonstrates, the heroic Santos Luzardo is torn between opposing emotional impulses that will

6 Unless otherwise noted, the remainder of the quotations in this chapter come, like this one, from Robert Malloy's 1948 translation.

continually influence his actions in the text.[7] This is driven home when, at the end of the same chapter, we read that, though Santos had begun his trip with the clear intention to sell the Altamira ranch, he is taken with the beauty of the Arauca and now contemplates a different endeavor, one "completely opposed" to his initial plans. This new enterprise is, of course, the civilization project that Santos Luzardo will enact throughout the novel, combining the unrelenting work ethic inherent to the descendants of the Luzardo family with "los ideales del civilizado, que fue lo que a aquéllos les faltó" (Gallegos 140) ["the ideals of a civilized man, in which they had been lacking" (Gallegos 29)]. In essence, Santos seeks to impose new methods of capitalist production, culled from his metropolitan education and symbolized in his efforts to erect fences on the plains, in order to effect progress in what are construed as antiquated practices of the rural economy. Nevertheless, as outlined above, this basic clash of the hero's stated goals so early in the novel introduces a contradiction in the melodramatic imagining that defines *Doña Bárbara*.

As Robert Heilman notes in *Tragedy and Melodrama: Versions of Experience* (1968), melodrama is a narrative format that strives to present unity between character and purpose, so producing a "wholeness" that lends coherency to narrative action. Heilman states that, "in the structure of melodrama, man is essentially 'whole'; this key word implies neither greatness nor moral perfection, but rather an absence of the basic inner conflict that, if it is present, must inevitably claim our primary attention." Heilman also comments that, in melodrama, man "is not troubled by motives that would distract him from the outer struggle in which he is engaged. He may indeed be humanly incomplete; but his incompleteness is not the issue" (79). Now, within the melodramatic framing of *Doña Bárbara*, Santos Luzardo does maintain a constant struggle against his enemy, Doña Bárbara, which upholds the wholeness of his purpose. But, we must note that the inner emotional turmoil that Santos experiences in re-conquering Altamira presents him as an increasingly complex character, so challenging basic concepts of melodramatic imagining. Santos's "incompleteness," to use Heilman's term, is indeed at issue as the greater symbolic conflict of the text is reproduced within his character; it is as if the overt allegorical

---

[7] With regard to this passage, Donald Shaw notes in *Gallegos: Doña Bárbara* (1972) that, "the alert reader at once perceives that this ambivalence is the root of his character, while his attractive appearance, his intelligence, and the courage shown in his confrontation with Melquíades at the *palodeagua*, are merely the conventional outer trappings of the fictional hero. Even before it is explained, his ambivalence has been translated into terms of plot" (52-53).

confrontation of civilization and barbarism of Gallegos's novel were projected upon the interiors of protagonist and antagonist alike (as we shall see, Doña Bárbara also faces contradictory emotions that problematize her melodramatic stability).[8] This dichotomic interior conflict repeatedly crops up in the text, offering possibilities for fusion of the two apparently-opposed concepts of social order, so highlighting the hybridity embodied in *Doña Bárbara*'s characters and the problematization of melodramatic aesthetics in Gallegos's novel.

Santos's internal grappling with his own dark side may be viewed as the inevitable presence of his new reality because, as Juan Pablo Dabove notes in *Nightmares of the Lettered City: Banditry and Literature in Latin America 1816-1929* (2007), "barbarism refers to the original violence in the constitution of the agrarian order. This barbarism is unmovable because it goes to the core of that agrarian order once we take into account that it was responsible for the transformation of nature into capital. But barbarism also refers to a particular mode of being in agrarian capitalism" (283). Indeed, as is evident in my analysis of the schism in Santos Luzardo's character, Dabove's study is formative in my understanding of the internal conflicts that riddle *Doña Bárbara*. Tracing banditry as a root of violence that defines the enterprises of both Santos Luzardo and Doña Bárbara, Dabove notes that, paradoxically, barbarism is at the core of agrarian civilization as it is represented in the rural environs of the text. This social coexistence of civilization and barbarism, I would argue, is exactly what problematizes and potentiates Santos's melodramatic character, destabilizing supposedly polarized modes of ethical and unethical conduct that establish him as a "good" character in the novel.

For instance, one obstacle that Santos Luzardo is forced to confront upon his return from Caracas to Altamira is the lack of confidence that his ranch hands show toward him. Because his style of dress and social etiquette immediately signal him as an urbanite and not a man of the country, a clear manifestation of melodramatic exteriorization of character, several of Altamira's employees are skeptical of Santos. A fortuitous occasion to prove his worth presents itself when, just after firing Balbino Paiba, Santos is able to show off his horse-handling skills by breaking a wild colt. Santos is well aware that horse-breaking is "la prueba máxima de llanería, la demostración de valor y de

8 By focusing on the duality of conflict in Gallegos's novel, the previously cited works by Donald Shaw and Javier Lasarte Valcárcel are central to the argument of this chapter as they are among the few critical works that delve into the complexity of characterization in *Doña Bárbara*.

destreza que aquellos hombres esperaban para acatarlo" (Gallegos 199) ["the great test of the cowboy, proof of the courage and skill these men were waiting to attribute to him" (Gallegos 97)], and he enters into the rodeo without hesitation, grabbing the reins, letting the skills honed in his youth take over, and gaining dominion over the animal and acclaim from his ranch hands.

Santos Luzardo has other opportunities in the novel to prove his cowboy skills, notably in a rodeo in which he lassoes and brings down an escaped bull, and, while he clearly comes out the winner of this test of his manhood, the episode creates dissonance within the basic melodramatic code of the novel. In showcasing Santos's rustic horse-handling skills, indicative of a dormant barbarity, this episode further problematizes Santos's character. Lest we forget, Santos's horse-breaking, an approximation to the wilds of the plains, occurs when he is in the midst of re-affirming economic interests by firing Balbino Paiba and restoring social hierarchy, so bringing ordered business to Altamira. To be sure, Santos's cowboy skills are intended to present him as a hybrid model of social being, equally capable of both the white-collar economic administration of Altamira, and of its basic hands-on production. But, his return to cowboying to a degree destabilizes the reforms that Santos attempts to enact, mixing his rank with that of the ranch hands whose job it is to break horses and comply with other manual tasks, and showing that for all his civilized mannerisms, he is eager to get his hands dirty.

These conflicting rustic and refined impulses, constantly in flux within Santos Luzardo, call into question the limits of classical melodramatic unity in representing his character. Following a melodramatic standard would necessitate that Santos be what the text offers as either civilized (urban) or barbarous (rural), but what scenes like this one illustrate is that he is somewhere in between the two.[9] This does not contradict Santos's heroic status in the text, but it does reveal that *Doña Bárbara* permits a great deal of flexibility in its melodramatic configuration of character. Contrary to basic melodramatic characterization, Gallegos's novel offers the possibility for the conception of characters who are not exclusively controlled by a single impulse, such as lust, revenge, or redemption. As Santos Luzardo's case illustrates, *Doña Bárbara* presents relatively complex characters that, even in their melodramatic conception, appear

---

9 In this sense, Gallegos's novel challenges the all or nothing reasoning of melodrama, in which characters are represented as definitively being one way or another and in which, as Peter Brooks states, "the middle ground and the middle condition are excluded" (*Imagination* 36).

to be caught in the throes of contradictory desires. This malleability of character is revelatory insomuch as it demonstrates that Gallegos's novel, which, given its ostensibly polarized, action-packed conflict, may well be considered a standard of Latin American melodramatic narrative of the twentieth century, is just as representative of melodrama as it is of the ambiguities of the narrative mode. In its depiction of the intricacies of postcolonial Venezuelan society, melodrama here offers far more than a static means of conveying concepts of good and evil. Rather, it is shown to be a dynamic narrative format through which social and psychological complexities are brought into focus, problematizing our understanding of ostensibly straightforward narrative action. This melodramatic complexity, embodied by Santos Luzardo, becomes increasingly evident as his insertion to life in the Arauca River valley continues.

As the novel progresses, Santos, still offering a civilizing ethos, complies with a series of modernizing measures on Altamira, the most important of which being the installment of a fence to create a border between the Luzardo's ranch and El Miedo. Yet, when Carmelito López, one of Santos's trusted ranch hands, is murdered and robbed of the feathers that he carried as payment for the barbed wire for Altamira's new fence, Santos Luzardo undergoes a decisive and patently melodramatic change that sees him eschew his progressive rhetoric. Demanding justice in the wake of Carmelito's murder, Santos travels to the district's municipal hub, San Pedro, to call upon Mujiquita, his former classmate and assistant to the local judge, to enact justice. Yet, when Mujiquita tows the party line, imposed by the local village's corrupt magistrate, Ño Pernalete, repeating the obviously fabricated tale that Carmelito died of a heart attack, Santos becomes convinced of the futility of his legal recourse. Instead of further attempts to pursue the issue through legal channels, Santos says to Mujiquita, "el atropello me lanza a la violencia y… acepto el camino" (Gallegos 395) ["I'm being driven to violence, and I'm accepting the direction" (Gallegos 346)].

Instead of insisting upon the rule of law as a means of exerting justice, a cornerstone of his civilizing project throughout the novel, Santos Luzardo instead decides to fight fire with fire, a decision significant inasmuch as it again demonstrates the plasticity of melodramatic characterization in the novel.[10] Santos,

---

10 As Pedro Díaz Seijas notes in his essay, "Aproximación semiótica al universo narrativo de *Doña Bárbara*," even when Santos Luzardo's acts border on reprehensible, they are ultimately vindicated by the character's implicit will to enact justice (202). This inherent goodness marks the representation of Santos Luzardo for a substantial part of the narration, in which the hero unquestionably acts, in the basic melodramatic logic of the novel, on behalf of the righteousness of modernity.

still the undisputed hero of the novel, gravitates to the barbaric, negative pole of the text by accepting the violent *modus operandi* of his enemy, Doña Bárbara; after all, it is she who relies on violence throughout the novel to achieve her goals, which categorizes Bárbara as one of the bad guys. This negative quality, then, paradoxically comes to characterize the novel's melodramatic hero as momentarily barbaric, so investing good with evil, a coexistence of contradictory values uncommon to classical concepts of melodrama. Further evidence of Santos's emerging dark side is found in his encounter with Doña Bárbara's henchmen, the Mondragones.

The Mondragón brothers occupy the Macanillal house that traditionally has served as a landmark delimiting the boundary between Altamira and El Miedo. Constructed atop stilts, the shack is highly mobile, and the Mondragones, at Doña Bárbara's request, frequently move the dwelling to appropriate more territory. Santos Luzardo has become tired of these encroachments on his land, and, after accepting violent tactics following his meeting with Mujiquita, he forcibly enters the shack and commands the Mondragón brothers to set it ablaze. In an attempt to defend their home, one of the brothers, el Tigre, reaches for his rifle, but Santos shoots him in the thigh. The only response from El León, the other of the Mondragón brothers, is to note, "cada hombre tiene su hora y el doctor Luzardo está desgastando la suya" (Gallegos 404) ["every man has his hour and Dr. Luzardo is enjoying his" (Gallegos 355)]. Upon returning to Altamira from this encounter, Santos insists that he is now on "another path," sensing that a new period of the "buen cacicazgo" or "enlightened despotism" is beginning at Altamira.

In these sequences of the novel in which the switch is flipped, so to speak, and Santos reverts back to the methods by which his ancestors had forcibly taken control of the Arauca River valley, we experience the melodramatic thrill of *Doña Bárbara*. Dramatic tension builds in the text to the point at which Santos's vindictive acts are the desired and pleasurable outcome of the text, allowing the reader to enjoy the reinstatement of a moral and social order that has been corrupted by Doña Bárbara and her lackeys.[11] Indeed, it feels as though

---

11 The excitement that the reader experiences in this instance is comparable to that felt by the spectators of cinematographic westerns. In Clint Eastwood's *Unforgiven* (1992), for example, the spectator also enjoys seeing the bandit William Munny (played by Eastwood) exact vengeance over corrupt sheriff Little Bill (played by Gene Hackman). Similar to what occurs in *Doña Bárbara*, what is glossed over is the fact that Munny must embrace evil and a violent past in order to right the moral balance of the represented world.

this almost *had* to happen, as we have witnessed the series of insults and injuries that Santos has suffered in his attempts to restore order. What is covered up, however, is that which has been highlighted above: in order for this exciting and satisfying chain of events to occur, Santos has to betray his own non-violent, civilized ethic. Santos's inconsistencies on this account are essentially excused by the reader as we give ourselves over to the melodramatic excitement of the text, delighting in vengeance disguised as justice, without fully noticing that the rules of melodramatic engagement are being bent. That is, in becoming emotionally involved in the text, we are willing to forget temporarily that Santos is employing those same violent tactics that he had sworn off, so that we may see the wicked be punished. We are willing to forgive these transgressions, as ultimately Santos Luzardo comes out unsullied by all of his efforts, though such is not his express intention.

In an attempt to discover the identity of Carmelito's murderer and the thief of his feathers, Santos Luzardo agrees to see one of Doña Bárbara's associates, Melquíades, at a late-night meeting in Rincón Hondo. Unbeknownst to Santos, Pajarote, a ranch hand from Altamira, follows him to assure his boss's protection. Pajarote's company proves to be crucial, as he murders Melquíades "*el Brujeador*," when he draws his gun on Luzardo. Santos, however, is unaware that it was in fact Pajarote who killed Doña Bárbara's messenger, as he too had fired on *el Brujeador*. Believing himself Melquíades's executioner, Santos feels that it is his duty to deliver *el Brujeador* to Doña Bárbara for proper burial, and, when leaving the lifeless body at El Miedo, Santos is crushed by the weight of his guilt. In spite of all his talk of asserting his rights and accepting his being pushed into violence, Santos Luzardo still attempts to suppress his hostility, and he is deeply ashamed of his barbarous regression. But, in the novel's denouement, Santos Luzardo discovers that he was not Melquíades's murderer: the bullet that killed the Doña Bárbara's henchman entered his left temple, an impossible shot for Santos, who was directly in front of Melquíades. Thus, Santos's assault on the Mondragones is his only true use of violence in the novel, which eases Santos Luzardo's conscience, permitting him to live out his happily-ever-after with Marisela, Doña Bárbara's daughter.

Furthermore, Santos's seemingly nick-of-time discovery that he did not kill Melquíades stands as another example of the melodramatic narrative techniques of *Doña Bárbara*. Commenting upon Sergei Balukhatyi's *Poetics of Melodrama* (1926), Daniel Gerould notes that stage melodrama often "makes dynamic use of a *secret*. The secret is the most powerful factor in the play's dynamics, permitting the melodramatist to hold the spectator's interest uninterruptedly throughout the performance" (*Formalist* 124). Similar to theatrical melodrama, in Gallegos's novel, this truth hidden from Santos Luzardo keeps the reader rapt until the facts are exposed. Yet, it is also through this revealed secret that Santos Luzardo is liberated by the melodramatic framing of the text: his failure to kill Melquíades preserves his moral authority and saves him from a full regression to the evil pole of barbarism. Thus redeemed as a "good" character, the civilizing agenda that Santos will impose at the novel's end is vindicated. But still, Santos Luzardo's will to violence illustrates a complexity in his character that displays the malleability of the melodramatic aesthetic of *Doña Bárbara*, a flexibility mirrored in the novel's depiction of its villain.

Doña Bárbara's position in the melodramatic matrix of the text is equal to, if not more problematic than that of Santos Luzardo. This becomes evident when we consider that, from the text's inception, Doña Bárbara retains the dual role of villain and victim. Bárbara's infamous double deals, witchery, sexual manipulations, and cutthroat violence are the stuff of local lore, easily identifying her as a textual villain whom Santos Luzardo must subdue. But, at the same time, as an adolescent, Bárbara is the victim of crimes that set her on her villainous path; it is because she has been victimized that she unrelentingly seeks revenge, misdirected as it may be, for the wrongs she has suffered. In fact, Doña Bárbara's thirst for vengeance may be read as having an even more basic origin: Bárbara was not only a victim of sexual violence, but she was also conceived by an act of that same form of violence. We read that Bárbara was "fruto engendrado por la violencia del blanco aventurero en la sombría sensualidad de la india" (Gallegos 141) ["fruit violently sown by a white adventurer in the shadowy sensuality of an indigenous woman" (my translation)], and this primary act of sexual violence marks an even earlier starting point for the circular pattern of violence in which Bárbara alternately will be victim and aggressor. In Doña Bárbara's simultaneous depiction as both villain and sufferer, then, a fundamental paradox is inscribed in Santos Luzardo's adversary, complicating the presumably straightforward dichotomic confrontation of the novel.[12]

[12] Lasarte Valcárcel notes that, "La presentación explicativa de la doble violación que lleva en el cuerpo la 'trágica guaricha' es, desde el comienzo, una invitación de la narración a su lector ideal a comprender al personaje no como una identidad esencialmente perversa, sino como el resultado de una historia" (179) ["the explanation of the double violation embodied in the 'tragic guaricha' is, from the start, an invitation in the story for the ideal reader to understand the character not as essentially perverse, but as the result of a personal trajectory" (my translation)].

When the reader first encounters the young Barbarita, she is presented as a fixture on a boat that travels the Orinoco River, trafficking in illicit goods. It is here where Barbarita meets the drifter Asdrúbal, the only positive male figure whom she has ever known and the only man who she has ever loved. Asdrúbal offers Bárbara the opportunity for advancement, teaching her to read and write, thus symbolically mirroring the civilizing actions of Santos Luzardo later in the novel when he attempts to educate Marisela. But disaster strikes when Barbarita falls prey to the same sexual violence that her mother was forced to endure: a mutiny on the ship leads to Asdrúbal's murder, Bárbara's gang rape, and her subsequent escape from the boat's crew before being sold to a leprous Syrian rubber trader.

The sexual violence that defines both Doña Bárbara's conception as well as her adolescent experience sets her on a path to avenge her honor, and, in this way, the novel retakes the melodramatic theme of vengeance that is crucial to Santos Luzardo's civilizing project. But, Barbara's vengeful acts seem somehow perverse, and thus her conquests appear different from those of Santos. After all, Santos Luzardo is at all times purportedly attempting to recoup what is his, seeking retribution for the offenses that he, his family, and his ranch hands have been made to suffer, which is consistently seen as an affirmation of justice, even when it goes beyond the letter of the law. On the other hand, though the young Barbarita is clearly undeserving of the violence and mistreatment that she receives, she avenges that violence by becoming a violent *caudilla*, dominating any male whom she encounters. She, thereby, is presented as a perverse element in the text. Bárbara's rage is misdirected and will never compensate her initial injuries. But, Doña Bárbara's thirst for vengeance is once again indicative of the Manichean reasoning active in Gallegos's novel, which would present a world in which one is either victim or aggressor, with no middle ground on which to stand.

The dichotomic logic of the text has fomented a critical reception, based in allegory, which understands Bárbara to be the incarnation of all things evil in the text. And, at the time of Santos Luzardo's arrival in the Arauca Valley, Doña Bárbara undeniably is entrenched as the underhanded boss of the region, having fortified her power through a series of treacherous acts. Upon arriving in the plains after her violent rape, Bárbara sets her sights on Lorenzo Barquero, Santos's cousin, and his ranch, La Barquereña. Through her alleged witchcraft and by enabling Lorenzo's alcoholism, Bárbara is able to swindle Barquero out of his rights to his ranch with a little help from a crooked lawyer named Coronel Apolinar. Doña Bárbara then quickly renames Barquero's ranch El Miedo and, just as quickly, murders Apolinar to consolidate control of her ill-gotten gains. Bárbara's past, however, is not entirely sealed off from her present reign: Marisela, the daughter she had with Lorenzo, serves as a constant reminder of her violent ascent to power and will cause Bárbara to recall her own youth as she battles Marisela for Santos Luzardo's affection.

This romantic subplot begins when Bárbara learns of Santos's appearance at Altamira and immediately associates Luzardo with the memory of her lost love, Asdrúbal, bringing about her patently melodramatic makeover. Instead of her basic ranch attire, she now wears a different dress, "descotada y sin mangas y adornada con cintas y encajes. Además llevaba el cabello mejor peinado, hasta con cierta gracia que la rejuvenecía y la hermoseaba" (Gallegos 205) ["low necked, sleeveless, and adored with ribbons and lace. Moreover, she had her hair better arranged, with a certain grace even, which made her handsomer and more youthful looking. (Gallegos 103-04)]. Bárbara's exterior change is meant to be representative of an interior, spiritual alteration operating in her character. However, a definitive change is not produced, as such ostensibly positive transformations in Doña Bárbara run contrary to their melodramatic framing. She is still presented as Santos Luzardo's textual adversary, even when her static evilness would presumably be mitigated in her exterior aspect.

Yet, even while Bárbara is progressively represented as embodying more superficially conventional feminine characteristics, she is alternatively described as androgynous and as a "marimacho" (Gallegos 153-54). In this way, Gallegos's novel presents Doña Bárbara as a complex figure whose conflicted gender becomes a means by which to gauge her degree of maliciousness, and this ambiguity present in Doña Bárbara is consistent with personal contradictions typical of classic melodramatic villains. As Juliet John observes in *Dickens's Villains: Melodrama, Character, Popular Culture* (2001), a function of melodramatic villains is to threaten the unity of character ascribed to melodrama's heroes. John comments, "melodramatic villains are thus not infrequently internally focused, guilty of self-violation as well as violation of the selfhood of others. Indeed, the dialectical emotional economy of the genre means externally focused violence is often synonymous with violence that is self-directed" (12-13). The villainous internal/external dialectic noted by John fits well with the portrayal of Doña Bárbara, as we witness that, within Doña Bárbara, "el hábito del mal y el ansia del bien" (Gallegos 363) ["evil habits and a yearning for goodness" (my translation)] are increasingly at odds as she continues to scheme to seduce Santos Luzardo. Even so, while the perception of Doña Bárbara as a clear melodramatic villain is initially supported by such explicitly presented clashes, it is important to note that the varying determinations that Bárbara assumes at crucial moments in the novel serve to illustrate the flexibility of the melodramatic aesthetic through which she is represented. Paralleling Santos Luzardo's attraction to dark, violent impulses, "algo similar, pero a la inversa, ocurre con doña Bárbara" (Lasarte Valcárcel 179) ["a similar, but inverted process occurs with Doña Bárbara" (my translation)], which becomes evident in the novel's conclusion, as Bárbara cedes to her desire for redemption.

By the novel's end, a significant change overcomes Doña Bárbara, forcing her to come to terms with her maternity and throwing the stability of polarized melodramatic characterization into question. As the tale draws to a close, Doña Bárbara, whose feminine aspect is now more pronounced than ever, gets rid of Balbino Paiba (the true author of Carmelito López's death) and travels to San Pedro to make reparations by turning in the feathers stolen by Paiba for Santos Luzardo to claim. She does so in hopes that, through this peace offering, Santos Luzardo will come to appreciate her. But, upon returning to El Miedo, Bárbara finds that all her ranch hands have abandoned her because she "no es la misma de antes" (Gallegos 462) ["is not the same as before" (my translation)]. On top of this, Bárbara discovers that Marisela, after a brief escape from Altamira in protest of Santos's indifference, has returned to the family ranch, this time as Santos's fiancée. The enraged Bárbara then grabs her revolver and sets out for Altamira with the express intention of killing her daughter. Yet, when Bárbara spies Marisela through the window, she sees her happiness, and memories of her romance with Asdrúbal envelop her in a strange new emotion. We read, "se quedó contemplando, largo rato, a la hija feliz, y aquella ansia de formas nuevas que tanto la había atormentado tomó cuerpo en una emoción maternal, desconocida para su corazón. 'Es tuyo. Que te haga feliz.'" (Gallegos 464) ["she remained a long time gazing at her happy daughter, and the longing for a new life which had so long tormented her took the form of a maternal sentiment, unknown to her heart. 'He is yours. May he make you happy.'" (Gallegos 434)]. Bárbara here experiences what the text offers as the dormant "noble sentiment" left by Asdrúbal so many years prior. In heeding that emotion, Bárbara bows out, abandoning the plains, with the suggestion that she may have even committed suicide, and leaving her ranch to her one and only heir, Marisela.

In this instance when Doña Bárbara recognizes Marisela as her daughter, she is shown to be immersed in a process of motherly purification, brought into line with the hegemonic moral order that *Doña Bárbara* upholds. Recognition is, in fact, a key component of melodrama, and, as Peter Brooks notes, melodrama "tends to become the dramaturgy of virtue misprized and eventually recognized. It is about the virtue made visible and acknowledged, the drama of recognition" (*Imagination* 27). In the context of Gallegos's novel, melodramatic recognition works doubly: making apparent Marisela's legitimacy as the rightful owner of El Miedo/La Barquereña, but also highlighting Bárbara's virtue in assuming her role as a mother.[13] Of course, Bárbara is still quite far from representing an idyllic picture of motherhood; simply deciding not to kill her daughter would not posit her as an exemplary matriarch. Yet she is vindicated in the sense that she seemingly sees the error of her ways, rectifying, if only slightly, her callous mode of being. In deciding not to kill Marisela, she gains a measure of sympathy from the reader, and, as such, motherhood offers Bárbara a means by which so many of her rotten deeds are mitigated as she exits the text.

In the novel's closing scenes, Bárbara returns to the Arauca River, and the ominous words "las cosas vuelven al lugar de donde salieron" (Gallegos 246) ["all things return whence they came" (Gallegos 430)], repeated by Doña Bárbara's spiritual contact, El Socio, seemingly could not ring more true. But, in Bárbara's retreat, Gallegos's novel recalls the initial state of purity stolen from Doña Bárbara that she can only now recoup. It was, after all, on the Orinoco where she seemingly lived the only happy moments of her life, a happiness that she may now attempt to rediscover. In this sense, the novel's finale paradoxically highlights the fact that Santos Luzardo's battle has been waged against a victim who should have received his sympathy and compassion, instead of his rebuke. As we shall see, this is a key difference between Gallegos's novel and Telemundo's recent *telenovela*, *Doña Bárbara* [2008].

That Doña Bárbara spares Marisela's life and retreats to a space of lost innocence manifests that the rules of melodramatic engagement are hardly presented as a black-and-white means of deciphering conflict in *Doña Bárbara*. Throughout the text, protagonist and antagonist assume varying degrees of melodramatic good and evil, all of which are tied up in the characters' conflicting relationships with their pasts. As Donald Shaw notes, Santos evolves from "the learned values of civilization back towards the instinctive *barbarie* of his forebears; Bárbara

---

13 Marisela's recognition will ultimately turn out to be an economic boon for her and for Santos Luzardo. As Juan Pablo Dabove notes "The novel does not suggest that Santos is, in fact, taking advantage of a situation whereby it was very easy for him to seduce the naïve girl and convince her that he was her knight in shining armor. Aside from Santos's sincerity, the real outcome of the romance is that Santos will legally become the owner of both Altamira and La Barquereña (the latter will disappear). The novel considers this a redemption" (283).

from her murderous hatred of the other sex, her witchcraft and avarice back towards the lost purity of her childhood" (31). These regressions are not, of course, complete, as such conclusive transformations would entirely reverse the melodramatic polarity of the text –Santos would end up the villain and Bárbara the hero. However, Santos's violent impulses and Bárbara's apparent return to a state of innocence demonstrate *Doña Bárbara*'s flexibility in conceiving melodramatic conflict. Santos Luzardo is presented as a hero who must embrace darkness in order to bring about a better tomorrow. And, while Doña Bárbara is presented predominately as a villainous character, her motives for vengeance are offered as a mitigating circumstance, and her ultimate maternal instincts show her to be a character that is not entirely unworthy of sympathy. Such variations in the basic polarized melodramatic conflict show a malleability of form at work in *Doña Bárbara*, problematizing the clear-cut universe of good and evil that melodrama is generally understood to represent.

The alterations of melodrama that occur in *Doña Bárbara* are finally reflected in the fact that, contrary to classical conceptions of melodramatic narration, the novel's finale does not offer a precise indication of the re-establishment of a clearly defined social order. As Peter Brooks notes, "melodrama starts from and expresses the anxiety brought by a frightening new world in which the traditional patterns of moral order no longer provide the necessary social glue. It plays out the force of that anxiety with the apparent triumph of villainy, and it dissipates it with the eventual victory of virtue" (*Imagination* 20). Accordingly, the virtue mentioned here by Brooks offers up a link to a previous form of social order that is threatened and desperately, melodramatically is in need of rescue. In this way, melodrama is often read as voicing nostalgia for a better, simpler time, a backward-looking desire for purity.

Given that in *Doña Bárbara* Santos Luzardo ostensibly restores the virtue of the Luzardos' reign to the Arauca Valley, Gallegos's novel may be perceived as typifying melodramatic axioms, which may not exactly sell the case for the progressive social itinerary that Santos Luzardo espouses. Without specifically mentioning melodramatic format, Alejo Carpentier notes this contradiction in Santos's rhetoric, critiquing the presentation of conservative social order achieved in *Doña Bárbara* by remarking that Santos Luzardo's modernization project provides little substance. Regarding the novel's closure, Carpentier questions:

> ¿Qué ha sucedido en realidad? ¿Se ha adelantado en algo? No. La antigua hacienda de los Luzardo ha vuelto a tener exactamente los mismos linderos que debió haber tenido siempre; vuelve a tener sus mismas dimensiones, vuelve el propietario a

> instalarse en su tienda, y todo el progreso que ha venido con Santos Luzardo, egresado de la Universidad Central de Caracas, es un rollo de alambre de púas. (26)
>
> [In reality, what has happened? Has there been any advancement? No. The Luzardos' hacienda again has the exact same borders that it once had, the owner returns to set up shop again, and the only progress that Santos Luzardo, graduate of the Universidad Central de Caracas, brought with him turns out to be a roll of barbed wire (my translation)].

Carpentier's comments highlight what may be read as a potentially problematic re-assertion of order, authorized by the melodramatic format of the text when the supposedly virtuous owner of Altamira regains power without regard for the changes that would allow for a more egalitarian advancement of the region on the whole. Though as Carpentier observes, a nostalgic sense of calm appears to be achieved in Santos's conquest in *Doña Bárbara*'s denouement, we may note that things are not quite the same as they had been in times past.

The conclusion of Gallegos's novel offers a glimpse of a complex transitional period in Venezuela's history concurrent to the composition of *Doña Bárbara*. As Fernando Coronil observes, under the Gómez regime, "the collusion between foreign oil companies and a regional caudillo brought together the most dynamic corporations of the capitalist world and the most characteristic form of rule in nineteenth-century Latin America" (83). *Doña Bárbara* embodies that dynamic relationship between customary forms of social governance and modern capitalism, offering an example of the amalgamation of multiple components of social existence represented in the text.[14] This combination of traditional governing authority with the demands of modern capitalism directly speaks to the allegorical dimensions of the text, and the commentaries of Nelson Osorio have illuminated the coexistence of civilization and barbarism in *Doña Bárbara*. Osorio notes that *Doña Bárbara*'s civilization/barbarism dichotomy, based as it is in writings of the Argentine intellectual Domingo Faustino Sarmiento, is not, in fact, posited in all-or-nothing terms. For Osorio, civilization and barbarism "deben ser entendidos aquí no como partes antagónicas de una antinomia irreductible sino como *tesis* y *antítesis* de una contradicción dialéctica. La síntesis, hegelianamente hablando, sería la superación de ambas, un mundo nuevo que habrá de

[14] To this end, Juan Pablo Dabove notes that *Doña Bárbara* presents Santos Luzardo as a commanding national intellectual capable of furthering "an economic system that is able to harmonize the homogenizing needs of modern capitalism with a respect for the uniqueness of the Venezuelan experience (one of the classic features of populism, at least as an ideal)" (271).

surgir de la conjugación de la *realidad* del Llano con los *ideales* de la civilización. La síntesis es, por consiguiente, una promesa, una esperanza" (74) ["must be understood, not as antagonistic parts of an irreducible opposition, but as *thesis* and *antithesis* in a dialectic contradiction. The synthesis, Hegelianly speaking, would be to surpass both factors: a new world that would come about from the conjugation of the *reality* of the llano with the *ideals* of civilization. This synthesis is, accordingly, a possibility, a hope" (my translation)]. This possibility for the simultaneity of competing modes of social order noted by Osorio is reflected throughout the text in the adaptations of superficially static conceptions of melodramatic characterization, but also in the final outcomes of the text.

The conclusion of *Doña Bárbara* showcases the amalgamation of civilization and barbarism, and of melodramatic virtue and guile, that defines the entirety of the novel, especially in Santos Luzardo's approval of knowingly-falsified information in the official verdict regarding the death of Melquíades, "*el Brujeador.*" Though Doña Bárbara is well aware of the fact that it was not Balbino Paiba who killed Melquíades, she suggests Paiba's guilt to her cowhands in order to get rid of a henchman who knows too much about her past dealings, knowing that they will seek him out to exact justice. After Doña Bárbara's ranch hands have wrongly avenged Melquíades's death, Bárbara attests to Paiba's guilt before Mujiquita and local justice Ño Pernalete, and, as far as they are concerned, the case is closed. When Santos Luzardo gets wind of this false testimony, his first instinct is to denounce Bárbara's version of the events, feeling that he and Pajarote (Melquíades's true assassin) were justified in killing "*el Brujeador*" because he was the first to draw arms. Pajarote, however, reasons to Santos that it is better to let sleeping dogs lie so as not to contradict Ño Pernalete, who is capable of taking revenge at a later time. Ultimately, Pajarote convinces Santos that, if this is the way that things have turned out, it must be God's way of punishing Paiba, who was guilty of a number of other crimes and even murders. When presented with such rationality, Santos can do no more than incredulously smile, apparently recognizing the futility of protesting the false tale that frees him of any culpability in Melquíades's death.

Santos Luzardo's silence here speaks volumes as to the final vision of justice represented in the text. Doña Bárbara's denunciation of Balbino Paiba occurs before the authority of the law, the legitimate state-sanctioned body whose justice Santos Luzardo has trumpeted throughout the majority of the novel. But, that accusation is a lie, one that Santos ultimately decides not to contest in spite of his knowledge of the truth. Santos thus allows manipulations of the legal system to go un-rectified, lending legitimacy to mob rule as a mode of exacting justice and showing that achieving state-sanctioned legality is less important than the "law of the *llano*." Evil barbarism becomes a way of enacting the goodness of civilization, the ultimate conjugation of melodramatic polarities in the novel. Santos's tacit approval of barbaric methods of justice are, after all, what make the melodramatic happy ending of the novel possible, evidenced in the relationship between Santos and Marisela.

The joining of these two characters at once serves to bring about a happy ending while simultaneously suggesting that the unharmonious social backdrop against which Santos's battle has played out will only be replicated in the future. So much may be observed in the fact that, in Santos and Marisela's union, each brings baggage indicative of a circular pattern of violence that is both interfamilial and sexual. Marisela is the illegitimate daughter of Doña Bárbara, and, like her mother, she was born, not of a loving relationship, but of what her mother perceived as a violent sexual imposition. Though Bárbara has disappeared from the plains, her legacy of sexual violence and the illegitimacy of her social control live on. Moreover, José Luzardo, Santos's father, murdered Sebastián Barquero, Marisela's grandfather. In this way, José Luzardo's violence, which Santos's mother attempted to flee by taking him to Caracas, is irrevocably woven into Santos's marriage.

Yet, beyond these problematic histories that will be united in Santos and Marisela's union, the reader observes irregularities in their union, which "is riddled with inequalities (class, race, and culture)" (Dabove 283). These problems are not highlighted in the novel because, as Doris Sommer notes, Santos and Marisela's marriage would serve a quite practical function in this national romance as Santos's "offer of legal and loving status to the disenfranchised mestiza shows Gallegos trying to patch up the problem of establishing a legitimate, centralized nation on a history of usurpation and civil war" (289). Perhaps paradoxically, *Doña Bárbara* presents this matrimony, with all of the social and historical baggage that it might imply, as the means to a happy ending. And, in spite of the celebratory tone of the final passages of the text, the complications embodied in Santos and Marisela's union cannot help but allude to a problematization of the represented family structure, a basic building block of Latin American melodrama.

As Carlos Monsiváis once noted, the centrality of family in Latin American society lends a particular staying power to melodrama, insistent as it is on the figure of family as a narrative constant.[15] Indeed, the family resides at the core

---

[15] Monsiváis comments that, "Yo creo que el melodrama hoy aún sigue tan fuerte –sobre todo en América Latina– porque la familia sigue siendo fundamental en la vida

of domestic melodrama in general, allowing for familial conflicts to embody greater social and political forces in society at large. As Nina Gerassi-Navarro observes regarding the family in Spanish American melodramas of the nineteenth century, "family happiness was a consequence not only of healthy feelings, but, more importantly, of specific political ideals that built and sustained the prosperity of a blissful home. Hence the private world of the home became deeply entwined with the public world of politics" (152). Similarly, in *Doña Bárbara*, domestic happiness is only possible when the socio-political conflict of the novel is resolved, and vice versa.

At the same time, broken families or the presence of illegitimate children –both formative factors in the tale told in *Doña Bárbara*– symbolically reach beyond the realm of the represented home, metaphorically offering commentary on the state of social affairs and a means of comprehending contemporary social structure. In *De los medios a las mediaciones: Comunicación, cultura y hegemonía* (1987), Jesús Martín-Barbero comments on this particularity of family in melodrama, suggesting that the familial complications of Latin American melodrama provide a matrix mirroring Latin American society inasmuch as "el enorme y tupido enredo de las relaciones familiares, que como infraestructura hacen la trama del melodrama, sería la forma en que desde lo popular se comprende y se dice la opacidad y complejidad que revisten las nuevas relaciones sociales." (*Comunicación* 131) ["the enormously complicated web of family relations which provides the basis for the plot of melodrama would be the perspective from which popular culture understands and speaks about the opacity and complexity of the new social relations of mass society" (*Communication* 119)]. As Martín-Barbero indicates, the family unit offers a means by which melodrama represents social issues to a public, frequently, if not predominately constituted by "popular" audiences. The centrality of family in melodrama and the social messages that that family is capable of encoding has great resonance in *Doña Bárbara*, ultimately offering a happy ending where these familiar/social conflicts are neatly resolved. This capacity for social commentary in Gallegos's novel is especially important since the text frequently has been adapted for film and *telenovela* productions geared toward popular audiences.

---

latinoamericana, como ya no lo es en Europa y como ya no lo es en Estados Unidos" (*Entrevista* n. pag) ["I believe that melodrama today is still strong –above all in Latin America– because the family continues to be essential to Latin American life, which it no longer is in Europe or in the United States" (my translation)].

Probably the best-known adaptation of *Doña Bárbara* is a film by the same name produced in 1943, for which Gallegos himself served as a screenwriter alongside the Mexican director Fernando de Fuentes. María Félix's performance of the title role, embodying the beauty and resilience of her hostile persona, for many, has come to epitomize the archetypical character. Gallegos's novel, however, has been adapted in several other occasions, most recently as a *telenovela* for the United States-based Telemundo network in 2008, set in a contemporary, but not specifically named, Latin American country.[16] And, beyond referencing the tremendous staying power that Gallegos's novel embodies, this recent *telenovela* also offers the opportunity to reflect on the continuity of melodrama between text and television adaptation. Indeed, the melodramatic aesthetics employed in each of the works share commonalities that disrupt the high/low dichotomy and question the validity of such categorization, even when the televised version of the text departs from the original's plot.

As is wont to occur in such adaptations, the novel's plot undergoes many changes, adding characters and subplots to fill the multiple hours of televised transmission. In this case, one of the major changes includes the presentation of Santos Luzardo's aunt, Cecilia, who also accompanies Santos at Altamira and plays a significant role in domesticating the plains. Another crucial plot change is observed when Santos is romantically torn between another new character, his metropolitan fiancée Luisana, and Doña Bárbara herself.[17] Indeed, the *telenovela*'s plot is predominantly dedicated to Santos and Bárbara's affair, as Santos feels a great deal of sympathy for Bárbara after learning of the brutal violence she suffered in her youth: exactly that compassion that was glaringly absent from the conflict in Gallegos's novel. This romance provides for much intrigue as Santos and Balbino Paiba battle for Bárbara's love and also as Marisela and Bárbara –who, in a departure from the novel, meet early

16 Almost all of the *telenovela* may be accessed on Telemundo's website (http://msnlatino.telemundo.com/novelas/Dona_Barbara). As mentioned in the introduction to this study, with regard to Telemundo's *Victoria*, the adaptation of *Doña Bárbara* is also indicative of the postcolonial heterogeneity of the *telenovela*. This is evident in that the leading roles of Santos Luzardo and Doña Bárbara are played, respectively, by the Peruvian Christian Meier and the Mexican actress Edith González.

17 In this way, the *telenovela* is more true to Gallegos's first version of *Doña Bárbara* (titled *La coronela*), in which, as Carlos Alonso notes, Santos returns to Altamira with his wife, Luisana, before confronting Doña Bárbara (initially named Guadalupe in *La coronela*) (*Regional Novel* note 27, 188).

on in the story and have frequent, conflictive contact– struggle for Santos's attentions. It appears for much of the story as if Bárbara, constantly employing her witchcraft to seduce Santos, will win out, especially when she becomes pregnant with Santos's child, which she eventually miscarries. But, because she systematically and brutally kills all of those men who raped her in her youth, Santos becomes convinced of the impossibility of a relationship with Bárbara, opting instead for Marisela.

However, obstacles abound on this front as well when Marisela, in initially feeling rejected by Santos, abandons Altamira. When she eventually returns, Marisela finds solace with another man, Gonzalo Zuluaga, one of Santos's old friends from his studies at university. Marisela's new romance ultimately fades when Santos re-enters the picture, but Gonzalo's addition to the story offers a new political dimension to the tale. A revolutionary whose movement is initially supported by Santos, Gonzalo eventually leads an insurrection against the government, only to become a corrupt politician involved in drug trafficking. Gonzalo's crooked dealings lead him to collaborate with those pirates guilty of Bárbara's rape, particularly one named El Sapo, bringing the *telenovela* to a crescendo when Santos and Bárbara are trapped by El Sapo. They ultimately turn the tables on the villain, vanquishing him and driving evil out of the *llano*.

In the conclusion of the *telenovela*, Bárbara, realizing the impossibility of her love for Santos, attempts to commit suicide in a marsh near La Chusmita, only to have Marisela save her. Marisela's act brings about a complete reconciliation of mother and daughter, and they share a tender exchange when Bárbara bathes Marisela, cleansing her of the swamp's mire and symbolically of their past feuds. Doña Bárbara then chooses to disappear down the Arauca, assuming the pseudonym "la doña de los ríos" and periodically helping out at a mission that gives her shelter in her initial escape from El Miedo. It is at that mission that Bárbara later dies peacefully of an illness accrued in her travels along the rivers. Santos and Marisela remain at Altamira and have three children, living out their happily-ever-after. In this way, both the novel and the *telenovela* coincide in offering a happy ending in which Santos and Marisela wed and Doña Bárbara is vanquished. But, to draw a more direct parallel between these two works that at times seem to be linked only in name, we may look to the melodramatic techniques that orient Gallegos's novel and its adaptation.

Beyond the use of any particular plot device or recurring motif, perhaps the most conclusive indicator of the shared melodramatics of the novel and the *telenovela* is found in the way each works to heighten the emotional environment of the tale. In each skirmish, in every romantic intrigue, in the sequential cliff-hanger endings of the novel's chapters and the *telenovela*'s episodes, the reader/spectator is drawn in emotionally and made to sympathize or become enraged. This emotional intrigue is what keeps us coming back for more, particularly in the case of the *telenovela Doña Bárbara*, whose serialized format –consisting of upwards of 150 episodes– hooks the spectator, placing him/her in contact with a tale that consistently fulfills narrative desire and offers the opportunity for pleasurable reception.

Jesús Martín-Barbero, however, notes that the Latin American *telenovela* offers something more than just a pleasurable process of reception, observing the social vindication that televised melodrama provides. As discussed in the introduction to this study, Martín-Barbero comments that the commercialization of the private sphere makes narration a means of reconciling personal and collective modes of perception. For Martín-Barbero, outmoded forms of storytelling embodied in melodrama, and the social recognition that it demands are that which:

> Le da sentido hoy al melodrama en América Latina – desde la permanencia de la canción romántica al surgimiento de la telenovela –, la que le permite media entre el tiempo de *la vida*, esto es, de una socialidad negada, económicamente desvalorizada y políticamente desconocida, pero culturalmente viva, y el tiempo *del relato* que la afirma y hace posible a las clases populares reconocerse en ella. Y desde ella, melodramatizandolo todo, vengarse a su manera, secretamente, de la abstracción impuesta por la mercantilización de la vida, de la exclusión política y la desposesión cultural. (*Comunicación* 245)

> [Gives meaning to the melodrama in Latin America –from the lasting impact of the romantic ballad to development of the *telenovela*. It is this anachronism that mediates between the time of the individual life– considered to be of no social significance, economically worthless, and a political unknown, but nevertheless culturally alive –and the time of the narrative which affirms this life and makes it possible for the popular classes to recognize themselves in this anachronism. This anachronistic perception of life, transforming into melodrama everything that it encounters, eventually gets revenge –in its own secret way– against the abstractions imposed on them by the commercialization of their lives, their political exclusion and their cultural dispossession. (*Communication* 226-27)]

For Martín-Barbero, then, televised melodrama offers a partial escape from the hegemonic drives of dominant contemporary culture. Melodrama encodes in its very narrative format a legitimation of a mode of conceiving social interaction, a recognition and affirmation of popular, emergent social sectors.

This recognition through melodrama is not, however, entirely without issue. As Horacio Legrás notes in *Literature and Subjection: The Economy of Writing and Marginality in Latin America* (2008), recognition must always be granted from without. Legrás observes:

> Although recognition seems to advocate the cause of the underdog, which to some extent it does, we must confront the fact that recognition is above all a strategy through which power reasserts itself in the minute details of the everyday. The recognition granted by the state (or by literature as a state apparatus) is never a gift, but a loan that is finally collected in kind. In this economy of reflexion [sic] and return, the state provides recognition in exchange for recognition. The recognizing activity of the state depends on the fact that the subjects receiving its favor must first recognize the state as the recognizing instance. In this structure, one cannot win legitimacy without consenting to sanction from above. Every recognition granted by the state further empowers the state's own imaginary constitution. In the end, the state's recognizing activity is an exercise in self-recognition. This structure does not pose major problems when the cultural makeup of the nation is relatively uniform, but it is destined to progress via waves of violence and suppression in those regions, like Latin America, where the heterogeneity of society cannot be easily reconciled with the centripetal impulses of nation-state formation. In such heterogeneous contexts, the false morality of recognition becomes even more blatant. (22)

Legrás's commentary has important implications for the very conception of melodrama in which recognition plays a fundamental role. Indeed, while, as Martín-Barbero observes, melodrama helps to carve out a spot for otherwise marginalized social discourses, we may note from Legrás's comments that it is only able to do so inasmuch as it is granted authorization by some governing body. In the case of the *telenovela* as a recognition of popular sectors' collective means of social participation, we must note that it is the television corporation that transmits and, perhaps more importantly, produces that which the public is able to recognize as their legitimizing discourse. This fact would seemingly return us to Walter Benjamin's observations in "The Work of Art in the Age of Mechanical Reproduction" regarding modern film's introduction of art to the masses and, subsequently, its revolutionary potential to make its public critical readers. Yet, as Benjamin notes, the means to produce film rested in the hands of the film industry, generally not of radical tendencies, and thus not likely to produce works of directly revolutionary content (231).

A possible escape from this paradigm is presented by Carlos Monsiváis in his consideration of the revolutionary potential of talk and reality shows. Monsiváis notes that these formats, while still using melodrama, begin to take over space once dominated by classic film and *telenovela*, giving people their fifteen minutes of fame. Monsiváis suggests that "al cabo del larguísimo periódico histórico en que el melodrama es la pedagogía sentimental y la guía para el manejo de las situaciones familiares y las crisis de la pareja, el público, o mejor, las infinitas manifestaciones individuales del público toman la palabra" (*No te vayas* 122) ["following an extended historical period in which melodrama was the chief sentimental pedagogy and the guide for handling family situations and couples' crises, the public, or better, the infinite individual manifestations of the public have the word" (my translation)]. As Monsiváis argues, the public re-appropriation of melodrama in given media formats would, in fact, work to weaken the social abyss separating sectors of production and consumption commented upon by Benjamin and Legrás since spectators-turned-participants would begin more directly to influence the production of the works in which it recognizes itself.

Nevertheless, we must note that, in the case of the *telenovela*, melodramatics straddle a difficult line, at once permitting the public's recognition of its own discourse, while at the same time only working with as much leeway as a larger governing body may permit. This fact then calls into question the real social impact possible in melodrama, be it televised or written. Does the representation of popular heroes provide for cohesion among members of oppressed social sectors, or is it just a false consciousness dispersed from above? Is the morality play of melodrama truly indicative of beliefs held by broad swaths of underrepresented factions of society, or is that ethos a packaged plan imposed by the governing elite? The answer to either of these questions would certainly vary by respondent. However, the fact that this debate exists draws our attention to the problematic of melodrama's reception among its public, whether in the written text or its mass reproduction.

But, the complications of melodramatic narrative in *Doña Bárbara* may be seen on an even more basic, structural level. Indeed, the fact that the story told in Gallegos's novel is ultimately about a fusion of old and new socio-economic practices problematizes the melodramatic structuring of conflict from its inception. As the text offers a hybrid model of civilized, capitalist modernization and barbarous, "traditional" agrarian order, it belies the stark good/evil binaries of the novel. As such, there is no definite triumph of Santos Luzardo's civilized goodness, nor a celebrated defeat of a purely evil, barbarous other. Modern capitalist practices and the established Venezuelan agrarian economy meet in a violent confrontation from which neither emerges unscathed, but where something new and yet without form is in configuration.

The staging of this fluidity is doubtlessly one of the greatest strengths of the text. Yet, the mutability of social structures in *Doña Bárbara* is also that which highlights the complexity of melodramatic framing in what has often been considered an overtly black-and-white conflict. As a classic example of Latin American melodrama, *Doña Bárbara* probes the limits of melodramatic narration and problematizes the static formulation of character, even when the reader is at all times aware of who is supposed to be good, who bad. Consequently, the dynamic conflict between good and evil shows that the supposed polarities of modernity and backwardness, of civilization and barbarism, are in constant flux. Melodramatic aesthetics in *Doña Bárbara* offer the possibility to consider the density of the social circumstances of the text, re-locating the impulses of good and evil as need be, a gesture radicalized in the text examined in the following chapter.

Suffering and Retribution: The Politicized Theatrics of *El tungsteno*

Martín Chambi's photograph *Víctor Mendívil y el gigante de Paruro* (1925) presents the spectator with an image that is at once unequivocal and paradoxical.[1] On the one hand, the social abyss that separates the two subjects of the photograph is clear: the young man whose suit and tie denote elegance and elevated social status is visibly disassociated from the anonymous giant whose traditional garments highlight his affiliation with the indigenous social sector. Yet, at the same time, the photo destabilizes the very social hierarchy codified in each subject's clothing. Beyond documenting the giant's physical dominance, the paternal gesture of the indigenous figure, placing his arm around the shoulder of the young dandy, suggests the protection offered by, and respect due to a venerated elder. The subordinate position of the young man is underscored by the perplexed gaze through which he observes the giant, an enigmatic stare that seemingly oscillates among various emotions: fear, respect, discomfort, and confusion. Ultimately, the ambiguity of the young man's contemplation cannot but suggest awe before the indigenous subject who, within the context of the photo, symbolically represents a threat to the hierarchy maintained in the social stratum of *señores* and *indios*.[2]

The expression of awe, the representation of social dichotomy, and the tension encoded in Chambi's photograph also constitute fundamental aspects of Peruvian literary *indigenismo* throughout the early twentieth century. While maintaining varying positive and negative perspectives toward the indigenous population, authors like Luis Valcárcel, Ventura García Calderón, José Carlos

---

1 I thank Professor Ricardo Viera, director and curator of the Lehigh University Art Galleries, for having facilitated my use of this image.

2 Chambi's photograph consciously plays upon the concepts of awe and social position, as Víctor Mendívil was, as noted by Esperanza López Prada and Amanda Hopkinson (see bibliography), the photographer's assistant. The social status represented by Mendívil and his perplexed gaze in this staged photo may be read, then, as artistic constructions of awe, as opposed to photographic documentation of an authentic reaction. This fact would establish a parallel between this work by Chambi and that of César Vallejo analyzed in this chapter with regards to each artist's perception of the possibilities of indigenous dominance.

Martín Chambi's *Víctor Mendívil y El Gigante de Paruro*, 1925.
(Reproduced with permission by Lehigh University Art Galleries)

Mariátegui, and Enrique López Albújar told tales of the glories of the *indio*, both past and present, and sometimes criticized his supposed vicious barbarism and superstition. For these authors and for many others, the distance that separated Mestizo and indigenous cultures constituted at once a social obstacle and a possibility to imagine and write about the national *other*. The case of César Vallejo (1892-1938) as an *indigenista* author is no exception to this rule. Of note, however, is the fact that Vallejo did have some direct contact with the realities of rural life and the agricultural economy that would serve to foment the social agenda of his narrative and theatrical works. As Jean Franco notes in *César Vallejo: The Dialectics of Poetry and Silence* (1976), Vallejo's experience as a functionary in the mines of Tambores and Quiruvilca, and later on the sugar plantation "Roma" in the Chicama Valley, exposed the author to the injustices suffered by Peruvian peasant workers (4-6). Vallejo would utilize these labor experiences as the basis for his novel *El tungsteno* (1931), which presents a confluence of *indigenista* preoccupations with the itinerary of revolutionary socialist literature.

El tungsteno may be classified under the somewhat nebulous, ample category of the "social novel," given the socialist realist aesthetic that governs the narration.[3] Divided into three somewhat uneven sections, Vallejo's novel tells a story of international industrialist exploitation in the Peruvian Andes. In order to communicate the socio-political message of the novel, Vallejo narrates a series of injustices including rape, forced labor, and murder. These wrongs are meant to illustrate the moral and physical degradation of two rural communities, Quivilca and Colca (represented as municipalities of the department of Cuzco), at the hands of a United States-based corporation called the Mining Society. As the reader comes to appreciate through the representation of moral corruption and the excessive use of violence in the text, *El tungsteno* relies upon a theatrical, polarized formulation of good and evil to define the limits of

---

[3] There is a certain anachronism here in reference to the socialist realist aesthetic of Vallejo's novel since the official precepts of this aesthetic imperative were not proposed until 1934 in the Congress of Soviet Writers. However, Vallejo's novel does coincide with the project of socialist realism as described by Terry Eagleton in *Marxism and Literary Criticism* (1976) when he writes that "the doctrine taught that it was the writer's duty 'to provide a truthful, historico-concrete portrayal of reality in its revolutionary development', taking into account 'the problem of ideological transformation and the education of the workers in the spirit of socialism'" (36).

social conflict in the novel, and to elicit sympathy for those made to suffer such extreme injustices.

To be sure, a melodramatic "theatrical substratum" (Brooks, *Imagination* xiii) is present in the narration of *El tungsteno*, as it strives to manifest the positive and negative attributes inscribed in the protagonists and antagonists of the ethical-political conflict of the text. The lexical exaggeration present in the narrative of the novel and the emotional gesticulation of its characters make it possible for each action narrated in the text to achieve an emphatic, definitive effect.[4] Most notably, the evildoers demonstrate their position through their boisterous imperialist rhetoric and through their visceral violent actions. Through this hyperbolic lexicon, *El tungsteno* presents conflicts in which characters' moral qualities, along with their polarized position in the novel's social conflict, are unequivocally demonstrated. The evil characters act as shameless profiteers while the meek, good characters are virtually helpless in the face of the wrongdoers' actions. Such positioning of the characters produces a recognition of virtue when it is attacked by evildoers, thus organizing an economy of suffering and retribution. Similar to what Linda Williams has observed in "race melodramas" in the United States, the oppressed sector's suffering becomes, paradoxically, a source of strength (43).[5] As the weak are made to anguish in *El tungsteno*, a bond of suffering is forged amongst them and also with the novel's audience, which sympathizes with the characters' tribulations. In this way, the persecution of the "good" characters and the abuses of power by the "bad" characters are narrated as emotional conflicts, illustrating a class dialectic that is easily legible to the reader.

But, in the exchange between emotion and social critique in *El tungsteno*, we may come to perceive a confusion of individual and collective concerns. The confluence of personal and communal grievances problematically subsumes the individual complaints of the novel's characters –along with the *indigenista* agenda of the text– into the project of the "proletarian novel." Thus, instead of expounding upon the multidimensional causality of social discord, the emotional excesses of melodramatic narration problematize any

---

4 Given this highly demonstrative narrative format, it may come as little surprise that Vallejo adapted portions of his novel for a theatrical piece entitled *Colacho hermanos o Presidentes de América*.

5 Williams comments, "American racial melodrama deploys the paradoxical location of strength in weakness –the process by which suffering subjects take what Nietzsche calls *ressentiment*, a moralizing revenge upon the powerful achieved through a triumph of the weak in their very weakness" (43).

singular political coherence that Vallejo's novel would attempt to demonstrate. This is evident given that a direct correlation is not achieved between the emotional motivations of the characters and the political project of the text, in turn obscuring what ought to be the happy ending of the novel. As such, what Vallejo's novel ultimately shows us is the central lack of coherence around which the political project of the novel revolves in its attempt to consolidate a multitude of actors and their individual concerns in a single ideological block.

It is likely this rather coercive means of communicating political directives that has produced the less-than-flattering critical reception of *El tungsteno*, and critics have often noted that Vallejo's novel –along with his theatrical works– is generally inferior to his poetic compositions, probably due in no small measure to the hyperbole and schematic nature of the former.[6] Nevertheless, it is worth noting that the perhaps simplistic representation of conflict found in *El tungsteno* coincides with that which Vallejo espoused to be the aesthetic of revolutionary art. In the posthumously published *El arte y la revolución* (written in 1931 but not published until 1973), Vallejo wrote that "la forma del arte revolucionario debe ser lo más directa, simple y descarnada posible. Un realismo implacable. Elaboración mínima. La emoción hel camino más corto y a quema-ropa. Arte de primer plano. Fobia a la media tinta y al matiz. Todo crudo, –ángulos y no curvas, pero pesado, bárbaro, brutal, como en las trincheras" (*Ensayos* 452) ["the revolutionary art form must be as direct, simple, and straightforward as possible. An implacable realism. Minimal elaboration. Emotion must be achieved by the shortest route, at point blank range. Art on a basic level. An absolute fear of ambiguity or hues of meaning. Everything must be raw, –angles and not curves. Heavy, barbarous, and brutal, as in the trenches" (my translation)]. This revolutionary aesthetic (which overlaps with what Vallejo defined as the "Bolshevik art" that he observed in his visits to the Soviet Union) would differ from what the author understands as "socialist art." In the latter case, the artist ought to possess "una sensibilidad orgánica y tácitamente socialista" (*Ensayos* 381) ["an organic and tacitly socialist sensibility" (my translation)] that intrinsically weaves socialist ideology into the art form itself. For Vallejo, revolutionary and Bolshevik art

---

6 On this point see, for example, Franco (158), Gutiérrez Girardot (143), or Podestá (17). Michelle Clayton also has recently argued in *Poetry in Pieces: César Vallejo and Lyric Modernity* (2011) that Vallejo's poetic works encode a dynamic embodiment of political and critical thought. Those politics are conveyed in a more direct lexicon in *El tungsteno*.

forms, on the other hand, are above all propagandist, and the revolution that they promote is located on a semantic level as opposed to a structural one.[7] *El tungsteno* manifestly obeys this aesthetic proposal, as it is impossible to ignore the overt brutality of its narrative, a figurative inhumanity that is meant to demonstrate a clear ethical dichotomy in the text.

Regarding the moral polarity of *El tungsteno* and the manner in which that schism supports an allegoric representation of national history, Juan Carlos Galdo notes:

> En la novela de Vallejo los personajes vinculados a la clase dominante son en su mayoría tipos planos y estereotipados que se limitan a actuar como inescrupulosos y envilecidos agentes del mal… Desde esta lógica que distingue sin matices entre el bien y el mal, claramente le corresponde a la clase dirigente el ejercicio de una conducta réproba, acorde en ello a las prácticas de explotación que, en efecto, implementaban en la realidad durante este periodo. (181)

> [In Vallejo's novel, the characters who are linked to the dominant class are by and large flat and stereotypical, limited to acting as unscrupulous and vile agents of evil… Following this logic that starkly distinguishes between good and evil, clearly the dominant class is charged with the exercise of malicious conduct, corresponding to the practices of exploitation that, in effect, they implemented in the reality of this period. (my translation)]

Following Galdo's line of analysis, it is interesting to note the parallel that may be drawn between the moral classifications that Vallejo offers in *El tungsteno* and the basic components of melodramatic characterization proposed by Peter Brooks. Brooks comments:

> Melodramatic good and evil are highly personalized: they are assigned to, they inhabit persons who indeed have no psychological complexity but who are strongly characterized. Most notably, evil is villainy; it is a swarthy, cape-enveloped man

[7] Similar to the revolutionary art that he advocated, Vallejo wrote "el arte bolchevique es principalmente de propaganda y agitación. Se propone, *de preferencia*, atizar y adoctrinar la rebelión y la organización de las masas para la protesta, para las reivindicaciones y para la lucha de clases. Sus fines son didácticos, en el sentido específico del vocablo. Es un arte de proclamas, de mensajes, de arengas, de quejas, cóleras y admoniciones" (*Ensayos* 380) ["Bolshevik art is principally for propaganda and agitation. It overtly proposes to stir and indoctrinate the rebellion and the organization of the masses in protest for their vindication and for class struggle. Its aims are didactic in the most specific sense of the word. It is an art of proclamations, of messages, of discourses, of complaints, of rage and of reprimands" (my translation)].

> with a deep voice. Good and evil can be named as persons are named –and melodramas tend in fact to move toward a clear nomination of the moral universe. (*Imagination* 16-17)

The melodramatic elements of characterization described by Brooks provide for the means of interpreting the schematics and hyperbolic distinctions between good and evil in *El tungsteno*, the ultimate indicators of the class conflict in Vallejo's provocative tale. *El tungsteno* constantly employs an emphatic lexicon in order to unequivocally demonstrate the boundaries of the moralized social milieu that it represents, painting characters as either heroes or villains with little (if any) gray area between the two. However, the employment of melodramatic aesthetics within the confines of a story that is quite evidently of revolutionary tendencies cannot but suggest a paradox, given that melodrama is frequently understood to be a conservative narrative form.

As discussed in the introduction to this study, melodrama rises from the ashes of the French Revolution when the incipient state sought to establish a clear moral base to its order. This was necessary, given that the Revolution had destroyed the divine link to the crown, and melodrama served in that void as a statist mode of disseminating models of ethical comport in the face of social chaos.[8] Subsequently, melodrama has often been characterized as attempting to protect and promote the status quo, which may share some points of contact with Gallegos's *Doña Bárbara* analyzed in the previous chapter, but would seemingly have little to do with the revolutionary discourse of *El tungsteno*. Yet, through the employment of melodrama in a radical political context, Vallejo's novel offers the possibility to appreciate another facet of melodramatic aesthetics: a progressive capacity contained within an outwardly-conservative narrative tendency. *El tungsteno* presents us with a narrative that, while employing an aesthetic mode that is generally viewed as conformist, adapts that format in order to question conservative politics contemporary to the novel's production. This use of melodrama, then, would serve to align *El tungsteno* with other Latin American authors of the "social novel" –like Jorge Icaza in *Huasipungo* (1934) or Jorge Amado in *Seara Vermelha* (1946), for instance– who utilized melodramatic aesthetics to give moral authority to radical politics.

Literary criticism, however, has not always been so quick to recognize the revolutionary capacity that melodrama or the social novel attempted to voice. As Ángel Rama noted in *Transculturación narrativa en América Latina* (1984),

---

8 On this point, see Brooks (*Imagination* 14-15), and Gledhill (*Investigation* 14-16).

by recurring to well-established literary techniques that play upon the reader's emotions, while at the same time failing to radicalize the novelistic format itself, the social novel presents a contradiction between its progressive politics and its conventional mode of expression. Rama observed:

> La novela social latinoamericana de los treinta... no discutió si estaba operando con una de las formas predilectas de la cultura occidental burguesa, limitándose a violentarla para que aceptara una ideología que respondía a las orientaciones de un pensamiento de izquierda (en el cual se mezclaba liberalismo, progresismo, tímidos escarceos marxistas) sin modificar demasiado notoriamente sus formas, apenas si simplificándolas en un régimen más marcadamente denotativo y lógico-racional... En tal comportamiento es posible discernir una secreta conexión cultural, la continuidad de una determinada concepción de lo real y de las formas literarias para traducirla, que sólo acepta variaciones de grado y no de sustancia, apuntando así a las contradicciones que presentan los nuevos grupos sociales que, sin embargo, pertenecen a la misma pauta cultural. (240-241)

> [The Latin American social novel of the 1930s... did not question if it was operating with the preferred forms of occidental bourgeois culture, only forcing that format to accept an ideology that responded to the orientations of leftist thinking (mixing liberalism, progressivism, and timid Marxist digressions) without modifying its structures, if only simplifying them in a system that was much more denotative and rational... In such activity it is possible to discern a secret cultural connection, the continuity of a determined conception of "the real" and the literary forms to translate it, which only accepts variations in degree and not in substance, and thus points to the contradictions presented by new social groups that, nevertheless, pertain to the same cultural paradigm. (my translation)]

Rama's assessment of the social novel's failure to radicalize form along with content, while lucid, is not without its critics as we shall see later in this chapter. However, Rama's observation that the social novel's progressive rhetoric is operative primarily on a sematic level is well taken. And, through Rama's critique, we may come to appreciate that it is, in fact, the semantics of melodrama that are deployed in the social novel, which is repeatedly demonstrated in *El tungsteno*. In order to communicate the urgency of the social issues conveyed through the social text, socially committed works take up the emphatic rhetoric of melodrama in attempts to draw attention to societal ills and the means to go about correcting them. Similarly, Vallejo's novel, through melodramatic aesthetics, goes out of its way to represent the worst impulses of the capitalist villains of the tale, so as to justify a rebellion against those enemies. The depravation associated with capitalism is evident, perhaps more than in any other passage of the novel, in the depiction of the rape and death of Graciela, a young woman from the highlands.

Graciela is the concubine of José Marino, owner of the local bazaar that serves primarily to satisfy the needs of the Mining Society. Mr. Taik and Mr. Weiss head the Mining Society, a conglomeration based in the United States, whose interest in the Andean region lies in its efforts to extract the metal for which Vallejo's novel is named: tungsten, as it is explained in the text, is needed by the United States military to produce arms as it prepares for its entrance into World War I.[9] José Marino and his brother, Mateo, for their part, are local entrepreneurs, members of the vilified petit-bourgeoisie, who are obsessed with enriching themselves and keeping the foreign industrialists happy as they pillage the Peruvian countryside. An important aspect of the Marino brothers' work consists of forcibly recruiting new workers for the tungsten mines, and it is during a farewell party for José Marino before he travels from Quivilca to Colca to recruit new laborers that Graciela's rape and death occur.

All of those invited to the party are somehow related to the functioning and administration of the mining operation, and, when they have all become drunk, José Marino decides to bet away his rights to Graciela during his absence in a game of dice. The insulting manner in which Graciela's liberty is gambled away, however, is just the beginning of the degradation that she is made to suffer. After the Commissioner Baldazari wins the dice game and, in turn, Graciela, José commands that Graciela be brought to the bazaar where the mine's administrators are celebrating. José then obliges Graciela to drink strong, homemade liquor so that Baldazari may enjoy his winnings. Graciela is rendered unconscious by José's alcoholic concoction, at which point her rape occurs:

> Al venir la noche, cerraron herméticamente la puerta y el bazar quedó sumido en tinieblas. Todos los contertulios –menos Benites, que se había quedado dormido– conocieron entonces, uno por uno, el cuerpo de Graciela. José Marino primero, y

9 Although I do not specifically develop this point, the historical conditions of the text provide a background to help understand Peru in the represented period, as well as Vallejo's militancy with regards to this situation. The Mining Society would apparently be a not-so-subtle reference to the Cerro de Pasco Mining Corporation that operated in Peru with United States' capital from 1901 to 1974 (Skidmore and Smith 191, 211). For a detailed analysis of this mining corporation, see Alberto Flores Galindo's *Los mineros de la Cerro de Pasco, 1900-1930: Un intento de caracterización social* (1974). With regards to the allegoric means by which Vallejo makes reference to foreign industrialism in Peru in *El tungsteno*, see the previously cited essay by Galdo.

Baldazari después, habían brindado la muchacha a sus amigos, generosamente. Los primeros en gustar de la presa fueron, naturalmente, los patrones míster Taik y Weiss. Los otros personajes entraron luego a escena, por orden de jerarquía social y económica: el comisario Baldazari, el cajero Machuca, el ingeniero Rubio y el profesor Zavala. José Marino, por modestia, galantería o refinamiento, fue el último. Lo hizo en medio de una batahola demoníaca. Marino pronunciaba en la oscuridad palabras, interjecciones y gritos de una abyección y un vicio espeluznantes. Un diálogo espantoso sostuvo, durante su acto horripilante, con sus cómplices. Un ronquido, sordo y ahogado, era la única seña de vida de Graciela. José Marino lanzó, al fin, una carcajada viscosa y macabra... (Vallejo, *Novelas* 250-251)

["As night came on, they closed the door tight and the store sank into darkness. And then, all those at the party –except Benites, who had fallen asleep– acquainted themselves, one after another, with Graciela's body. First José Marino and then Baldazari had generously offered the girl to their friends. The first to tear into this warm flesh were, of course, the bosses, Mr. Taik and Mr. Weiss. The other characters then got into the act, in the order of their social and economic rank: Commissioner Baldazari, the treasurer Machuca, the engineer Rubio, and the schoolmaster Zavala. Out of modesty, gallantry, or delicacy, José Marino went last. He accompanied himself with a demonic commotion. He spewed forth into the darkness cries and exclamations absolutely hair-raising in their filth and depravity. And throughout this harrowing performance he kept up an obscene chatter with his accomplices. A choked, muffled snore was the only sign of life from Graciela. José Marino finished with a hideous phlegmy laugh... (Vallejo, *Tungsten* 42)[10]]

Shortly after her rape, Graciela perishes. But this particular passage –which takes special care to note the surveyor Leónidas Benites's abstinence so that he may later be presented as a positive component of the uprising that would occur at the novel's end– and the final ramifications of this sexual violence succinctly illustrate the theatrical representation of evil in the text. A "demonic" violence, depicted in hyperbolic, patently melodramatic language, so as to highlight the grotesque nature of the scene, takes shape in the actions of José Marino and his companions, all associated with the Mining Society.[11] It is

---

10 All translations of *El tungsteno* come from Robert Mezey's edition of the novel.

11 On this point, Serge Salaün comments that Vallejo's novel reproduces "hasta la caricatura el lenguaje pintoresco (pero revelador de una comunicación pervertida, basada en la incultura, la codicia, los instintos primarios, la violencia social, etc.)" (81) ["to the point of caricature picturesque language (but revelatory of a perverse communication, based in a lack of culture, in avarice, in basic instincts, in social violence, etc.)" (my translation)]. The picturesque language to which Salaün refers is precisely the poetics of melodrama that attempts to demonstrate beyond a shadow of a doubt the morality, or lack thereof, in each of the novel's characters.

worth noting that this is not the only scene of the novel in which evil is defined by means of sexual violence or perversion. The Marino brothers share Mateo's concubine, Laura, who is pregnant with a child that she believes belongs to José. There also exists a sordid rumor about Judge Ortega, a powerful and corrupt functionary in Colca, inferring that perhaps he had practiced necrophilia with his deceased lover. There is, thus, a marked insistence to define the moral poles of the tale by means of sexual practices, which, in the case of the dominant class, are sanctioned and represented as perverse. Accordingly, the reader is invited to associate the infamy of sexual violence with the social violence exercised against Peru through imperialist exploitation. This jump from personal violence to a systematic national one, which would call for an allegorical reading of the novel, is not unfounded, given that the agents of aggression on both a micro and macro level are one and the same.

And, this portrayal of ubiquitous evil is furthered in the violence inflicted upon two indigenous conscripts, Isidoro Yépez and Braulio Conchucos, whose military "enlistment" is presented through melodramatic hyperbole similar to that found in the depiction of Graciela's rape. Braulio is torn unmercifully from his family and forced to march from the countryside to Colca alongside Isidoro, while suffering blows inflicted by military overseers. Because of the frenetic pace of the march, during which the conscripts are essentially dragged by mules, Isidoro soils himself, and Braulio drops dead from exhaustion and the beatings he suffers. The whole of this passage is recounted with a macabre overtone that takes advantage of every opportunity to demonstrate the depravity of the military guards and the abject suffering of the indigenous victims. This dichotomy is further driven home in the fact that Isidoro Yépez and Braulio Conchucos's forced enlistment is approved by the sub-prefect Luna and the authority granted to the rest of the Draft Commission, composed of local fat cats: Mayor Parga, Judge Ortega, Dr. Riaño, and a wealthy landholder named Iglesias. Although these men are Peruvian functionaries and citizens, their loyalties lie above all with the United States. This much is evident when, after slaughtering the protesters united against the mistreatment of the indigenous conscripts in the Colca's main plaza, the local authorities drunkenly celebrate, toasting until daybreak: "¡Vivan los Estados Unidos! ¡Viva la Mining Society! ¡Vivan los norteamericanos! ¡Viva Wilson! ¡Viva míster Taik! ¡Viva míster Weiss!... ¡Abajo los indios!" (Vallejo, *Novelas* 307) ["cheering the United States, the Mining Society, the North Americans, cheering Wilson, Mr. Taik, Mr. Weiss,... and damning the Indians in the same breath" (Vallejo, *Tungsten* 106)].

Tellingly, the "Indians" referenced here are presented throughout the novel as being a defenseless, innocent mass, incapable of standing up for themselves.[12] As mentioned above, it is this indigenous suffering that allows the reader to side with these vulnerable characters, so showcasing melodrama's particular knack of representing *indigenista* stories. Indeed, *indigenismo* truly is an ideal artistic location for melodramatic aesthetics because the moral void necessary for melodrama parallels the narrative void that distances the reader from the represented communities in the *indigenista* text. That is, just as melodrama, via an affective, ethical discourse, seeks to fill a moral abyss born of modernity, the gap separating the *indigenista* author and audience on one side and the real socio-historical conditions of the *indio* on the other must also be bridged by the moralizing and often exoticizing discourse of *indigenismo*. This fact serves as a constant in a great number of *indigenista* works and would serve to draw a direct, but perhaps not immediately evident, connection between Vallejo's novel and the works of Clorinda Matto de Turner. As Ana Peluffo demonstrates in *Lágrimas andinas: Sentimentalismo, género y virtud republicana en Clorinda Matto de Turner* (2005), the use of tear-jerking aesthetic devices serves as a central means of illustrating nationalist principles in the works of the Matto de Turner. Vallejo travels a similar aesthetic route, only to much more radical ends. The melodramatic sentimentality of *El tungsteno*, grounded in compassion, may induce the reader to tears but also to rage, so providing for identification with the novel's defiant indigenous hero, Servando Huanca.

Indeed, in order to underline the Mining Society's status as a purveyor of evil, there must be a counterweight of goodness in the text, thus establishing an equilibrium of narrative conflict. This balance is found in the heroic representation of Servando Huanca, the indigenous laborer and agitator, whose greatest action in the novel is to spearhead a failed attempt at insurrection in defense of Isidoro Yépez and Braulio Conchucos. Huanca, a blacksmith by trade, is quite clearly differentiated from those indigenous inhabitants of Colca and Quivilca because of his birth in the northern Peruvian mountains. Huanca is presented as "un tipo de indio puro: salientes pómulos, cobrizo, ojos pequeños, hundidos

---

12 On this point, it is relevant to note that the Sora Indians in the novel are infantilized, presented as being simplistic and childlike. Consequently, Roberto Paoli noted that Vallejo's *indigenista* text must be considered in light of the particular social and artistic context of the 1920s and 30s. At this point in time, when the first sociological analyses like that of Mariátegui were emerging, the *indio* was still highly romanticized and viewed through the nostalgic lens of a lost past that would hopefully be revived in the future (342).

y brillantes, pelo lacio y negro, talla mediana y una expresión recogida y casi taciturna" (Vallejo, *Novelas* 290) ["a type of pure Indian: high cheekbones, coppery skin, small eyes deep-set and glittering, straight black hair, medium height, and a reserved, almost taciturn demeanor" (Vallejo, *Tungsten* 87)]. The omniscient narrator's physical description of the indigenous leader makes use of a stereotypical ideal of a "pure Indian" for the effect of idealization, which, in Huanca's case, directly connects to the revolutionary politics he espouses:

> Servando Huanca se dolía, pues, y rabiaba, más por solidaridad o, si se quiere, por humanidad, contra los mandones – autoridades o patrones – que por causa propia y personal. También se dio cuenta de esta esencia solidaria y colectiva de su dolor contra la injusticia, por haberla descubierto también en los otros trabajadores cuando se trataba de abusos y delitos perpetrados en la persona de los demás. Por último, Servando Huanca llegó a unirse algunas veces con sus compañeros de trabajo y de dolor, en pequeñas asociaciones o sindicatos rudimentarios, y allí le dieron periódicos y folletos en que leyó tópicos y cuestiones relacionadas con esa injusticia que él conocía y con los modos que deben emplear los que la sufren, para luchar contra ella y hacerla desaparecer del mundo. Era un convencido de que había que protestar siempre y con energía contra la injusticia, dondequiera que ésta se manifieste. Desde entonces, su espíritu, reconcentrado y herido, rumiaba día y noche estas ideas y esta voluntad de rebelión. ¿Poseía ya Servando Huanca una consciencia clasista? ¿Se daba cuenta de ello? Su sola táctica de lucha se reducía [a] dos cosas muy simples: unión de los que sufren las injusticias sociales y acción práctica de masas. (Vallejo, *Novelas* 291)
>
> [Servando Huanca grieved, then, and raged against the bosses or civil authorities more out of solidarity or, if you will, humanity, than out of any personal motive. He also became aware of the social and comradely nature of his pain in the face of injustice, through having discovered it equally in the other workers when they talked among themselves of crimes and abuses committed against the rest. Finally, Servando Huanca came, at various times, to join with his companions of work and pain in little guilds or rudimentary unions, and there he was given newspapers and pamphlets in which he read of cases and controversies touching on that injustice he knew so well and on the methods that those who suffer it should use to struggle against it and to abolish it from the earth. He was convinced that it was essential to protest injustice constantly and fiercely, whatever form it took. From then on, day and night, his wounded and single-minded spirit mulled over these ideas, this determination to resist. Could Servando Huanca now be said to possess class consciousness? Was he aware of it? His only tactic in the struggle came down to two very simple things: a union of those who suffer social injustice, and practical mass action. (Vallejo, Novelas 87-88)]

Through Huanca's description, Vallejo is able to combine the *indigenista* aspect of *El tungsteno* with the aims of the proletarian novel, perfectly matching an idealized representation of nascent class-consciousness. We may draw, then, a parallel between *El tungsteno* and *Siete ensayos de interpretación de la realidad peruana* (1928), by José Carlos Mariátegui, which also posits social vindication for Peruvian indigenous sectors through socialist ideology, and in which Mariátegui commented extensively on Vallejo's poetry in *Los heraldos negros* (1919) and *Trilce* (1922).[13] Similarly, both Vallejo and Mariátegui combine concepts of race and politics in an attempt to suggest a revolutionary archetype capable of bringing about change in a world plagued by injustices. Notably, this archetype is formulated in an emphatic lexicon in *El tungsteno*, brimming with rhetorical questions and ethical contrasts that intrigue and provoke an emotional reaction from the reader. In this sense, Servando Huanca is subject to the same melodramatic emotionality as that which is utilized to present the negative characters in the novel.

The portrayal of these opposed social figureheads shows that melodramatic confrontation is, by and large, externalized in *El tungsteno*, as members of divergent social classes, nationalities, and ethnicities embody contrasting positions in which their moral perspectives are encoded. Yet, in Vallejo's novel, there is also one case in which the moral battle is waged within a single character. In fact, the melodramatically-tinged spiritual dilemma of Leónidas Benites may be read as the starting point for the entirety of *El tungsteno*, as Vallejo first published this passage of the novel as a short story entitled "Sabiduría" in José Carlos Mariátegui's *Vanguardista* journal *Amauta* in 1927. As such, Benites's

---

13 The confluence of socialist and *indigenista* projects was common in Peru throughout the 1920s and 30s, given the instigative nature of such positions. And, as Antonio Cornejo Polar comments in *Literatura y sociedad en el Perú: La novela indigenista* (1980), "En las décadas de los años 20 y 30 el indigenismo se inscribió decididamente dentro del vasto movimiento anti-oligárquico que por entonces tuvo variadas manifestaciones. Ciertamente, en sus mejores realizaciones, trascendió con soltura este nivel, hasta confundirse con los requerimientos de un proyecto revolucionario de signo socialista, pero si el marco de referencia es el movimiento en su conjunto, hay que reconocer que su horizonte genérico fue el de la lucha contra la oligarquía, en especial contra su sector más primitivo, formado por los grandes terratenientes serranos." (27) [In the 1920s and 30s, *indigenismo* was decidedly inscribed within the vast anti-oligarchic movement that had various incarnations at that time. At its best, *indigenismo* certainly transcended this level, combining with the requirements of the revolutionary socialist projects. But, if our frame of reference is *indigenismo* as a whole, one must recognize that its generic horizon was the battle against the oligarchy, especially against its most primitive sector, made up of the large landholders of the sierra (my translation)].

ethical conflict, accented by invocations of religious iconography, serves as an important narrative base for the moralizing tone and the outsized narrative stylings of the novel.

Benites's melodramatized delirium occurs when, in spite of his meticulous hygienic practices, the surveyor becomes ill. In fevered hallucinations, Benites sees visions of the Sacred Heart of Jesus juxtaposed against allusions to his ethically questionable tasks as a surveyor for the Mining Society, and in his sometimes illicit dealings with José Marino. Along with Marino and the engineer Baldomero Rubio, Benites is complicit in manipulating the Sora Indians to forfeit their rights to their land. On some level, Benites feels guilt for his deeds, as his hallucinations suggest. Believing that he faces his final judgment, he clamors before Christ "¡Señor! ¡Apaga la lámpara de tu tristeza, que me falta corazón para reflejarla! ¿Qué he hecho de mi sangre? ¿Dónde está mi sangre? ¡Ay, Señor! ¡Tú me la diste y he aquí que yo, sin saber cómo, la dejé coagulada en los abismos de la vida, avaro de ella y pobre de ella!... ¡Señor! ¡Yo fui el pecador y tu pobre oveja descarriada! (Vallejo, *Novelas* 238-39) ["Lord! extinguish (sic) the lamp of Your sadness, for I haven't the heart to reflect it! What have I done with my blood? Where is my blood? Dear Lord! You gave it to me and look how I left it clotted in the depths of my life, unwittingly, miserly with it, poor with it. Lord! I was the sinner, I was Your stray sheep!" (Vallejo, *Tungsten* 29)]. Once again the text stages another moral dilemma in a characteristically emphatic lexicon. Tellingly, this time the conflict is presented as occurring in the interior world of a bourgeois character, torn between his desire for social and economic benefit and his Christian ethics. And this Christian –and more specifically Catholic– substratum of Vallejo's tale may be viewed as a prevalent element of Latin American melodrama in general. As Carlos Monsiváis notes in the essay, "Se sufre, pero se aprende: El melodrama y las reglas de la falta de límites," in Latin America, "el melodrama depende en lo fundamental del (lento) proceso de secularización del siglo XIX y el traslado parcial de los sentimientos religiosos a la vida privada" (100)" ["melodrama fundamentally depends upon the (slow) process of nineteenth century secularization and the partial transfer of religious sentiment to private life" (my translation)]. In *El tungsteno*, Benites's crisis illustrates this confluence of individual actions and the religious connotations projected upon them. In this way, melodrama serves as an ethical guidepost, directing the social conscience of the novel's would-be intellectual.

Jean Franco has questioned if Benites's crisis –Benites being Vallejo's grandmother's surname– may not indeed be a caricature of Vallejo himself, who takes up a radical posture only after having worked in the administrative branches of mines and haciendas (156-57). Franco's investigation insightfully presents the contradictions inherent to Vallejo's project, which may in turn suggest a problematic that is inherent to *indigenista* authors in general. Such writers, along with authors of radical socially-oriented works, would find themselves in the uncomfortable position of writing in favor of the oppressed, but always from a position of privilege. As becomes evident in Vallejo's novel, that distance between the author and the subjects that he represents would ostensibly be bridged by the compassion and sympathetic representation of the plight of the underprivileged. But, Vallejo's sentimental recourse ultimately may be viewed as a problematic means of forging a class-based coherence between disparate social sectors, when, as we shall see, such direct ideological bonds are tenuous at best.

Such complications, however, have not hindered literary criticism's attempts to evaluate *El tungsteno* in terms of its literary innovation, grounded in the strength of its nuanced ideological presentation, and John Beverley's reading of Vallejo's novel exemplifies this approach. In reference to Ángel Rama's previously-cited critique of the conservative nature of the social novel, Beverley comments:

> El que cree que *El tungsteno*... reproduce los esquemas logocéntricos de la narrativa burguesa decimonónica simplemente no ha leído el texto, que es uno de los más extraños y difícilmente clasificables en la narrativa moderna latinoamericana, o lo ha leído a través de cierto prejuicio de lo que iba a encontrar. *El tungsteno* representa un esfuerzo para encontrar una forma narrativa capaz de representar en la literatura el fenómeno del imperialismo, las nuevas relaciones humanas que implica, los conflictos de transculturación a que da lugar, su transformación de la forma de subjetividad burguesa, el nuevo mundo social del capital financiero, el trabajo mecanizado, la tecnología. (*Novela social* 173)

> [He who would believe that *El tungsteno*... reproduces the logocentrism of nineteenth century bourgeois narrative simply has not read the text –which is one of the strangest and most difficult to classify in modern Latin American narrative– or has read it from certain prejudices of what he was going to find. *El tungsteno* presents an attempt to find a narrative form capable of representing the phenomenon of imperialism, the new forms of human relations that it implies, the conflicts of transculturation that it stages, its transformation of bourgeois subjectivity, the new social world of capital finance, mechanized labor, and technology. (my translation)]

Beverley goes on to state that a close reading of *El tungsteno* utilizing the tools of sociological, Marxist, feminist, and post-structural analysis would reveal "una obra no menos intricada (y problemática) que, por ejemplo, *Paradiso*"

(*Novela social* 175) ["a work no less intricate (and problematic) than, for example, *Paradiso* [by José Lezama Lima]" (my translation)]. To conclude his comments, Beverley expresses his hope to see the project of the Latin American social novel renewed in the publication of economically accessible popular editions, or by means of their representation in "guiones de cine, teatro popular, fotonovela, telenovela o radionovela." (*Novela social* 176) ["film scripts, popular theatre, photo-novels, *telenovelas*, or radio shows" (my translation)], so as to reach the "público lector popular, obrero" (*Novela social* 175) ["reader in popular sector, the worker" (my translation)].

Beverley's line of analysis is complex, as he attempts to elucidate the cryptic nature of *El tungsteno* and the social novel in general, while at the same time promoting its resurrection in the most accessible –and, not coincidentally, the most traditionally melodramatic– forms of popular art. But, in his call for a return to popular art forms, Beverley would seemingly invoke the latent melodramatic structure of *El tungsteno* and the capacity of that structure to make the complexity of social change intelligible. Social transitions expressed through melodrama are all the more clear, given that they are made, first and foremost, emotionally accessible to a wide, popular audience (as opposed to an aesthetically-complex format intended for a more specialized academic audience). As Thomas Elsaesser notes, melodrama offers the possibility for popular culture to translate and comprehend social change in the terms of private, emotional events (47).[14] Thus, melodrama may provide, as Jesús Martín-Barbero suggests, a means by which popular culture may secretly exact revenge against the exclusive practices of hegemonic dominant social discourse (*Comunicación* 245).[15]

As such, melodrama serves as the aesthetic mode that lets us understand the confluence of what Rama saw as conservative, and of what Beverley views as the revolutionary or new radical aspect of the social novel. Following Rama's comments, we gain insight into melodrama's employment within conventional narrative formats. But, in Beverley's approach to the social novel, we see how that same format allows for the representation of radically heterogeneous social contexts, potentially couched in melodramatic aesthetics. Accordingly, we may paradoxically view melodrama as being at once conservative and radical in nature: it simultaneously employs well-established literary techniques and questions the status quo. In this context, melodrama stands as a recognizable

---

14 For Elsaesser's full quotation, see the introduction to this study.

15 For Martín-Barbero's full quotation, see the previous chapter.

narrative strategy that serves to rescue human experience in the face of the commodification of social relations in the international marketplace. Without question, the affirmation of humanity against the dehumanization of international capitalism is a fundamental characteristic of *El tungsteno*. Yet, in spite of melodrama's acumen for social critique, similar to that which was observed in the previous chapter's analysis of *Doña Bárbara*, the solidity of moral polarity in Vallejo's novel is ultimately compromised when melodrama is employed in attempt to consolidate the text's political message.

El tungsteno's conclusion narrates the organization of an uprising that is offered as a logical and inevitable response to the series of injustices depicted throughout the novel. In this way, Vallejo's novel would comply with what Antonio Gramsci –in reference to Ibsen's *A Doll's House*– proposed as a basic function of popular narrative or a "theatre of ideas": "the representation of passions related to social behaviour, with dramatic solutions which can depict a 'progressive' catharsis, which can depict the drama of the most intellectually and morally advanced part of a society, that which expresses the historical growth immanent in present social behaviour itself" (372). But, following Gramsci's reasoning, it would seem that Vallejo's execution would be lacking, given that, as Gramsci states, "this drama and these passions, though must be represented and not expounded like a thesis or a propaganda speech. In other words, the author must live in the real world with all its contradictory needs and not express feelings absorbed merely from books" (372-73). Contrary to Gramsci's proposal, it is precisely in the cathartic moment of *El tungsteno* that the programmatic explanation of the novel's political agenda manifests the incoherence present in the revolutionary project.

The third and final segment of the novel takes place in a decrepit ranch and presents the clandestine meeting of three characters: the indigenous hero Servando Huanca, the surveyor Leónidas Benites, and the ranch's owner, the mine's anonymous timekeeper, who proclaims to be the lover of the now deceased Graciela. In the representation of this encounter, Vallejo utilizes a propagandistic tone against which Gramsci warned when Servando Huanca states:

> Los patrones y millonarios franceses, yanquis, alemanes, ingleses, son más ladrones y criminales con los peones de la India, de Rusia, de la China, del Perú, de Bolivia, pero son también muy ladrones y asesinos con los peones de las patrias de ellos. En todas partes, en todas, pero en todas, pero en todas, hay unos que son patrones y otros que son peones, unos que son ricos y otros pobres. Y la revolución, lo que busca es echar abajo a todos los gringos y explotadores del mundo, para liberar a los indios y trabajadores de todas partes. (Vallejo, *Novelas* 313)

> [The French bosses and millionaires, yanqui, German, English, what you will, are worse thieves and criminals with the peasants of India, Russia, China, Peru and Bolivia, but they're greedy and murderous enough toward the lower classes in their own countries. Everywhere, and I mean everywhere, some men are bosses and others are workers, some men are rich and others poor. And the revolution, what it's after is to overthrow all the gringos and exploiters in the world and free the Indians everywhere. (Vallejo, *Tungsten* 112-13)]

As is clear in Huanca's diatribe, the revolution simply does not permit intermediary positions. There are rich and poor, bosses and workers, clear oppositions that the revolution seeks to destroy. These dualities are not, however, the only means by which the final scene of the novel attempts to present a melodramatically-clear vision of conflict and the justifications for it.

Another example of the melodramatic structuring in *El tungsteno*'s conclusion is the presence of the timekeeper in the climax of the novel. Since Vallejo's novel plays upon the economy of suffering and retribution in order to arrive, in theory, in a triumph of virtue over villainy, the very inclusion of the timekeeper may suggest another typical melodramatic motive that has a decisive, yet problematic, role in the political action of the novel: the revenge of an offended lover. This romantic subplot, tied to indigenous uprising, is a tried-and-true technique that can also be found in Alcides Arguedas's *Raza de bronce* (1919) and in Sergei Eisenstein's film *¡Que viva México!* (1932, 1979). Similarly, in *El tungsteno* the romantic motive is utilized to manifest the justice of the novel's rebellious project. This fact is clear when we consider that the timekeeper –a nameless, minor character who is barely mentioned previously in the novel in the back story of Graciela's arrival to Quivilca– is now positioned as a character central to the revolutionary project. That is, the forced incorporation of the timekeeper in the novel serves as an element by which the reader may identify with the tale since the topics of romance, suffering, and lover's revenge form an emotional bridge between the text and its audience. These affectively charged experiences are legible to the novel's audience, and, for that reason, they forge an emotional rapport with the reader.

In spite of the rhetoric and structural simplicity of this final scene, the secret meeting importantly illustrates the plurality of motives that join the characters in their desire to rise up against the Mining Society. As noted above, Servando Huanca's motives for rebellion are, for all intents and purposes, purely political. Leónidas Benites, on the other hand, opts to attend the clandestine meeting only after having lost his job with the Mining Society. The possibility of Benites's affiliation with Huanca's uprising is, thus, principally based in personal motives, evident when the surveyor proclaims, "¡Yo me vengaré!" (Vallejo, *Novelas* 323) ["I swear, I'll get even!" (Vallejo, *Tungsten* 124)]. Like Benites, the timekeeper offers deeply personal motives for his participation in Huanca's project, declaring, "¡A mí me han de pagar lo que hicieron con la Graciela! ¡Ah! ¡Por éstas!... ¡Gringos, jijos de puta!..." (Vallejo, *Novelas* 323) ["And me, me! They owe *me* for what they did to Graciela. Ah, those bastards, those gringo sons of bitches!" (Vallejo, *Tungsten* 124)].

In this way, it becomes evident that there is a plurality of individual complaints that serves to unite the group. However, it is important to note that the distinct personal motives are formulated against a common enemy, and the fact that there is only one enemy makes the melodramatic framing of strife all the more effective. As Peter Brooks notes, "the ritual of melodrama involves the confrontation of clearly identified antagonists and the expulsion of one of them. It can offer no terminal reconciliation, for there is no longer a clear transcendent value to be reconciled to. There is, rather, a social order to be purged, a set of ethical imperatives to be made clear" (*Imagination* 17). In *El tungsteno*, the fact that there is an unequivocal enemy facilitates the melodramatic framing of an insurrectionist group capable of battling the evil Mining Society. But, at the same time that melodramatic dichotomy generates in the novel a problematic confluence, if not an outright confusion, of political and personal imperatives.

In Vallejo's novel, each personal protest comes to form part of a greater general complaint, conceived, with the aid of Huanca's incendiary speech, as being somehow inherently political. The fusion of the political and the personal is plain in the closing lines of the novel, when the timekeeper finds himself alone following his meeting with Huanca and Benites.

> No podía dormir. Entre los pensamientos y las imágenes que guardaba de las admoniciones del herrero, sobre "trabajo", "salario", "jornada", "patrones", "obreros", "máquinas", "explotación", "industria", "productos", "reivindicaciones", "conciencia de clase", "revolución", "justicia", "Estados Unidos", "política", "pequeña burguesía", "capital", "Marx", y otras, cruzaba esta noche por su mente el recuerdo de Graciela, la difunta. La había querido mucho. La mataron los gringos, José Marino y el comisario. Recordándola ahora, el apuntador se echó a llorar.
>
> El viento soplaba fuera, anunciando tempestad. (Vallejo, *Novelas* 324)

> [He could not sleep. Among all the words and images he retained from the blacksmith's exhortations, words like *labor*, *wages*, *workday*, *bosses*, *exploitation*, *industry*, *commodities*, *grievances*, *class consciousness*, *revolution*, *justice*, *United States*, *petit-bourgeois*, *capital*, *Marx*, and so on, there passes through his mind that

night the memory of Graciela, the dead girl. He had loved her very much. The gringos had killed her, they and José Marino and the Commissioner. Remembering her now, the timekeeper began to weep.

Outside, the wind was rising, portending storm. (Vallejo, *Tungsten* 125)]

As this passage illustrates, *El tungsteno* ultimately offers a confusing mixture of private motives and revolutionary politics, which serves the very practical function of explicating the text's social message: Marxist abstractions of social conflict find an unmistakable target, and personal motivations justify the impending struggle.[16] Significantly, this message carries a strong emotional connotation, abiding by an economy of melodramatic persecution and justice, and again identifying the Mining Society as an agent of evil against whom a moral and political battle must be waged. Yet, additionally, it becomes clear that, among those who would participate in this battle against evil, there is a somewhat forced, uncomfortable gathering of various concerns under the flag of a supposedly coherent collective, when in reality such a collectivity is not originally conceived ideologically.

The unity of the imminent uprising in *El tungsteno*'s conclusion reflects the hegemonic consolidation present in mass revolutionary movements. Examining Rosa Luxemburg's analysis of "spontaneity," in *Hegemony and Socialist Strategy: Towards a Radical Democratic Politics* (1985), Ernesto Laclau and Chantal Mouffe note:

> In a revolutionary situation, it is impossible *to fix the literal sense* of each isolated struggle, because each struggle overflows its own literality and comes to represent, in the consciousness of the masses, a simple moment of a more global struggle against the system. [...] Thus in a revolutionary situation, the *meaning* of every mobilization appears, so to speak, as split: aside from its specific literal demands, each mobilization represents the revolutionary process as a whole; and these totalizing effects are visible in the overdetermination of some struggles by others. (10-11)

16 This combination of sentimental and political motives has not, however, always convinced critics of Vallejo's novel. Jean Franco notes, "In these final paragraphs, the language of class-consciousness appears abstract and meaningless. The timekeeper's suffering cannot be alleviated by his dedication to the cause, though socialism may eventually create a new society. Thus Vallejo never indicates that socialism will be the panacea for all suffering –only for the suffering that arises from exploitation" (158). Significantly, Lisiak-Land Díaz comments that such a conclusion "nos induce a pensar que son los sentimientos los que instigan la revolución y no una verdadera conciencia de clase" (61) ["makes us think that it is emotion that instigates the revolution and not a true class consciousness" (my translation)].

This spontaneity, then, may be viewed as contributing to a larger hegemonic process, since, as Laclau observes, "a class or group is considered to be hegemonic when it is not closed in a narrow corporatist perspective, but presents itself as realizing the broader aims either of emancipating or ensuring order for wider masses of the population" (*Emancipation[s]* 43). But, for Laclau, this hegemony, which may be employed toward either conservative or radical ends, need not necessarily carry a negative connotation and may, indeed, offer a productive contingency that unites disparate actors to work toward a shared general goal.

In the spontaneous process outlined here, the tenuous grouping of many individual complaints into a single movement implies a necessary forgetting –or at least a deferment– of the particular concerns of the rebellious masses, in order to achieve the greater good of revolutionary mobilization. Likewise, in *El tungsteno*, the revolutionary project also groups together the distinct complaints and motivations of multiple characters in order to respond to the generalized evil of the Mining Society. But, in so doing, the characters' individual complaints must be brought into line with the greater goal of the group: regime change and a new social order. In this sense, the revolutionary process in *El tungsteno* is founded atop a fault line of sorts: the possible agency of revolutionary action is potentially jeopardized, since the personal emotional conflicts of the text, presented in vivid melodramatic language, shape the revolutionary project, rather than expressly political motives or class-consciousness (with the exception of Servando Huanca).

Yet, something still gets done. In spite of the fact that disparate complaints voiced in *El tungsteno* are perhaps haphazardly united, *they are united*. This may be viewed as a central strength of Vallejo's novel, as it shows that, if this revolutionary situation were indeed to come to pass, the multiplicity of complaints and the very fragmentary nature of protest itself could be turned into a radical potential. Whether battling the Mining Society for personal or for political aims, the various actors here are still rising up against the Mining Society and laying out a prospective plan of action for the reader. In this way, *El tungsteno* complies with the propagandist function that Vallejo viewed as central to revolutionary art forms.

However, we would be remiss to not acknowledge that the linkage between personal and political aspects of Vallejo's novel works to evidence a central void that, paradoxically, serves as the basis for the social imperative outlined in *El tungsteno*. This void or essential lacking is the absence of a stable project, but, at the same time, a core, a shared space for a general uneasiness present in all the particular complaints of the text. It is, to use Laclau's terminology, an "empty signifier" that activates the hegemonic processes of the possible revolutionary mobilization of the text. This void, around which all of the individual complaints of the text are formulated, then becomes an absence necessary to give voice to revolutionary rhetoric. And that rhetoric is potentiated through melodrama, making the political message of the novel accessible by means of a highly emotional lexicon. The affectively charged melodramatics of Vallejo's novel essentially work to erase or, at the very least, to cover up any ideological inconsistency that the text may present. That is, melodrama serves to mask the lack of explicit political unity at the core of the revolutionary uprising by emphatically showing the reader the social ills that must be combated. And, in over-writing the depravities of evil, melodrama forges that emotional connection to the reader that makes us read with our hearts, not only our minds, taking the side of the unjustly oppressed "good guys." In Vallejo's novel, melodrama, then, exercises a force similar to that of hegemony, since it identifies a singular antagonist against which all characters, independent of their personal motives, must battle. Melodrama, thus, functions as an aesthetic horizon containing the diverse complaints against the Mining Society, all of which are organized in the portrayal of the protagonists' and antagonists' versions of morality, or lack thereof. In this way, the novel demonstrates a balance of suffering and retribution through which *El tungsteno* attempts to illustrate the concept of social and poetic justice.

Servando Huanca and the movement that he represents are, thus, reinforced and presented as a model of resistance in the face of international capitalism. The melodramatic idealization of the heroic indigenous leader and his political project show, beyond a shadow of a doubt, Vallejo's attempt to present an alternative to industrialist exploitation in an autochthonous Peruvian model. Following the trends of social art in Peru and in Latin America at large at this moment in history, Vallejo was inspired by the indigenous figure as a possible agent of resistance. But, in order for Vallejo's indigenous hero to comply with his vision for future success, the author was forced to impose a Marxist rhetoric upon his protagonist. The European origins of this rhetoric are evident, thus manifesting a tension between the indigenous subject and the means by which to represent him. As Manuel Burga and Alberto Flores Galindo have noted in *Apogeo y crisis de la República Aristocrática* (1980), the indigenous millenary uprisings that shook southern Peru from the final decades of the nineteenth century to 1923 –a period that includes the historical moment represented in Vallejo's novel (approximately 1917)– essentially lacked political orientation (*República* 198-199). The authors view this as one of the primary causes for the ultimate failure of these rebellions to bring about any quantitative social change for the indigenous sectors of southern Peru. And, this historical reality would seem to run counter to the politically-romanticized representation of indigenous leadership as it is presented in *El tungsteno*.

Indeed, the very selection of indigenous sectors as the chosen representatives of national advance highlights the peculiar position of *indigenista* authors like Vallejo. As Jorge Coronado observes in *The Andes Imagined: Indigenismo, Society, and Modernity* (2009):

> When indigenismo is understood beyond its desires to improve the lot of the region's indigenous peoples and placed, rather, at the intersection of nationalist, classist, and racial contentions and difficult birth of modern society, the contradictions between indigentista texts and discourses and their titular objects become glaring. At this intersection, the disconnect between indigenismo's representational goals and its real effects become visible. This disconnect raises the question of why indigenista writers and artists would choose the indio, arguably the representative of some of the most backward aspects of Andean society as it relates to modernization, to communicate ideas about how the Andes should enter into and reap the benefits of modern future. (11)

Coronado concludes that an important part of the discursive projection of *indigenismo* had to do with the opportunity it offered to *indigenista* artists to conceive of new forms of communal identity in the Andes, so offering the potential for new articulations of nationalism and regionalism (11). In spite of the ideological imposition of *El tungsteno*'s *indigenista* agenda, the perception of indigenous sectors as the group intended to further national advancement cannot but suggest the fascination with which Vallejo –and socially-minded intellectuals of the period along with him– perceives indigenous culture.

On this point, it is possible to draw a parallel between the awe contained in Víctor Mendívil's gaze in Martín Chambi's photograph, analyzed at the beginning of this chapter, and that awe with which Vallejo represents Servando Huanca in *El tungsteno*. As is evident in Chambi's photograph, there is a clear distinction between the would-be lettered urbanite and the indigenous subject. In Vallejo's novel, this distance persists, this time between the representation of the indigenous figure and the lived social and ideological conditions of the native population. However, *El tungsteno* attempts to bridge that gap with a political rhetoric potentiated by emotionally heightened language that represents indigenous suffering and the subsequent, inevitable rebellion. In thus conceiving the indigenous subject, his heroism, codified within melodramatic poetics, is shown to be the product of a heterogeneity of potentially conflicting discourses that coincide in a romanticized vision of the *indio*. Conflicting social discourses, this time purposely played against one another, are fundamental to the melodramatics of the text examined in the next chapter.

What More Can One Man Do? Disillusionment and Conformity in *El amor brujo*

In *Kafka: Toward a Minor Literature* (1975), Gilles Deleuze and Félix Guattari outline the basic characteristics of what they call minor narrative. Those attributes include a deterritorialized language –a "major" or dominant language contorted and enhanced by minority members of a given society–, an overriding political immediacy of narrative action, and an essentially collective quality of the narrative work that vindicates otherwise repressed attempts at individual enunciation (16-18). And, while the context in which Deleuze and Guattari apply their critical postulates differs from the social and political milieu of the works of Roberto Arlt (1900-1941), these same analytical posits illuminate several crucial aspects of the Argentine author's works. In tune with the philosophers' concept of the "minor," Arlt's characters grapple with language and "legitimate" forms of knowledge, the anxiety imposed by a restrictive social and political hierarchy, and the conflicted aspirations of collective advance.[1] Indeed, as Beatriz Sarlo notes in *Una modernidad periférica: Buenos Aires 1920 y 1930* (1988), from the perspective of a first generation immigrant, Arlt's fiction

1 The concept of "minor" uses of language coincides particularly well with the analysis of Arlt's works. Minoritarian parallels may be found in Ricardo Piglia's foundational essay "Roberto Arlt, una crítica de la economía literaria," and, more recently, Alan Pauls has commented on the Arltian language machine, seemingly an allusion to another aspect of Deleuze and Guattari's philosophical works. Pauls notes that "La lengua arltiana, lengua de niño o lengua maquínica, es un amalgama de piezas discordantes, una olla o una probeta en la que se metamorfosean jergas, idiomas prestados o robados, lenguas extranjeras, discursos filosóficos y científicos, literaturas altas y bajas, todo un flujo de elementos heterogéneos y conflictivos que nunca terminan de solidificarse y que permanecen, siempre, abiertos a nuevas irrupciones" (316). ["Arltian language –the language of a child or a machinistic language– is an amalgam of discordant pieces, a pot or test tube in which slang, borrowed or stolen language, foreign languages, philosophic and scientific discourses, and high and low literatures all metamorphose in a flow of heterogeneous and conflictive elements that never completely solidify and remain always open to new irruptions" (my translation)].

presents a continual quest for knowledge and power denied to those residing in the periphery of social and political acknowledgement.

Arlt's illusory Buenos Aires is populated by sinners and saints, madmen and ideologues, prostitutes and moralists, executioners and victims, all of whom inhabit the margins of urban society, eking out a meager existence while aspiring to grandiose futures. These characteristics of Arlt's narrative are readily identifiable in *El amor brujo* (1932), Arlt's fourth and final novel, which retains the dubious honor of being the author's "mala novela" ["bad novel"].[2] Indeed, *El amor brujo* is often shunned, if not entirely unrecognized in the discussion of Arlt's works. While it would be impossible to conclude definitively why readers have reacted so negatively to *El amor brujo*, it is evident that Arlt takes a somewhat different route to conveying his tale in this novel. *El amor brujo* in a sense avoids certain truculent situations to which his audience had grown accustomed, instead representing a mundane middle class engineer in a most humdrum tale of romance. Likewise, *El amor brujo* ostensibly eschews prolonged apocryphal reflections upon the prospects for a radical social reordering of Argentine society, a move more in tune with *El juguete rabioso* (1926) than with *Los siete locos* (1929) and *Los lanzallamas* (1931). *El amor brujo* focuses instead on the individual's capacity to manipulate social protocol to his own ends. The social procedure under scrutiny in the text is the regulation of amorous relationships through marriage, offering a malicious assessment of the family engendered by the supposedly loving couple ensnared by matrimony.

The very concept of marriage vexed Arlt, much like it vexes the protagonist of *El amor brujo*, Estanislao Balder, and he revisits the topic in short stories like "El jorobadito" and "Noche terrible," as well as in early theatrical writings like *Prueba de amor*. Each of these works presents amorous relationships (always heterosexual) and marriage as elaborate traps –often controlled by a conniving would-be mother-in-law– from which an overwhelmingly male set of characters must escape by any means necessary. The depiction of marriage as an ambush on happiness was culled from Arlt's own lived experience as he believed that he had been lured under false pretenses into what became a highly problematic marriage to Carmen Antinucci.[3] Arlt nevertheless parlayed his conju-

---

[2] On the negative critical reception of Arlt's final novel, see Larra (36), Flint (63), and Jarkowski (111).

[3] Regarding Arlt and Antinucci's relationship, see Sylvia Saítta's excellent biography *El escritor en el bosque de ladrillos: Una biografía de Roberto Arlt*.

gal discontent into fodder for not only for his literary, but also his journalistic career, commenting on the pitfalls of matrimony in several of his *Aguafuertes porteñas*, which were published contemporary to the appearance of *El amor brujo* (Saítta 112).

It was also during this period that Arlt demonstrated his most clear association with communist and revolutionary politics through his collaborations with the periodicals *Actualidad. Económica, política, social*, and *Bandera roja*.[4] Arlt, however, generally maintained ambiguous political affiliations, as shown by the frustrated attempts of scholars over the years to definitively associate him with either the Florida or Boedo literary schools between which he oscillated.[5] And, while the discussion of Arlt's political affiliations is relevant and certainly necessary for the proper analysis of his texts, the object of this chapter is not to attempt to associate the author with one particular political ideology or another as has been done in so much previous criticism of Arlt's works.[6] Rather, what is of interest here is the analysis of exactly how Arlt takes on dominant conventions –both social and literary– in *El amor brujo,* critiquing them through the manipulation of the melodramatic norm.[7]

---

4 Alongside a marked interest for the *lumpenproletariat* in his fictional writings, it is due in large part to these journalistic endeavors that Arlt frequently has been associated with radical social sectors and communist politics in Argentina of the early twentieth century. As Sylvia Saítta has noted, it is in *Actualidad*, directed by Arlt's friend and fellow author, Elías Castelnuovo, where Arlt had a more sustained presence, working with Castelnuovo to form the short-lived *Unión de Escritores Proletarios* (Union of Proletarian Writers) in 1932. That same year, while writing for the left-leaning publication *Bandera roja*, Arlt's opinions would become the object of some controversy as he –according to the official communist line that oriented the periodical– displayed a misunderstanding of Marxist social critique, exposing his own bourgeois intellectualism (Saítta 154-68).

5 With regard to the Florida versus Boedo dispute, José Amícola comments that Arlt never truly fit with either group, thus leaving himself open to a wider breadth of readers (101). Christopher Towne Leland also notes that Arlt's affiliations with the groups were more personal than ideological in nature (97).

6 As Jorge Ruffinelli notes, in this line of the ideological analysis of Arlt's works, Raúl Larra, Óscar Massota, Diana Guerrero, and Beatriz Pastor have provided pivotal investigations (See bibliography).

7 Here I follow Ruffinelli's lead when he notes in his analysis of *El juguete rabioso*, "lo que importaría en esta instancia determinar no es tanto la inserción de la novela dentro de un discurso que la excede y que sería el de la ideología pequeño-burguesa, como la determinación del tránsito que va y viene desde y a esa ideología y esa novela" (16-17) ["what is important to determine in this instance is not so much the insertion of the novel in a discourse that exceeds it and that would be that of petit

The story told in *El amor brujo* is presented through the distorted lens of sentimental narrative, mockingly employing commonplace recourses of melodramatic aesthetics to underline the conservative deliberateness of those artistic conventions. That is, melodrama provides the aesthetic devices necessary to the construction of this urban sentimental tale. Yet, in this ironic critique, a fundamental paradox is inscribed in the text: the novel at once parodies the techniques of melodramatic storytelling and relies on those same aesthetic recourses to convey its tale. In seizing upon the techniques of conventional romantic tales that promote dominant social trends, Arlt shows the status quo to be propped up by a false morality embedded in the social etiquette of the middle class. The critique of narrative style, then, constitutes a form of social evaluation, without necessarily venturing into the realm of explicit social realism.[8] Differing from works by Boedo authors like Leónidas Barletta, for example, *El amor brujo* itself is not caught up in partisan rhetoric, which is not to say, however, that *El amor brujo* does not seek to comment forcefully upon social polemics of his day. So much was clear from the moment when Arlt announced the future publication of *El amor brujo* in the often quoted prologue to *Los lanzallamas*, in which he complains about the constraints of the working author who has little time for questions of style in his works, himself preferring to write as if it were a violent blow to the jaw.[9]

But, contrary to his claimed ignorance of narrative method, Arlt displays a hyper-awareness to the literary techniques involved in representing his tale by landing his literary "cross" in *El amor brujo*. The novel itself functions as a

---

bourgeois ideology, but the determination of the transit that comes and goes to and from that ideology and that novel" (my translation)].

8 In this sense, *El amor brujo* shares a commonality with *Los siete locos* and *Los lanzallamas*. As David William Foster notes, "a basic ingredient of *The Seven Madmen*... is an element of fantasy and surrealism quite disconsonant with the 'committed' literature of social realism" (26). Likewise, *El amor brujo* maintains a distance from partisan social commentary as it presents a continual play on fiction and Balder's fantasies of liberation and revenge.

9 What is less often noted but which bears an impact on *El amor brujo* is the epilogue to *Los lanzallamas*, in which Arlt thanks the novelist Carlos Alberto Leumann for the suggestion of the novel's title. Arlt had a rather strange way of expressing his gratitude, as *El amor brujo* would seemingly parody key elements of Leumann's novel *La vida victoriosa* (1922). As is the case in Leumann's novel, Arlt's protagonist is an engineer, married and with child, who seeks an impossible love in the Tigre district of Buenos Aires. But, instead of taking this romance seriously as Leumann does in his allegoric national romance, Arlt derides the conventions of sentimental narrative.

compendium and a sardonic play upon the melodramatic devices of sentimental literature. True to the most stereotypical sentimental tale, Estanislao Balder seeks the life-changing event of falling in love. Balder's dream of a fresh and pure romance –complicated by the fact that he is already married to another woman– ends in deception when he concludes that his would-be soul mate, a schoolgirl named Irene Loayza, is not the virginal lover he believed her to be. However, it is through the process of disillusionment, itself an inversion of anticipated melodramatic bliss, that the force of *El amor brujo* is found: even when embitterment sets in as Balder progressively discovers Irene's flaws and eventually separates from her, the devious protagonist begins to act histrionically as if he were in love so as to further his romantic plot.

Through his melodramatic actions, Balder is easily able to prey upon the desires and convictions of his enemies, but only because he knows all too well the frivolous melodramatic morality that he attributes to the bourgeoisie. This is due to the fact that, no matter how hard he resists, Balder is a member of that same social class, abiding by the same value system as his enemies, which will ultimately doom his undertaking. And in the very frustration of his ambitions, Balder's tale displays the limits of melodramatic reasoning, as his actions showcase melodrama from both within (his apparently genuine desire for love) and without (his simulation and conscious critique of love). Instead of accepting melodramatic emotion as a functional instrument of narrative within both the story and the rapport between reader and text, Arlt's novel auto-reflexively showcases the mechanisms through which melodramatic affectivity is produced and to what ends by presenting a character that must knowingly perform his role in the story.

Self-conscious representation in *El amor brujo* revels in offering impediments to the overt devices of the melodramatic aesthetic and, in turn, problematizes the framing of any sort of social commentary from a melodramatic perspective. Arlt's novel directly questions what would happen if the good and evil polarities so crucial to melodrama –as exemplified in the ostensive structuring of Gallegos's *Doña Bárbara* and Vallejo's *El tungsteno*– were located in just one character. How might melodramatic poetic justice be presented if the text actively works against identification between the protagonist and the reader? Is social commentary via the melodramatic narrative model even plausible, given the limited scope of melodrama's aesthetic devices? These issues that reside at the core of *El amor brujo* make it a work central to the consideration of melodrama in twentieth century Latin American narrative as it lays a groundwork for the future questioning of melodrama, both in the latter works analyzed in this study and well beyond.

The allure of melodrama comes under fire, in fact, from the very outset of *El amor brujo*. Even before the dramatic action of Arlt's novel begins, an epigraph by Oscar Wilde posits the critical inclination of the novel. Wilde's quote states that, "The worst of all vices is that of frivolity; all that reaches one's consciousness is just" (my translation).[10] *El amor brujo* proposes an alternative to the "frivolous" aesthetics of melodramatic sentimentality, and Wilde's quote quite literally sets the stage for the critique that is about to unfold. Indeed, the concept of staged events plays a crucial role, as is readily evident in the title of the first segment of the novel "Balder va en busca del drama" ["Balder Sets Out in Search of Drama"]. In the novel's first fragment, a flash-forward, the reader finds Balder pleading his case to court Irene to her mother, the sinister yet morally-affected Susana Loayza. Balder's requests are met with Susana's incredulous replies that she would never permit her daughter to be courted by a married man, leading Balder to false exaggeration and posturing at his request's denial. The oddity of this initial scene becomes evident as the novel progresses, immediately backtracking to the chronological beginning of the story, and so underlining the opening anecdote's structural implication for the novel.

By beginning *in medias res*, *El amor brujo* immediately puts the cart before the horse and defies a basic norm of realist, sentimental storytelling, given that dramatic action in this narrative style typically starts from the beginning and ends at the finale. The actions represented in the text, then, follow their logical sequence, evolving and maturing "naturally" as love is discovered, faces doubt and challenges, but eventually comes to fruition. By beginning with a flash-forward, *El amor brujo* shows that there is nothing "natural" about fictional romance, and, by bracketing off and decontextualizing this initial scene, *El amor brujo* shows itself to be pure artifice from the start. Balder's search for drama, then, represents a scene of farce within a greater work of fiction, offering an imaginary threshold that the reader must breach in order to access the story told in *El amor brujo* and underlining the fact that the tale at hand is not an organic expression of reality.

To highlight this crucial aspect of *El amor brujo*, it is of use to consider Arlt's novel in light of Jacques Derrida's discussion of *parergon* (that which is supplemental or ornamental) in *The Truth in Painting* (1987). Derrida argues here that the frame, the supplement to the painted canvas, is essential inasmuch as it reveals a lack residing in that artistic work. That is, the painting is not

---

10 Because no translation of *El amor brujo* exists, all translations of the text in this chapter are my own.

in and of itself inherently art. The artistic object becomes such when it is set off by its frame, making that edging at once auxiliary and indispensable to the work itself. When read in the terms of *El amor brujo*, Derrida's commentary illuminates the basic sentimental *lack* that Arlt attempts to underline as residing at the core of the sentimental novel. The criticism that Arlt levels against sentimental narrative is that it holds no depth, that it is frivolous, and that it needs to be supplemented by critical commentary. The initial scene in the novel provides just that, an ancillary ground against which all other action in the novel may be considered and which in itself contributes a complexity to the text that is often absent from the standard, straight-forward sentimental tale conveyed through melodramatic aesthetics. By divorcing Balder's story from reality, by giving it a frame, Arlt neutralizes that liminal space between reality and fiction that melodramatic sentimental narrative attempts to inhabit.

The reader's conscious entrance into the realm of fiction constitutes an immediate affront to melodramatic aesthetics, as drawing readers' attention to the artificiality of the story compromises his or her capacity to empathize with the character. There are, to be sure, a multitude of other complications for empathy with Balder. But, by placing an emphasis on the fictionality of the novelistic scene, the reader does not grow to know and identify with the protagonist as is desirable in the employment of melodrama; we as readers do not enter into the novel under the illusion that this story, however fanciful it may be, could in fact happen in real life. Rather, one instantly is aware that Balder is nothing more than a character –actually a character that is playing a role in his own story– and that he is only capable of actions in the fictional world that he inhabits.

El amor brujo, then, offers a departure from the typical *folletín* narrative so popular in Buenos Aires throughout the early twentieth century, while at the same time ironically conserving certain essential characteristics of serial literature. As is frequently noted, Arlt's style is heavily influenced by serial literature, and clearly the Rocambolesque aspirations of Silvio Astier in *El juguete rabioso*, along with the narrative structuring of *Los siete locos*, *Los lanzallamas*, and *El amor brujo*, denote an homage to the *folletín*.[11] However, contrary to serial works of sentimental literature, which constituted a most overt form of social education via emotional identification in Buenos Aires at the beginning of the

[11] On this point, excellent criticism abounds. See Beatriz Sarlo's already cited *Una modernidad periférica: Buenos Aires 1920 y 1930*, Ricardo Piglia's *Crítica y ficción* (1996), Fernando J. Rosenberg's *The Avant-Garde and Geopolitics in Latin America* (2006), or Paula Kathleen Speck's doctoral dissertation *Roberto Arlt and the Conspiracies of Fiction*.

twentieth century, Arlt's tale immediately interrupts the affective connection between reader and character, so problematizing social-sentimental commentary. As Beatriz Sarlo notes in *El imperio de los sentimientos* (1985) regarding serial fiction published in *La Novela Semanal* and *La Novela del Día*, the sentimental tale was effective inasmuch as it presented love as the overriding, all-absorbing topic of the text. The theme of love, however, also provided a means of socialization as it educated the reader about the pitfalls of dangerous desires that threaten social and moral order and which are destined for failure (Sarlo 22, 170). In order for these rules to be successfully communicated, an affective rapport between reader and text must be established, and this is precisely the melodramatic norm that *El amor brujo* disrupts from the outset.

Still another early departure from a typical employment of melodrama in *El amor brujo* –as well as a common feature of Arlt's novels– is found in the presence of an external commentator who functions as Balder's interlocutor and confidant. This chronicler, as he will refer to himself, is a privileged spectator who has conversed with Balder directly at a point in time subsequent to the events represented in the novel and who is ultimately responsible for the organization of the text. He does, however, purport not to interfere with the information that he presents, reminding the reader that "deber de cronista es exponer hechos, no hipótesis" (Arlt, *Amor* 39) ["the chronicler's task is to present facts, not hypotheses"]. Yet, as was the case in the disjointed introductory segment of the novel, the chronicler's presence and voice simultaneously inside and outside the text serves as an obstacle to melodramatic identification that interrupts the flow of the tale, diminishing melodrama's capacity to beguile the reader. The chronicler is still granted virtually unfettered access to Balder's perception, and, when needed, he incorporates extracts from Balder's diary into the text.

The assimilation of these journal selections into the text represents a curious amalgamation of writing formats, adding a complexity that is uncharacteristic of standard melodramatic narrative. This is even more apparent inasmuch as it is in these diary entries that Balder shows his true colors, expressing his repulsion at Irene's simplistic concepts of romantic contentment and at her mother's petty attempts to trap him in marriage. Not easily recognizable as the writings of a smitten lover, Balder's diary clearly presents the protagonist as on the offensive, and it would appear that he does not care who knows it. The unabashed style in which Balder constructs his diary has direct melodramatic implications, given that, while writing in this most intimate of formats, Balder is clearly aware of the theatrical nature of his prose. The diary is by definition a highly personal writing arena, composed by and for a single individual. In his journal, however, Balder is acutely aware of the fact that his musings will be read by others, which is to say that his writing is at once personal, private, public, and theatrical. Regarding the stupor in which he finds himself while awaiting the life-altering event of meeting Irene, he at one point invokes his public, stating, "como ven ustedes, no me adorno con el epíteto de imbécil, gratuitamente, ni modestamente" (Arlt, *Amor* 48) ["as you all can see, I do not refer to myself with the epithet of imbecile gratuitously nor modestly"]. Through this type of interjection in his journal, Balder transcends the space of personal writing, performing himself before an implicit audience, which, on one hand, makes perfect sense within the realm of melodrama: gesturing before an audience forms a cornerstone of melodramatic exposition. Yet, on the other hand, when Balder's diary launches into diatribes against Irene, her mother, and the social class that they represent, his writing is most out of tune with melodramatic styling. Customarily, a sentimental tale rooted in melodramatic emotion simply ought not to have a rogue protagonist who acts detrimentally toward a woman with whom he is purportedly in love. Yet, Balder's penchant for melodramatic performance in his diary comfortably meshes with another form of writing found in Arlt's novel: theatrical script.

The most detailed example of these theatrical textual intrusions is found in a conversation between Balder and his wife, Elena, where Balder explains that his reason for abandoning his family is to be with Irene. This segment of the text entitled "Cuando el amor avanzó" ["When Love Had Advanced"] is among the most melodramatic passages of *El amor brujo*.

> Alcoba conyugal. Balder y su esposa Elena. Tinieblas. Palabras que chasquean rencorosas.
>
> Balder: Quiero a esa criatura y no la dejaré, ¿entendés? No la dejaré nunca.
>
> Elena: ¿Para qué me sacaste de mi casa?
>
> Balder: No te he sacado. Pero en el supuesto caso que lo hubiera hecho, ¿querés decirme qué me has dado? Vida gris… eso. Desde que nos casamos. Reproches. Luchas.
>
> Elena: Sos un perro, callate. (Arlt, *Amor* 126)

> [The married couple's bedroom. Balder and his wife Elena. Shadows. A dialogue brimming with hostility.
>
> Balder: I love that girl and I won't leave her. Do you understand? I won't ever leave her.
>
> Elena: Why did you even take me from my home?
>
> Balder: I didn't take you anywhere, but in the case that I had, what did I get out of it? Ever since we married, a dreary existence, nothing more. Accusations and fights.
>
> Elena: Shut up, you bastard.]

By first presenting apparent stage directions and later a script to be enacted, this fragment of the novel offers readers a preview of Arlt's future endeavors as he would turn his creative focus to theater following the publication of *El amor brujo*. Indeed, the entanglement of sentimental and theatrical narratives in Arlt's novel is facilitated by the common melodramatic foundation that the two narrative forms share: lest we forget, melodrama itself is born of theater. In *El amor brujo*, melodramatic sentimentalism, be it amorous or resentful as it is in this instance, is shown as emotionally exaggerated and worthy of dramatic representation. This is driven home by the intrusive, unsettling manner in which the theatrical text is interjected in the novel.

Indeed, those blocks of theatrical script –like Balder's diary, the chronicler's annotations, and the novel's flash forward introduction– are blatantly disruptive to the flow of sentimental narrative. Arlt's novel causes the reader to grapple with the text's multiple narrative voices and contrary scriptural formats time and time again, drawing attention to its very fissures, which disturb the continuity of the tale and break any possibility for melodramatic enchantment. And, if I have insisted upon the structural complexity of *El amor brujo*, it was to demonstrate the social critique that the text embodies through its commentary on narrative form. Arlt views writing as a means of social existence, and, to this end, Ricardo Piglia notes that "para Arlt la sociedad está trabajada por la ficción, se asienta en la ficción. [...] Hay una crítica muy frontal de Arlt a lo que podríamos llamar la producción imaginaria de masas: el cine, el folletín, y sobre todo el periodismo son máquinas de crear ilusiones sociales, de definir modelos de realidad" (*Crítica* 25) ["for Arlt, society is formed and affirmed through fiction. [...] Arlt offers a direct criticism of what we might call the imaginary production of the masses: film, *folletín* (serial literature), and above all journalism, are machines that create social illusions and define models of reality (my translation)]. Because *El amor brujo* presents melodramatic sentimentality as a form of imagining and maintaining the status quo, an evaluation of the sentimental tale's narrative mechanics constitutes the possibility of considering the social practices and the institutions that are perpetuated by melodramatic sentimental narrative.

By becoming aware of the methods of conveying sentiment, the reader is invited to consider the overarching social narratives that are reinforced by the sentimental tales, which are the object of scrutiny in *El amor brujo*. And, because of the interruption of the anticipated sequence of events in the sentimental tale, Arlt's novel places the mechanisms of melodramatic sentimentality on display, insisting that those working parts of narrative must be observed individually as they are presented out of order and in general dissonance. Arlt's technique thus shares a commonality with Bertolt Brecht's theatrics of alienation.[12] With regards to the production of alienation among the spectators, Brecht wrote, "as we cannot invite the audience to fling itself into the story as if it were a river and let itself be carried vaguely hither and thither, the individual episodes have to be knotted together in such a way that the knots are easily noticed" (201). Similar to Brecht's theatrical practice, Arlt's novel strives to expose the knots in its construction, and it does so to a similar end. In Brecht's estimation, the manifestly fragmented format of his theatrical representations offered the public the opportunity to reflect on the provisional nature of rules governing social conduct, so leaving "spectators productively disposed even after the spectacle is over" (205). Arlt's novel works in a comparable fashion as its active engagement with the reader through constant narrative estrangement seeks to provoke an analysis, and indeed a criticism, of the social conventions that he puts on display.

Instead of utilizing sentimentality as a means of social education, Arlt produces a social critique in *El amor brujo* through the objectification of sentimentality. That is, it is not the tale itself, but the simultaneous conscious reflection upon the tale and the mode through which it is expressed that produce social evaluation. This fact would indicate an exasperation of the sentimental narrative model and of the melodramatic aesthetics that give form to it, which gives way to parody in *El amor brujo*.[13] And, in *El amor brujo*, that parody is manifested explicitly in the caricature of the sentimental male protagonist, Estanislao Balder. Balder, however, is not parodied simply in the sense that his character is singled out for ridicule or criticism, but rather in an overt doubling of his character through which narrative irony is manifested. This doubling technique is a most effective means of creating estrangement in the text, presenting a character that, in a Brechtian sense, stands "in a valley and [makes] a speech in which he occasionally changes his views or simply utters sentences which contradict one another, so that the accompanying echo forces them into confrontation" (Brecht 191).

---

12 Ángel Núñez, in *La obra narrativa de Roberto Arlt* (1968), was among the first to observe the affinity between the works of Brecht and Arlt, particularly in his analysis of *El amor brujo* (24-29; 59-95).

13 Paula Speck has commented that, in Arlt's fiction, parody is necessary once the techniques of a given genre become conventional, offering up "literature as a drug, the temptation to passive and irresponsible reading" (208-09), similar to Cervantes's *Don Quixote* or Gustave Flaubert's *Madame Bovary*.

With Balder, the reader is presented with an unstable character who demonstrates diametrically opposed impulses, which confound the clarity of the text: he vacillates between loving or hating Irene, embracing or fleeing from marriage to her. There are, indeed, two Balders in the novel: the melodramatically affected gent in search of love and the vicious trickster bent on demonstrating his superiority to the bourgeoisie that he loathes. Balder would then seemingly embody both hero and villain, problematizing the most basic polarity of melodrama and so muddling the entire structure of the plot. This incoherence between Balder's pure and his malicious amorous impulses fails to resonate with basic melodramatic characterization, as it shows that he is not a "whole" character. To disentangle these contradictory and alternating positions, which are presented at varying intensities throughout the text, the reader must consider Balder as exemplifying, on the one hand, melodrama from within (a hero longing for love, typical of sentimental narrative) and, on the other, melodrama from without (a rogue who offers a questioning of, and distancing from the sentimentality of his other).

The first of these two positions, Balder as the wide-eyed lover, is the lesser-developed of his postures. It is nevertheless important because Balder immediately construes romance as a means of escaping his monotony and of accessing a higher plane of being. In Balder's perception, society is corrupt not because of the way in which the individual demonstrates a perversity in his or her personal actions, but because each individual does not live up to his or her full potential. His conception of morality, at least in the initial passages of the novel, is based on moving past conceptions of social convention, so as to achieve a sublimity beyond the limits of social hierarchy. Significantly, Balder seeks a life-altering romantic experience to achieve this higher plane.

Balder's amorous adventure begins chronologically when, while waiting on a train platform, he spots the coquettish young Irene, who does not shy away from the stranger's gaze. Forgetting his previous engagements, Balder then boards Irene's train, approaches her, and spouts forth a barrage of maudlin reflections to a mostly-mute response from the bewildered sixteen-year-old girl. Balder states, "yo sé que estoy infringiendo todas las reglas de convivencia social al tutearte. Existe un protocolo y yo he prescindido instantáneamente de formas y protocolos. ¿Por qué? Quizá la necesidad de manifestarte mi fiesta interior... pero ante vos me gusta mostrarme como un pequeño animalito feliz... sí, eso, Irene; un pequeño animalito feliz de haber encontrado a su diosa" (Arlt, *Amor* 27) ["I know that I am infringing on all the rules of social etiquette by speaking to you so informally. There is a protocol, and I have instantly dispensed with forms and protocols. Why? Maybe it's my need to demonstrate to you my internal jubilance... but before you I like to present myself as a happy little animal... yes, Irene; a little animal that is happy to have found his goddess"]. It is important to note that, in this instance –already complicated by the flash forward that precedes it, showing Balder as an actor in a romantic farce, and, of course, by Irene's youth– Balder's romantic impulse is what determines his actions. The reader is thus firmly ensconced in the realm of sentimental fiction, in which love is the sole topic of interest. This textual situation is immediately stifled in the following segment of the novel, entitled "El fuego se apaga" ["The Flame Burns Out"].

In only their second meeting, Balder becomes convinced that his love for Irene was nothing more than an illusion, but he still continues to press the issue. After forcedly conveying his excitement upon their meeting and praising Irene's goodness, only to find that they have nothing more to say to one another, Balder believes that his dream of love is dead. But, at this critical juncture in the novel, Balder initiates the performance that will call into question the authenticity of his actions throughout the remainder of the text. While waiting for Irene to finish the piano lesson that had brought her from her home in the Tigre district of the city to downtown Buenos Aires, Balder waits in a nearby café and plots a course to "asegurar su conquista" ["assure his conquest"]:

> Después de cavilar un instante, redactó dos carillas de amor mentiroso, "destinadas a excitar la imaginación de la jovencita y sus vulgares sentimientos de chica de familia". Incluso le decía que "se imaginaba él y ella, cuando fueran ancianitos, rodeados de muchos hijos". Esto es simplemente repugnante y absurdo. Balder, además de encontrarse casado, no quería hijos, y por otra parte, no sentía ningún apego a la vida del hogar. Sentíase llamado a destinos más altos, pero en esta circunstancia procedió como un jugador, matiz que entraba en su temperamento, tratando trabajosamente que el estilo de la carta fuera lo suficiente estúpido como convenía a la mentalidad que revelaba Irene. (Arlt, *Amor* 38)
>
> [After a moment's hesitation, he wrote two pages of deceitful love, "destined to excite the imagination of the young girl and the vulgar sentiments engrained through her upbringing." He even wrote that, "he imagined the both of them, when they were older, surrounded by many children." This is simply repugnant and absurd. Balder, in addition to already being married, did not want children, and felt no inclination toward a home life. He felt a higher calling, but, in this circumstance, he proceeded as a gambler, a role that suited his temperament, laboriously crafting the style of the letter so that it was sufficiently stupid to fit the mentality that Irene displayed.]

The chronicler's participation in the text through quotations and appraisals of Balder's experience makes the protagonist's cynicism clear. His stated intent is to lie to Irene so as to further his agenda, and it is notable that his means of trickery is the written word. In the same sense that sentimental fiction dupes its public into believing far-fetched tales of love, Balder seeks to ensnare Irene in a romantic tryst, writing at a level that is "sufficiently stupid" to appeal to her intelligence.

From this moment forward, each and every one of Balder's actions is under the reader's scrutiny, as we are aware that Balder is leading a double life. Representing what I termed above as a perspective on melodrama from without, Balder quite consciously undertakes his mission to seduce Irene, but not merely for the sake of fulfilling his sexual impulses. Balder's project in romancing Irene and working his way into her family is to patently demonstrate the moral vacuity of the Loayzas, an exemplary middle class family. In tricking Irene and her mother Susana, who hopes for the economic gains and social status that Balder and Irene's marriage would bring about, Balder seeks to expose the senselessness of their reliance on the social conventions so dearly held by the middle class. Marriage, in fact, comes to serve as a catchall target for Balder's continued criticisms of the bourgeoisie throughout the novel. Balder's consistently nebulous commentaries on class all pass through the lens of matrimony (and the families it produces), a convention essential to the maintenance of what the protagonist views as a deplorable middle class and its values system. But, beyond the mention of the restraints imposed by marriage, *El amor brujo* never analytically delves into the actual political perspectives that are imposed by the middle class through matrimony at this moment in Argentine history. That is, Balder's pent-up social rage finds a target in marriage, and he cyphers all of his commentary against the hegemonic values of the middle class through that particular social affiliation. This saves the novel from delving into any dense political analysis of the rise of the Unión Cívica Radical, the political fortune of Hipólito Yrigoyen, or his forced removal from office by General José Uriburu in the years preceding the publication of Arlt's novel. All of these elements combine to demonstrate the volatility of an Argentine middle class that was unable to forge a coherent social base, a shortcoming that Arlt critiques in Balder's commentaries on matrimony.

In order to expel his anger, Balder takes up what he calls the "camino tenebroso y largo" (Arlt, *Amor* 18) ["the shadowy and long path"]. But, for Balder, the shadowy path is not a typically subversive process of vengeance; it is not working against the grain in a conventionally nefarious plan. Rather, Balder's dark path is that which represents a route to ultimate happiness in conventional sentimental narrative: courtship that leads to matrimony. *El amor brujo* inverts the standard melodramatic scheme, demonstrating the status quo to be that which is sinister and Balder's subversive actions to be the exercise of goodness and justice. It is on this dark path that Balder takes up a full repertoire of melodramatic elasticity, performing emotional histrionics that indicate, not what he thinks, but that which a sentimental protagonist would or ought to do in his position. By mocking the Loayza's morality through exaggeratedly playing to their every whim, Balder ultimately proposes to set their ethical code on its head, vengefully making an example of the family that had attempted to trap him through the ritual of matrimony. And, in this, the underlying project of the text is brought to the fore as Balder's histrionics permit him to mock and criticize middle class morals and their normative institutions.

In fact, in the introductory fragment of the novel in which Balder seeks permission from Susana Loayza to court her daughter Irene, he enters the Loayza's home reflecting to himself that "la comedia ha comenzado" (Arlt, *Amor* 11) ["the comedy has begun"]. It is from this consciously falsified position that Balder emotionally pleads to Susana that he and Irene are bound by destiny and that nothing will stand in the way of his love for the schoolgirl. This instance demonstrates that there is little to indicate any sincerity between Balder's thoughts and his actions. But, more importantly, beyond the love that Balder professes, an immensely prohibitive social roadblock is placed before his relationship with Irene. Indeed, Susana Loayza's primary concern regarding Balder is the fact that he is a married man. Balder's only response to Susana's trepidation is to affirm that he is married, but separated, and that he will soon begin the legal process of divorcing his wife. This seems to be enough for Susana, who concedes that, if he were divorced, then she would consider permitting Balder to court Irene, with the ultimate aim of seeing the two happily married.

Sensing that his emotionally histrionic plea might have gotten more than he had bargained for, Balder seeks an immediate line of escape from the situation by noting the absurdity of his own enterprise. When Irene's friend, Zulema, who had engineered the meeting between Susana and Balder, expresses her joy at the prospect of Balder and Irene's marriage "en un romanticismo de película barata" ["in the romantic register of a B movie"], the reader observes Balder's reflections:

> "Esta mujer es una burra. No se da cuenta que propone un sacrilegio. La Iglesia no admite el divorcio en el matrimonio consumado. Doctrina definida por los cánones 5, 6 y 8 del Concilio de Trento." Y contestó:
>
> - La Iglesia no admite el divorcio, señora. El único que en realidad tolera es aquel que en Derecho Canónico se define como "quat thorum et abitationes", es decir separación en cuanto a habitaciones.... (Arlt, *Amor* 17)

> ["This woman is an idiot. She doesn't realize that what she proposes is sacrilegious. The Church does not permit the divorce of consummated matrimony. Doctrine defended by canons 5, 6, and 8 of the Council of Trent." And he responded:
> - The Church does not permit divorce, ma'am. The only thing that it recognizes is that which in Canonical Law is defined as "quat thorum et abiatationes," that is, separation with regard to domicile...]

It is here that the reader is able to clearly perceive the absurdity that defines the entirety of Balder's actions. From the very beginning of the novel, he is conscious that his union with Irene, even if it were only as melodramatic soul mates, would be socially condemned forever in the sense that it could not be normalized. This fact is the first evidence that, for all of Balder's rage against the middle class, he still governs his actions –cynically or not– according to the precepts of bourgeois normativity, chief among which is obedience to legal and religious conventions.

The commentary Arlt's novel makes on the guidelines regarding matrimony and its dissolution thus references what was certainly a hot-button issue in Argentina throughout the early twentieth century. As Asunción Lavrin notes in *Women, Feminism, and Social Change in Argentina, Chile, and Uruguay, 1890-1940* (1995), "divorce was debated and defeated in the Argentine Congress on seventeen occasions from 1888 to 1932" (236). In fact, the debate on divorce is all the more current a topic in *El amor brujo*, given that, during the year in which Arlt's novel was published, "a bill allowing complete dissolution [of marriage] was approved by the Chamber of Deputies and forwarded to the Senate which shelved it and successfully resisted all urging from the Deputies to discuss it" (Lavrin 236). The overriding factor that had prevented suspension of the marital contract in Argentina was the Catholic Church's position that marriage maintained a special sacramental status and was not simply a civil contract, this being true even in the instances in which a civil union had been formed without any religious ceremony. In spite of this fact, Argentine judges during the late 1920s considered cases of legal separations, though such deliberations never definitively terminated the marital contract.[14] But, some Argentines did work to obtain legal divorces by seeking them beyond the national

---

[14] On this point, Lavrin notes that, in 1929, "[jurist Juan Carlos Rébora] argued that the existing Argentine jurisprudence on 'divorce' allowed the judges determining separation cases between 1926 and 1929 to engage in serious inconsistencies between the theory inscribed in the Civil Code and reality" (239). Though divorce remained illegal in Argentina until 1987, litigations on separations did carry some legal weight regarding the dissolution of marriage.

border in Uruguay, where divorce was legalized in 1907, creating a peculiar situation in which Argentine nationals could leave their country to dissolve their marriages (Lavrin 241). At that point, divorced persons could, in theory, remarry. But, in practice, many couples eschewed the step of acquiring a foreign divorce, remaining married to their initial partner but marrying another spouse outside of Argentine territory. As Mala Htun comments in *Sex and the State* (2003), couples would return to Argentina with a foreign marriage certificate from countries like Uruguay or Mexico, paying a lawyer, who "then took these foreign marriage certificates to local offices of the civil registry to obtain a local marriage certificate. These local certificates were important socially, not legally (since no court would recognize them), for they demonstrated to peers and colleagues that, even though Argentine law did not permit it, the stable union had been converted into marriage somewhere" (97).

Anxiety regarding the immutability of marriage becomes a driving force of *El amor brujo*, as Balder is already trapped in an unhappy marriage. The prospect of love with Irene presents, if only for a moment, the possibility of true love free from intrusion by any governing institution. Balder seeks the melodramatic ideal of a pure, reciprocal love, questioning why he and so many like him continue to be enslaved by the limitations imposed by marriage. Balder analyzes the domestic situation of his colleagues at work, which appears to be much like his own: they had married young only to take up mistresses, never intending to ever leave their wives out of fear of becoming bored once again by the monotony of another monogamous relationship. In turn, Balder also sympathizes for the wives in these relationships, who also experience the loneliness and boredom of their spouses. In Balder's estimation, women, like men, are unjustly limited by marriage, but their punishment is even crueler in the sense that they lack the wherewithal to effectively cheat on their husbands, remaining "encadenadas por escrúpulos que la educación burguesa les había incrustado en el entendimiento [...]" (Arlt, *Amor* 58) ["enslaved by scruples that bourgeois education had incrusted in their mentality"].

Balder believes that these marital conditions produce families in which no real understanding exists, and that forms of popular entertainment in which melodrama abounds anesthetize the unhappiness resulting from such conjugal situations. Regarding women ensnared in loveless marriages, the text states that, "para substituir la ausencia de vida espiritual (el religiosismo en su forma de culto es olvidado por las mujeres en cuanto éstas se casan) iban al cine. Leían escasas novelas fáciles, más se interesaban por las intrigas de las actrices de la pantalla, y cavilaban sus escándalos y los de sus galanes, cuyos adulterios ofrecían a estas imaginaciones reducidas pero hambrientas, un mundo extraordinario" (Arlt, *Amor* 58) ["in order to make up for the absence of spirituality (religiosity in its cult form is forgotten by women as soon as they marry) they went to the movies. They read simplistic novels every now and then, but were more interested in the intrigues of film actresses and dreamt of their scandals, and also those of the leading men whose adulteries offered an extraordinary world to their limited but insatiable imaginations"]. Along with stoking prohibited romantic desires, these tales bolster aspirations to consume. We read that contemporary film "planteaba como única finalidad de la existencia y cúspide de suma felicidad, el automóvil americano, la cancha de tenis americana, una radio mueble americano, y un chalet standard americano, con heladera eléctrica también americana" (Arlt, *Amor* 63) ["presented the only reason to go on living and the absolute height of happiness in the American automobile, the American tennis court, an American radio, and a standard American chalet with an American refrigerator"]. In this way, popular narrative forms, particularly film, are presented in *El amor brujo* as a means of escapism through which bourgeois normativity is communicated and maintained. Passion may be consumed through fiction, so as to supplant any devious desire in the spectator, and ideals of materialistic wellbeing similarly may be disseminated through the popular medium. It is not a great leap to recognize in *El amor brujo*'s critique of these popular narratives the traces of melodrama with its insistence on emotional provocations (frequently based in romance) and the impulse to maintain the status quo by commonly presenting hegemonic ideals of contentment, material or otherwise.

With these narrative conventions in mind, Arlt's novel takes up several basic mechanisms of melodramatic narration and mockingly plays upon their effectiveness. For example, Balder fails to live up to the melodramatic standard of attractive outward appearance: in the novel's initial physical depiction of him, he looks like a defeated, poorly-shaven man with a bad haircut. Apart from this fact, however, Arlt's antihero parodies the stereotypical protagonist of melodramatic sentimental narrative in his utter lack of action for a prolonged period of the story. After Balder's two initial encounters with Irene, she then disappears from his life after failing to appear at her piano lessons in downtown Buenos Aires. Balder dreams of their future encounter in the Carnaval celebrations in the Tigre district of the city, but he fails to muster the energy to actually attend the festivities for two consecutive years. In other words, far from being a take-charge melodramatic lead, Balder suffers from paralysis that prevents him from taking even the most minimal steps to secure a relationship with Irene. Instead, Balder waits for an "extraordinary event" that will shake him out of the monotony of his dull life, which does in fact come about by the most melodramatic of means.

Some two years after Balder and Irene's last encounter, Balder receives a phone call from Irene's friend, Zulema, inquiring as to whether he is the engineer Estanislao Balder who had given a newspaper interview two months prior regarding the skyscrapers of the future. As luck would have it, that interview arrived in Irene's home when it was used as newspaper wrapping for bread purchased from a local bakery. Upon seeing this fated article, Irene decides that she simply must find the man whose love letters she had clung to over the past two years. This improbable set of circumstances leaves Balder questioning, "¿entonces la vida era semejante a una película de cine?" (Arlt, *Amor* 70) ["is life like the movies?"]. Could his very existence indeed be guided by the fantastic serendipity common to popular cinema? In this instance, Arlt's critical reflection upon popular film continues as these events unfold in the most tongue-in-cheek manner, winking at the reader while presenting him/her with these most implausible circumstances.[15] In true melodramatic form, the written document with the missing shred of evidence is that which permits Balder and Irene to be reunited. Such developments add theatrical flair to an almost-missed opportunity for romance, which is all the while presented in *El amor brujo* as a preposterous melodramatic convention.

However, the exaggerated dramatics that shine through in this instance should not be entirely unexpected, as the environs in which the entirety of the tale develops maintain a rarified air of theatrics. In fact, both Irene and Zulema are specifically associated with art and performance: Irene is an aspiring pianist who trains at the national conservatory, and Zulema is a chorus girl who ultimately acquires work in the Teatro Colón. As such, even beyond Balder's overt gesticulation, theatricality gives shape to the entirety of the represented world, as each character is linked to performative arts and surroundings in some way.[16] And, that border between performance and the "real" upon which Balder so frequently encroaches is also breached in the representation of Zulema's obsession with 1920s silent film star Rodolfo Valentino.

---

15 And the convention being mocked in this instance is one that is commonplace in melodrama where, as James L. Smith notes, "Awful Secrets are always revealed and The Missing Papers found. These necessary documents provide endless excitement" (36).

16 On this point, Aden W. Hayes has noted that there is a direct parallel here between the bourgeois comedy that Balder lives and the theatrical environs of the tale, each with its corresponding lack of profundity in character (61-62).

Zulema's infatuation with Valentino is detailed when her husband, a mechanic named Alberto, explains to Balder that, for a time, his wife had become so taken with Valentino that their home was overrun by photographs of the actor and that he once had to lock Zulema in the house to prevent her from going to the theater to see Valentino's films (a punishment from which she escaped). Alberto's explanation of Zulema's behavior, however, occurs only in light of the fact that a different Rodolfo has appeared on the scene to disastrous ends for Zulema and Alberto's marriage. Zulema's obsession with Rodolfo Valentino is transferred onto a second Rodolfo –this time a dancer performing in the Teatro Colón– with whom she has had an affair, leaving Alberto emotionally crushed by her infidelity. In this instance, the spheres performance and entertainment have bled over into the "real" world represented in the text, by Zulema's fascination with an iconic figure. She consumes this idealized image and imposes it upon her immediate surroundings in an attempt to live out a romance with an icon of the silver screen. *El amor brujo* thus demonstrates the detrimental influence of popular culture, as it impresses desires and creates unrealistic and superficial ideals of contentment. Moreover, in the proliferation of Rodolfos, the novel displays a healthy dose of sarcasm regarding the limited repertoire of characterization in the melodramatic aesthetic imagination, which lacks the creativity to construct varied, complex characters.[17]

A similar scorn for the limitations found in melodramatic tales is displayed in the fact that the love triangles represented in *El amor brujo* (Balder, Elena, and Irene; Alberto, Zulema, and Rodolfo) follow a very similar trajectory, scarcely deviating from a standardized tale of marriage, boredom, intrigue, betrayal, and emotional turmoil.[18] The two married couples' relationships become stagnant and are then thrown into question when affairs challenge the precept of monogamy and, in turn, standard concepts of middle class happiness. Even so, the drive to perpetuate the figure of the happy family is at the core of Alberto and Zulema's desire for Balder and Irene to formalize their relationship. Shocked by Alberto's conservative nature in his attempts to see him marry, Balder reflects that "este obrero que tiene la obligación moral de ser

---

17 Another example of this limitation may be found in the fact that Irene's first boyfriend's name was *Walter*, which is not staggeringly different from *Balder*. Also, Balder believes that Irene's sister *Simona* looks like a "*mona*" (monkey). This play on names in the novel stands as a clear critique of the limitations of the melodramatic aesthetic imagination.

18 Rita Gnutzmann has also noted the parallel in which Balder's deceit of Elena serves as a model for Zulema's deceit of Alberto (79).

revolucionario me viene a conversar a mí que soy un ingeniero, de la necesidad de respetar los convencionalismo[s] sociales. Qué lástima de no estar en Rusia. Ya lo habrían fusilado" (Arlt, *Amor* 117) ["this working-class man who has a moral obligation to be a revolutionary is telling me, an engineer, about the need to respect social conventions. It's a shame we are not in Russia where he would have been executed by now"]. Alberto, however, is not as thoroughly conservative as Balder makes him out to be.

In fact, Alberto, like Balder, purports to be quite liberal in his understanding of relationships between men and women. So much is clear in the closing fragment of the novel in which Alberto seeks out Balder's advice upon discovering that Zulema is having an affair with Rodolfo the dancer. But, when Alberto asks Balder if he believes Zulema to be capable of being unfaithful, Balder's tactless response exposing the obviousness of the affair furthers Alberto's melancholy. Because of Zulema's frivolous chatter throughout the novel and her excessive admiration of the two Rodolfos, Balder has come to believe her to be capable of the most deceitful behavior, and he also supposes that Alberto had cynically condoned Zulema's actions. Alberto, however, claims to have never felt threatened by Zulema's infatuations because of the tacit understanding the two shared. Alberto tells Balder that he and Zulema had agreed that, if she ever fell in love with another man, instead of sneaking around behind his back, she should simply let him know and he would then let her out of their marriage. Balder's immediate response is to judge Alberto as a naïve fool for having taken Zulema at her word. Yet, like Alberto in his iconoclastic spirit, Balder also pretends to uphold unorthodox positions on sexual freedom for both men and women alike.

As discussed above, Balder claims to feel sympathy for women who are enslaved by marriage and are unable to live out their desires because of the social prohibitions regarding feminine sexual freedom. But, at the same time, Balder is beset by notions of feminine purity through virginity and is horrified when realizing in his first encounter with Irene that she, like all other women, is a sexual being. Subsequently, Balder becomes obsessed with finding out if Irene is a virgin. When he initially interrogates her and Irene responds that she has never had sex, however, Balder reflects "qué desgracia. Para mi felicidad, hubiera sido preferible que tuviera un amante" (Arlt, *Amor* 85) ["what a shame. It would have been better for me if she had had a lover"]. Just as the reader observes in Balder's pantomime throughout the text, which comes dangerously close to actually participating in those social practices that he loathes, the protagonist is again caught in a double movement in which he at once desires and abhors the social conventionalism he confronts. While Irene's virginity represents that melodramatic maxim of purity, an idealized quality that Balder desires, it also shows a dependence upon a value system that Balder purportedly disdains. Accordingly, Irene is shown to be a slave to the social conventions that Balder attacks but to which he also paradoxically aspires.

In Balder's confusion, he seeks to have everything both ways: he desires a pure, virginal lover (the conformist, melodramatic ideal), while at the same time searching for an iconoclastic companion who refuses to abide by dominant social conventions (the subversive counter-melodramatic model). And, in dealing with Irene's virginity, Balder's actions are just as contradictory as the ideals that he possesses. Because he believes Irene's claims of virginity, at least initially, he feels obliged to confess to her that he is a married man because not to do so would be a stain on the impeccable purity of his young lover. Yet, in his confession to Irene regarding his civil status, Balder shows that he also abides by the dominant social values that he supposedly despises. After all, if he truly wanted to represent an affront to the system via his relationship with Irene, he could have simply violated the ethical code of bourgeois values by carrying on their affair without telling her about of his marriage. Yet, because he does not do so, Balder demonstrates that his obedience to social protocol is entirely too well engrained.

Balder's contradictory situation comes to a head in the closing segments of the text, as it is here that he seeks to prove definitively the baseness of the Loayza's values by demonstrating the falsity of Irene's claims to virginity. In his final encounter with Alberto, Balder, having already sent a letter to Irene breaking off their affair, explains to the mechanic why his relationship with his young lover has come to an end. Much to Balder's apparent dismay, after he and Irene make love for the first time, he claims to be convinced that Irene is not the virgin that he believed her to be. In relaying the details of the situation to Alberto, Balder maintains that Irene's hymen was not intact before they made love, leading him to new heights in his melodramatic histrionics:

> [...] Irene ha hecho la comedia de la virginidad. Me ha engañado terriblemente. ¡Queriéndola como la quería! ¿Para qué me mintió? ¿Con qué necesidad? ¿No es estúpido, infinitamente estúpido lo que ocurre? Piense usted, que yo me he mostrado ante ella comprensivo desde el primer día de nuestro trato. Habré mentido en detalles secundarios. En lo esencial fui verídico, cuando no siéndolo hubiera ganado mucho más. Y ella en compañía de la cínica de su madre a cambio de una hipotética virginidad me exigía rotundamente el divorcio. (Arlt, *Amor* 204)

> [(...) Irene has made a mockery of virginity. She has cruelly tricked me. And me, loving her as I did! Why did she lie to me? For what reason? Isn't it stupid, infinitely

> stupid what is happening here? Consider the fact that I have shown myself to be understanding of her from our first meeting. I may have lied in secondary details, but in the basics I was truthful even when I would have gained much more through lying. And she and her cynical mother demanded that I divorce in exchange for a hypothetical virginity.]

In putting all the blame on Irene for her lies, Balder conveniently sidesteps the matrimonial trap that he believes Irene and Susana Loayza intended for him, since the next logical step for the couple following Balder's separation would have been remarriage to Irene. Balder's pretext works perfectly, as it allows him to maintain his high moral ground, showing himself to be an offended lover while washing away any sense of guilt that he may harbor from this sordid affair. But, as the text immediately reveals, Balder's explanation to Alberto is only half the story.

After the mechanic leaves Balder, criticizing him for his "prejuicio de la virginidad" (Arlt, *Amor* 205) ["virginal prejudice"], Balder is visited by his "Fantasma," a voice of conscience that communicates with him throughout the text and questions his motivations. In this instance, Balder's inner voice reveals a particularly important piece of information, stating, "Balder, le ocultaste al mecánico el cincuenta por ciento de lo que ocurrió. ¿Por qué no le dijiste que ayer, después de que Irene se fue, llegó tu esposa y te reconciliaste con ella?" (Arlt, *Amor* 207-08) ["Balder, you hid from the mechanic fifty percent of what happened. Why did you not tell him that yesterday, after Irene left, your wife arrived and you worked things out with her?"]. Balder simply rationalizes that his reconciliation with his wife is of little consequence, given Irene's lie. But, the Fantasma glibly responds, "¡Magnífico, Balder!, no discutamos. Te asiste la inhumana razón del jugador. Apostaste a un naipe, la mentira de Irene, y no has perdido" (Arlt, *Amor* 208) ["Magnificent, Balder! Let's not argue then. You are aided by the unflinching reason of a gambler. You bet a card, Irene's lie, and you haven't lost"], suggesting that Balder's escape from the situation was more a stroke of luck than reason based in ethical objection.

After this anti-climactic conclusion, the reader may ask what the point of Balder's gesticulation and criticisms leveled against the Loayzas has been. Indeed, we are essentially left off where the story began, with Balder, likely unhappily, alongside his family. But, in reaching this humdrum "(un)happily ever after," the reader must recognize that Balder does, in part, reach his goals of attacking the Loayzas. In seducing Irene and later abandoning her on moral grounds, Balder most definitely wreaks havoc on Susana Loayza's designs for her daughter's eventual marriage, and, by the logic of Balder's stated goal of attacking middle class marital and familial conventionalism, it would be safe to say that he has achieved his objective. But, paradoxically, in order to attain that goal, he must betray his own revolutionary ethic and return to his own family, an example of that same structure of which he is so critical and which he attempts to destroy throughout the novel.

By *El amor brujo*'s end, then, Balder is shown to be more a conformist than an antihero of the melodramatic sentimental narratives that he mockingly imitates throughout the text. In the novel's conclusion, the reader finds Balder pleading for melodramatic recognition while taking up the flag of bourgeois morality to demonstrate his superiority to Irene. This melodramatic recognition, as discussed in Chapter two, would be a hidden virtue eventually acknowledged, and Balder certainly wants to be appreciated as a victim who has been unjustly persecuted by the Loayza women's lies and evil plot. But, in this final twist of the text, perhaps just another of Balder's ruses, the possibility of destroying the "long and shadowy path" once and for all is definitively compromised. That is, Balder's appeal for recognition serves to demonstrate, not the triumph of his subversive mission, but the frustration of any attempt to deviate from the norm. By returning to his family and ostensibly upholding the moral standard that he invests in virginity, Balder embraces those conventions of bourgeois society that he had set out to destroy, presenting himself as the standard-bearer of middle class morality. Clearly this is a dramatic departure from Balder's cynical musings throughout the novel. Yet, as the entirety of Balder's enterprise indicates, he is caught in a double movement in which he seeks a new form of social existence while still clinging to the social protocol of the bourgeoisie and so failing to comply with a Nietzschean model of moving beyond standardized concepts of good and evil. Balder's actions, then, mirror the very structure of the novel as it at once criticizes melodramatic sentimentality and relies on the sentimental format to convey its tale. In Balder's disaster, we see the very problematic of the text in its call for a change, but one thought, perhaps impossibly, from outside of its own discursive confines.

Still, the ultimate failure of Balder's quest serves to illustrate the limitations of melodramatic textual reasoning by enacting a direct critique and, indeed, a politicization of the sentimental format. Arlt's novel strives time and time again to show the foolishness of melodramatic techniques in sentimental narrative, which comes to a head in the forced and deliberately-unfulfilling happy ending. Here, Arlt quite clearly calls into question the objectives and effectiveness of melodramatic narration, investing the sentimental format with a social commentary that interrogates the authority of middle class normativity. *El amor brujo* offers a process through which sentimental narrative is politicized, which may be best understood when read through the prism of Walter Benjamin's "The Author as Producer."

In his essay, Benjamin asserts that the work of art, in order to be politically productive, must not merely appease its public by appealing to a particular ideological tendency, but must also delve into the question of form, furthering an examination of the work's quality as an artistic object. Such an endeavor interpellates the public, making them grapple with artistic form, transforming them from "readers or spectators into collaborators" (Benjamin, *Producer* 233). To illustrate this point, Benjamin significantly discusses Bertolt Brecht's epic theatre and the process of alienation discussed above. We may similarly note that in Arlt's manipulation of the sentimental format and the melodramatic aesthetics by which it is shaped, the author complies with Benjamin's charge of inducing the reader to become a collaborator. That reader is forced to question the social conventions put on display when the content of the tale and the very structure of *El amor brujo* refuse to be easily consumed as yet another product of mass-produced melodramatic narrative.

In the prologue to *Los lanzallamas*, Arlt quite directly states his literary intentions: "Crearemos nuestra literatura, no conversando continuamente de literatura, sino escribiendo en orgullosa soledad libros que encierran la violencia de un 'cross' a la mandíbula. Sí, un libro tras otro, y 'que los eunucos bufen'" (Arlt, *Obras I* 386) ["We will create our literature, not endlessly conversing about literature, but writing in proud solitude books that embody the violence of a cross to the jaw. Yes, one book after another, and 'let the eunuchs scoff'"]. It is not difficult to discern here Arlt's aggressive take on literature, a literature of urgency, and that he is only lightly concerned with entering into any sort of literary debate. But, what the reader finds in *El amor brujo* –and what we would have likely found in the novel's sequel *El pájaro de fuego*, which Arlt promised but was unable to deliver– is a tale that very thoroughly engages in a highly literary, though equally social exchange. Through writing a story so intimately aware of its own methods of production, Arlt inserts his novel into a historical and social debate on sentimental narrative and the melodramatic techniques through which it is produced. In doing so, Arlt offers the reader something entirely new and indeed revolutionary: a love story in which a character reflects upon his lines and cynically crafts his gestures so as to reach the desired effect among his public. Such aesthetic innovation defies contemporary sentimental norms and sets the stage for postmodern debates that would occur decades after Arlt's death. As such, *El amor brujo* does nothing short of setting the melodramatic order on its ear, questioning the legitimacy of conveying "whole" characters and, in turn, the social conventions that those characters would embody. This problematization of the very narrative and social capacity of melodrama is reflected in the remaining chapters of this study.

Romance, Intrigue, and More in *Gabriela, Cravo e Canela*

From his early politically dogmatic works to latter carnivalesque novels that have inspired *telenovela* and film adaptations, the writings of the Brazilian Jorge Amado (1912-2001) offer an intriguing view of the changing face of Latin American melodrama. Over the course of his long literary career, Amado's writings gradually move from a world that is portrayed in stark contrasts of tyrants and the oppressed to one illustrating a more sweeping cast of characters, inhabiting a more complex social environment. Yet, throughout his vast body of works, Amado's stories never cease to critique the social norms that buttress a problematic status quo, or to embody essential characteristics of melodramatic narration. Given Amado's extensive catalogue, the attempt to define where the author's transition from one mode of writing to another –if it is indeed legitimate to cite such a transition in the first place– has become a point of critical contention. Nevertheless, the work that consistently stands out as a decisive point of reference in Amado's literary trajectory is *Gabriela, Cravo e Canela (Crônica de uma Cidade do Interior)* (1958) [*Gabriela*], one of Amado's first works to illustrate a certain taming of his overt political rhetoric, while at the same time demonstrating a concerted interest in representing the contradictions wrought by the forces shaping Brazilian national history.[1]

Literary critics have amply noted the softening of the left-leaning politics that define Amado's writing prior to *Gabriela*, and Bobby J. Chamberlain finds Amado's political discourse so subdued that he goes as far as to state, "*Gabriela* had nothing of the partisan polemics to which Amado's readers had been accustomed" (9). Chamberlain notes that in *Gabriela* Amado makes extensive use

1 Miécio Táti's early work *Jorge Amado: Vida e Obra* (1961) called into question the legitimacy of reading *Gabriela* as different from Amado's foregoing works as the basic elements of social and political commentary remain a constant (160-61), an approach that Nelson Cerqueira also develops in *A Política do Partido Comunista e a Questão do Realismo em Jorge Amado* (1988). However, in general, critics are wont to see *Gabriela* as a watershed moment for Amado as evidenced in the commentary of Jean Roche (194), Joanna Courteau (43), and Constância Lima Duarte (165-66). Essays by Ivia Alves and Renata Nascimento also have illustrated superbly the changing perceptions and critical focus upon *Gabriela* from the novel's publication up through its film and television adaptations.

of irony and parody, not directly leveling accusations against villainous characters as he had done in earlier works like *Cacau* (1933) or *Suor* (1934), but instead making picaresque tongue-in-cheek comments about the social and political dealings of the emergent rural city of Ilhéus, Bahía (29-32). Chamberlain's approach to reading *Gabriela* is highly productive, as it does not definitively elude the political content of the text, but finds it re-framed in a subtler, though no less effective formula. The body of criticism on *Gabriela*, however, shows how the political subtext of the novel may be obscured by the text's dual focus on the romance between Nacib Aschar Saad and Gabriela, and on the political strife between Mundinho Falcão and Ramiro Bastos.

Nacib and Gabriela's relationship serves as one of the principal stories that structures the tale, which is historically situated in 1925, thirty-three years before the production of the novel itself. The couple's relationship takes flight after Nacib, in need of a cook for his bar Vesúvio, hires Gabriela, an immigrant who is fleeing drought in the northeastern hinterland of the *sertão*. Nacib quickly becomes enamored of Gabriela because of her good looks, eager sexual disposition, and superior cooking, and the two eventually wed. Marriage is not, however, a happy situation for Gabriela as the social rules that she must endure as a respected wife of Ilhéus clash with her free spirit. The couple carries on until Nacib discovers that Gabriela has been cheating on him with Tonico Bastos, notary and the son of local political boss Colonel Ramiro Bastos. Nacib dissolves the marriage but refuses to enforce the local tradition of murdering the unfaithful wife and her lover. Following their separation, when Nacib again finds himself in need of a cook for a new restaurant he plans to open, he is eventually convinced to hire Gabriela. The novel closes as the two lovers re-kindle the romance they maintained before their marriage, thus eschewing constrictive local norms on "proper" behavior for a couple and serving as a model of social progress.

Concurrent to the narration of Gabriela and Nacib's tale, a political battle for control of Ilhéus is played out between Mundinho Falcão and Colonel Ramiro Bastos. This conflict pits progress, embodied in Mundinho's plans for economic and industrial modernization, against the stagnancy found in Ramiro's antiquated political governance. Mundinho relocates to Ilhéus from São Paulo to become an exporter of cacao, and eventually decides to run for the Bahian congressional seat. His opposition is the old guard, personified by Colonel Ramiro Bastos whose riches violently amassed in cacao farming came to dominate local politics in the years when Ilhéus was yet an untamed territory. When Mundinho's plans to bring a dredge to remove the sandbar blocking the local harbor interfere with Ramiro's long-standing political pledges in the port city of Salvador, a political firestorm is unleashed, threatening to return Ilhéus to an archaic epoch of armed political confrontations. Yet in the end, following Ramiro's timely death of old age, Mundinho is assured his political future when all signs indicate that he will usher in a new era of progress.

These two intertwined tales –along with a host of sub-plots played out among a cast of minor characters– make up the extensive narration that is *Gabriela*. Yet what is interesting to note is the way in which these stories, taken together, work to reformulate basic functionalities of melodrama. While still relying on a plot that is easily re-cast in patently melodramatic film and *telenovela* formats, *Gabriela* takes on many basic assumptions of melodramatic formulation. For instance, an ostensibly polarized conflict between progress and backwardness is still present, as viewed in the clash between Mundinho and Ramiro, and yet there is paradoxically no clear-cut "good" or "bad" character. As such, apparently divergent social positions are not represented as corresponding to diametrically opposed moral stances as is common in classic melodrama. Rather, in Amado's novel, dichotomized melodramatics are still used as a frame of reference, but now with an apparent understanding that the complexity of the social situation depicted in the text does not allow for a stock representation of the triumph of good over evil, virtue over villainy, the new over the outmoded. In this way, *Gabriela* consistently and effectively represents the very heterogeneity that defines the social milieu of the text, while employing nuanced melodramatic narrative devices.

Paralleling this social complexity, the novel's unconventional romantic tale leaves us with lingering questions, even while presenting us with a seemingly happy ending. When Gabriela and Nacib are reunited at the novel's end, we may recognize the commonplace union of lovers that serves as a hallmark of melodramatic success. However, that reunion in *Gabriela* is, in fact, an un-union, so to speak, since we witness the couple's legal separation earlier in the novel. Gabriela, then, returns to being a mistress instead of a formally-recognized partner to Nacib, which is presented as an improvement in her situation, but is not without its own unsettling outcomes.[2] In both Manichean character-

---

2 I allude here to Roberto Reis's insightful reading of *Gabriela*, to which I will refer throughout this chapter. Reis rightly notes that the denouement of *Gabriela* problematically sees the feminine protagonist regain "sua alegria, feliz na condição de mulher de cor, boa de cama e mesa, oprimida e objeto do prazer sexual dos homens" (20) ["her happiness, content in her condition as a woman of color, good in bed and in the kitchen, oppressed, and an object of male sexual pleasure" (my translation)].

ization and romantic intrigues, tried and true melodramatic devices that commonly serve to provide clear-cut conclusions are problematized. At the same time, however, a definitive conclusion to the text favorably ties up all of the novel's loose ends in a patently happy ending.

Gabriela thus presents us with a sweeping melodramatic story that calls into question basic aspects of its very framing. There is not, however, a conscious attempt to parody the rules of melodramatic engagement as there was in the case of Roberto Arlt's *El amor brujo* as seen in chapter three. Instead, similar to the case in chapter one's analysis of Rómulo Gallegos's *Doña Bárbara*, the players consistently exceed their roles, presenting complexities that push the boundaries of melodramatic characterization, being at once progressive and conservative, as is demonstrated by Mundinho or Gabriela's characters. And yet, contrary to Gallegos's novel, the failure of Amado's characters to remain within the boundaries of melodramatic narration does not happen seemingly without intention. Instead, breakdowns in melodramatic functionality in *Gabriela* may be understood as having to do with Amado's historical critique, which informs the text's socio-political perspective. Indeed, given that the period represented in Amado's novel pre-dates its publication by thirty-three years, the author writes from a distance that allows him to position himself as an observer of history and also as a participant in a different phase of national literary development. Amado's position within Brazilian literature of the period may be better understood when read alongside Antonio Candido's essay, "Literatura e Subdesenvolvimento" ["Literature and Underdevelopment"] (1970) since the critic's ultimate postulate of translating social strife into a mode of representation helps us understand the modification of melodrama in *Gabriela*.

In his essay, Candido seeks to delineate between what he views as two inter-related periods in the development of national literatures: one that displays what he terms as a "consciência amena de atraso" (142) ["mild consciousness of backwardness" (125)], and another that offers a "consciência catastrófica de atraso" (142) ["catastrophic consciousness of backwardness" (121)]. For Candido, in works of the mild consciousness of backwardness, "o escritor partilhava da ideologia *ilustrada*, segundo a qual a instrução traz automaticamente todos os benefícios que permitem a humanização do homem e o progresso da sociedade" (146) ["the writer shared the *enlightened* ideology, according to which schooling automatically brought all the benefits that permitted the humanization of man and the progress of society" (125)]. As Candido details, intellectuals of this period looked to Europe to provide that idealized notion of intellectual enlightenment, which in turn leads to imitations of cultural models that seemed out of touch with the realities of Latin America and perhaps may even have been obsolete within the imitated European context; Candido cites the Uruguayan Juan Zorrilla de San Martín's foundational poem, *Tabaré* (1888), as an example. Candido then notes the social novel of the 1930s and 1940s and specifically works of *indigenismo* by the Ecuadorian Jorge Icaza and early regionalist works by Amado himself, as being precursors to the consciousness of underdevelopment. These precursors, while not entirely abandoning European modes (naturalist influences, for example), would focus their attention on the social concerns of their national environs, looking inward and not outward, so to speak, for subject matter. In the final phase of the consciousness of underdevelopment, Candido groups a diverse mix of authors –Juan Rulfo, José María Arguedas, João Guimarães Rosa, Alejo Carpentier, Mario Vargas Llosa, and Augusto Roa Bastos, among others– who have internalized their respective nations' underdevelopment and have given an autochthonous voice to their national literature. As such, works by the authors of this final period constitute, as Candido comments with regard to Vargas Llosa's *La casa verde* (1965), the "fase recente de alta consciência técnica, onde o pitoresco e a denúncia são elementos recessivos, ante o impacto humano que se manifesta, na construção do estilo, com a imanência das obras universais" (158) ["modern phase of high technical consciousness, in which exoticism and denunciation are latent in relation to the human impact that is displayed, in the construction of style, with the immanence of universal works" (136)].

Set against the work of subaltern and cultural studies, Candido's understanding of a national voice within literature is problematic, as are some of his assertions regarding popular culture –both as folklore and mass media– which he would seemingly view as subordinate to what he terms "erudite literature" (123). Moreover, Candido's apparent underlying intent to establish the validity of Latin American letters within the sphere of the universal would only serve to revive the debate between Julio Cortázar and José María Arguedas preceding the latter's tragic suicide. Yet Candido's commentary on the political commitment perceptible in a literary consciousness of national underdevelopment is useful in understanding the transformation of melodrama at work in *Gabriela*, which lays bare the political underpinning of the text. In contrasting the two states of a consciousness of underdevelopment examined in his essay, Candido comments:

> Na fase de consciência de país novo, correspondente à situação de atraso, dá lugar sobretudo ao pitoresco decorativo e funciona como descoberta, reconhecimento da realidade do país e sua incorporação ao temário da literatura. Na fase de consciência

> do subdesenvolvimento, funciona como presciência e depois consciência da crise, motivando o documentário e, com o sentimento de urgência, o empenho político. (158)
>
> [In the phase of "new country" consciousness, corresponding to the situation of backwardness, it gives a place, above all, to the decoratively picturesque and functions as a discovery, a recognition of the reality of the country and its incorporation into the themes of literature. In the phase of the consciousness of underdevelopment, it functions as a premonition and then as a consciousness of crisis, motivating the documentary and, with a feeling of urgency, political engagement. (136)]

In other words, works bearing a consciousness of the crisis of underdevelopment move beyond a representation of the exterior features of a given national environs and translate the dynamics of social discord precisely into a means of representation, a tension woven into the very language and characterizations of the text. In Amado's case, consciousness of social crisis, transformed as a crisis of representation, becomes evident in *Gabriela*'s manipulation of melodramatic aesthetics.

Melodrama, traditionally considered to be one of the most stable narrative formats available to the author, is fundamentally problematized so as to represent more plausibly the fluidity and inherent instability of social processes operative in the national milieu of *Gabriela*. Patent representations of good and evil that can be located in singularly focused characters give way to ambiguous players, who, while still directly referencing the positively –and negatively–attributed social order, introduce doubt as to the authenticity of their characters. Similarly, romance does not offer us a closed ending indicative of the continuity of marital structure that foments social growth, but rather a relationship whose very stability rests upon its evasion of socially-sanctioned legitimacy. As a result, melodrama becomes less and less a means of understanding the world as black and white in *Gabriela*; the shades of gray that complicate the text appear as a function of Amado's maneuvering of the melodramatic norm.

It is fruitful to read the complex social viewpoint of *Gabriela*, expressed through the melodrama, within the context of Amado's evolving political stance contemporary to the novel's publication. Literary critics and historians have documented Amado's forays into Brazilian politics and his repeated political incarcerations, as well as his international travel and self-imposed and officially-mandated exiles caused by his ties to communist politics in Brazil.[3] The author's 1945 election to the Communist party's Chamber of Deputies of

---

[3] Chamberlain's work quoted above offers a succinct recounting of Amado's political biography.

São Paulo may well mark the height of Amado's official political activity previous to the publication of *Gabriela*, yet, at the time of *Gabriela*'s publication, Amado had suffered a falling out with the party.[4] Amado's conflict with those among the communist ranks was due in no small part to how those in the party interpreted the author's latest work, and, as Nelson Cerqueira observes, *Gabriela*'s new narrative format drew the ire of Marxists who accused Amado of bourgeois revisionism and of presenting a decadent worldview (7). Yet, what critics on the Brazilian left viewed as an abandonment of Amado's political principles may be more productively read as a change in the author's literary style. Amado's transition in expression becomes evident when we view the manner in which social conflict is melodramatically framed throughout *Gabriela*.

When compared to Amado's dogmatic political texts, such as *Seara Vermelha* (1946), the political polarization in *Gabriela* would appear to be more neutralized, so much so that it almost ceases to be a driving narrative force. This is not entirely the case, but it is true that opposing social and political forces in the novel meet on an unstable ground, as is evident in the confrontation between Colonel Ramiro Bastos and Mundinho Falcão in the rapidly developing provincial city of Ilhéus. Ilhéus, in fact, serves as an ideal space for the transitional aesthetic of *Gabriela*, as the city itself is caught in the throes of economic and cultural evolution. The text states that "progresso era a palavra que mais se ouvia em Ilhéus e em Itabuna naquele tempo" (Amado 32) ["*progress* was the word heard most often in Ilhéus and Itabuna at that time" (Amado 11)], and the townspeople of Ilhéus are enchanted by new buildings, new streets, well-kept public gardens, buses connecting the region, night clubs, a movie theater, and functions at the local Progress Club.[5] Ilhéus is not, however, a complete model of civic maturation, as we read that "ainda se misturavam em suas ruas êsse impetuoso progresso, êsse futuro de grandezas, com os restos dos tempos da conquista da terra, de um próximo passado de lutas e bandidos" (Amado 33) ["the streets still revealed, along with the progress and future greatness, some remnants of the recent past, of the time of bandits and bloodshed" (Amado 12)]. In this culturally and temporally hybrid provincial city, alongside the trucks carrying cacao in Ilhéus's business center go donkeys loaded with the same merchandise.

---

4 Interestingly, José Paulo Paes comments that the fall of Stalinism and its subsequent questioning from within the international communist political community offered Amado and other leftist authors the possibility to explore new literary formats (27).

5 Unless otherwise noted, all English translations of *Gabriela* come, like this one, from James L. Taylor and William L. Grossman's 1962 edition of the novel.

Businessmen and professionals mix with hired guns from the backlands, and cold-blooded murder in the street is still almost as commonplace as a society function in the Progress Club. Yet the most apparent holdover from Ilhéus's past is the entrenched political strongman, Colonel Ramiro Bastos.

Ramiro, with a great deal of skepticism, has closely witnessed the increasing influence of "progress" in Ilhéus, and was in his own time a purveyor of development in the city, cultivating public gardens and sewers and encouraging the construction of new and, above all, attractive homes. Indeed, much of Ramiro's attempt to improve Ilhéus remains superficial, which does not take away from the crucial role that he had played in the early development of the town. Having arrived in Ilhéus at a time when "era fácil mandar. Bastava ter força" (Amado 265) ["it used to be easy to rule. All you needed was force" (239)], Ramiro amassed his riches in the cultivation of cacao, an agricultural product of great import in the growth of Bahia.[6] Cacao served to foment an economic boom in Bahia in the early twentieth century, but also to consolidate political power in the figures of the colonels, the arcane title granted to the landed gentry that references a family's military past but holds no contemporary rank.[7] In *Gabriela*,

---

[6] Though cacao was an important export crop for Brazil throughout the nineteenth and twentieth centuries, its significance pales in comparison to coffee. As E. Bradford Burns demonstrates, during the last decade of the nineteenth century, coffee accounted for 64.5% of national exports, whereas cacao made up only 1.5% (196). Coffee's dominance continued well into the twentieth century, and, as Burns notes, "coffee in 1960 was still the dominant crop, accounting for 17 percent of the area under cultivation, 15 percent of farm income, and 50 percent of the exports" (475). However, due to climatic and geographic conditions, cacao was the crop of choice in Bahia, and, as Mary Ann Mahony notes, "Unless southern Bahia farmers were completely unresponsive to prices –which seems unlikely– they must have been planting cacao rather than coffee because they earned more money for doing so despite the better prices for coffee. That was probably because cacao produced so well with so little labor, while coffee in southern Bahia was very labor-intensive because of the ripening schedule. When we take into consideration the amount of money and labor required to produce cacao in Bahia, in comparison with coffee or any other crop, it seems clear that the return on cacao must have been greater than that on the other crops" (194). Indeed, cacao seemed to be a natural choice for agriculture in Bahia, and those who produced the crop were able to quickly obtain riches and, in turn, political influence in the region.

[7] E. Bradford Burns succinctly describes the role of the colonels as the following: "The landed class exploited the countryfolks' ignorance and isolation to augment their power. The patriarchal chiefs of the landed gentry customarily bore the title *coronel*, a title derived from the service they or their forebears gave to the National Guard. They firmly controlled the countryside. Ownership of immense tracts of

Colonel Ramiro Bastos exemplifies the underhanded aspects of an outmoded political hierarchy, longing for the days when he could employ violent methods to achieve his goals, sending out hired hit men to eliminate his political obstacles. Yet resorting to violence was oftentimes not necessary as Ramiro could rely on his fellow colonels to back his measures and to instruct their employees and acquaintances to do the same. Indeed, this trafficking of influences appears as one of the most insidious aspects of the colonels' power. In throwing their weight behind Ramiro and his contacts in the Bahian capital, Salvador, they maintain a stranglehold on Ilhéus's future to ensure that it remains both politically and financially beholden to external interests, while enjoying the kickbacks that they receive from the arrangement. This trafficking of influence will eventually come to be Ramiro's undoing when some of his trusted allies decide to back Mundinho Falcão for federal congressman, as opposed to Ramiro's incumbent candidate, Vítor Melo.

As such, given that both Ramiro and Mundinho are equally dependent on the sway of the colonels to sustain their political power, Ramiro's counterpart in the seemingly polarized political conflict uncomfortably parallels a great many traits for which Ramiro and the colonels are obliquely lampooned in *Gabriela*. Though Mundinho, the bearer of progress and a would-be virtuous figure of the novel, aspires to new political goals, he engages in the same trafficking of influence and political violence as engaged in by Ramiro, using his political sway to further his economic interests in Ilhéus. Thus, the emphasis Mundinho places on promoting new forms of capitalism in Ilhéus shows that the exporter does not propose any alteration of the social structure already in place, except for a new and improved mode of capitalistic development, a transition to a new phase of capitalism.[8] In this sense, the supposed social advance-

---

land conferred on them authority over the people dependent on that land. With their economic advantages and social prestige, they also exercised local political control. Some employed private armies to enforce their will, others hired the backlands bandits for that purpose. Friendship or familial ties with local, state, and national politicians and with neighboring *senhores de terras* buttressed the power structure of each *coronel*" (279-80).

8 Here I again concur with Robert Reis's assessment of *Gabriela* when he notes the convoluted transition of power in the novel. Reis comments that, "embora se implante algum progresso em Ilhéus, a verdade é que os coronéis não deixarão de todo o poder e é lícito supor que dificilmente Mundinho Falcão venha a ser um político distante daquele que no passado haviam reinado na cidade" (19) ["though some progress is established in Ilhéus, the truth is that the coronels do not entirely leave power and it is safe to suppose that it will be difficult for Mundinho Falcão to be-

ment embodied in Mundinho's political project fails to clearly distinguish itself from the violent control of Ramiro's reign, which problematizes the melodramatic formulation of conflict in the novel.

As Peter Brooks succinctly notes, "what we most retain from any consideration of melodramatic structures is the sense of fundamental bipolar contrast and clash. The world according to melodrama is built on an irreducible manichaeism, the conflict of good and evil as opposites not subject to compromise" (*Imagination* 36). Following the melodramatic logic of the two polar opposites that will collide in the text, Ramiro is intimately linked with an antiquated system of politics, while Mundinho is identified with innovation and progress. For all intents and purposes, the two characters are set on a clear path to melodramatic confrontation, and their quarrels and differences are formative to the text. But, importantly, in *Gabriela*, Amado strays from both a dogmatically evil portrayal of the colonel and a glorified vision of the modern businessman turned politician. Though Ramiro is associated with a flawed political order, one which will not be entirely erased at the novel's end, he is presented more as being out of touch with the city's needs than being entirely morally corrupt. Conversely, Mundinho is demonstrated to be more responsive to the needs of the people of Ilhéus but clearly not immune to the ills that Amado presents as inherent to the union of politics and business.

Accordingly, throughout *Gabriela*, we see Ramiro and Mundinho, not as two entirely opposed models of social and civic duty, but as competitors for control of the growth model of the cacao industry in Ilhéus, as it were. And, it is here where we are able to perceive Amado's nuanced take on melodrama in *Gabriela*. Ultimately, the role of whether the capitalist or the communist character is the positive or negative figure ceases to be a concern as it might have been in Amado's earlier works. Rather, through reading *Gabriela*'s neutralized vision of conflict, that the good are not entirely perfect and the bad are not precisely evil, we may come to note a grudging recognition of the permanence of the political and economic models that are represented in the text. Such acknowledgement, however, does not constitute an endorsement; through neutralizing the melodramatic polarity of *Gabriela*, Amado presents a different form of critique –a satirical, but no less poignant, political analysis– from what he had offered in his earlier works. In *Gabriela*, when melodrama no longer paints a dramatically contrasted view of virtue and villainy, it manifests a criti-

---

come a different politician from those that had previously reigned in the city" (my translation)].

cal perspective on the limited scope of possibility for social change. Amado's perception of the restricted prospects for social reconfiguration becomes apparent in the depiction of *Gabriela*'s ostensibly innovative political leader, Mundinho Falcão.

Mundinho comes from a politically influential family whose wealth was amassed in the São Paulo coffee industry. But, unlike his brothers Lourival and Emílio, Mundinho escapes ties to the family business to relocate in Ilhéus, in great part fleeing an infatuation with his brother Lourival's wife, Madeleine. Yet, the destination of Ilhéus is not chosen by happenstance. For Mundinho, Ilhéus "não era uma terra qualquer. Ali crescia o cacau. Onde melhor aplicar o seu dinheiro, multiplicá-lo? Bastava ter disposição para o trabalho, cabeça para os negócios, tino e audácia" (Amado 61) ["was not just any land. Cacao grew here. Where could he better invest his money? All one needed here was boldness, good sense, a head for business, and a willingness to work" (Amado (40)]. Expressing his motivations in terms quite similar to those of the colonels of the region, Mundinho arrives in Ilhéus scheming to get rich and feeling that he possesses the audacity and drive to accomplish his goals. Yet, in a key difference from Ramiro, Mundinho is not an actual cacao farmer, but is solely involved in the exportation phase of cacao. It is, thus, to his advantage to ensure the most effective means to distribute the local staple, which effectively links Mundinho's political and economic motives. Appropriately, then, Mundinho's political campaign promises the removal of the sandbar blocking the local bay, which inhibits Ilhéus's and the politician's export capacity. Mundinho seeks to cut out the middleman, shipping directly from Ilhéus and canceling Salvador's involvement in the exportation of Ilhéus's cacao. Such a project threatens to alter the local political hierarchy from which the colonels have reaped so many benefits, but Mundinho is anxious to stake his claim, and he, like Ramiro, is not afraid to use intimidation to reach his goals.

In the same trip to Rio de Janeiro in which he announces his political intentions to his family, Mundinho pays a call to the Ministry of Transportation and Public works, demanding an engineer to evaluate and fix the issue with Ilhéus's port. When the Minister responds that political ties to the Governor of Bahia impede what is Mundinho's doubtlessly noble cause, Mundinho retorts:

> O governador é um velho, o genro um ladrão, não valem nada. Fim de govêrno, fim de clã. Vais ficar contra mim, contra a região mais próspera e poderosa do Estado? Burrice. O futuro sou eu, o governador é o passado. Além de que, se venho a ti, é por amizade. Posso ir mais alto, bem sabes. Se falar com Lourival e Emílio tu receberás ordens do Presidente da República para mandar o engenheiro. Não é verdade?

> Gozava aquela chantagem com o nome dos irmãos aos quais, por nenhum preço, pediria fôsse o que fôsse. (Amado 64)
>
> [The Governor's an old man, his son-in-law is a thief, they're not worth a damn. It's the end of their clan and the end of their regime. Are you going to stand against me, against the most prosperous and powerful region in the state? That would be stupid. I'm the future, the Governor is the past. Besides, if I come to you, it's just out of friendship. I can go a lot higher, as you well know. If I speak to Lourival and Emílio, you'll get orders for the President of the Republic to send an engineer. Isn't that so?
>
> He enjoyed this bit of blackmail, especially in view of the fact that under no circumstances would he have asked his brothers for this or any other favor. (Amado 43)]

Issuing threats and throwing around his (feigned) political influence, even before he has formally decided to mount a campaign for Bahia's congressional seat, Mundinho from this early point in the novel begins to employ political tactics that are not entirely unlike those utilized by the colonels of Ilhéus. In this sense, even more credence may be given to passages in the novel that draw parallels between the two political opponents, stating that "na voz de mando do exportador, parecia a voz do Colonel Ramiro Bastos quando mais môço, ordenando sempre, ditando leis" (Amado 108) ["the note of command in the exporter's voice; it sounded like the voice of Ramiro Bastos when he was younger, always giving orders, laying down the law" (Amado 87)], and that Mundinho "falava agora quase com o mesmo tom de voz de um coronel dos outros tempos" (Amado 341) ["sounded almost like a colonel of the old days" (Amado 313)]. These similarities between Mundinho and Ramiro and their implications for the melodramatic structure of the text shine through in decisive moments of the political campaign for Bahia's federal congressional seat.

The most important event leading up to Mundinho's ultimate triumph over Ramiro's candidate, Vítor Melo, reflects the central problem of trafficking of influence in which both political opponents engage throughout the novel. As Mundinho's campaign heats up, the candidate battles Ramiro to gain Colonel Aristóteles Pires's support. A local political boss controlling government operations in Itabuna, Aristóteles had been a longtime supporter of Ramiro Bastos. But, the colonel had become increasingly frustrated by Ramiro's neglect of Ilhéus's nearby neighbor, and when Mundinho visits Aristóteles to make his political pitch, he is rewarded with the influential landowner's support. Ramiro, however, makes Aristóteles pay dearly for this perceived betrayal. While inspecting work on the sandbar, accompanied by Mundinho, Aristóteles is struck by a bullet that ultimately fails to kill him. Yet, in spite of this last-ditch attempt for control,

Ramiro's days of political influence come to an abrupt end. As Aristóteles convalesces and formally announces his support for Mundinho, Ramiro disappears from the political horizon and from Ilhéus entirely, gently dying in his sleep. After a gigantic funeral procession and ceremony, Mundinho is left as the last man standing in the Ilhéan political struggle, and his plans for social advancement proceed unimpeded. Work on the sandbar is completed, and a new era of prosperity is set to open in Ilhéus. All's well that ends well, or so it would seem.

Gabriela, however, does leave doubt in the reader's mind as to how substantial a change has really occurred at the novel's end. Near the conclusion of the novel, in a conversation with Ramiro Bastos's right-hand man, Coronel Amâncio Leal, Mundinho tips his hand and shows that, for all the civilization that he is set to bring to Ilhéus, he still knows and relies upon the power of barbarism. Amâncio comes to make peace with Mundinho, and he opens by saying:

> —Estava preparado para virar Ilhéus pelo avêsso. Pela segunda vez. Quando eu era moço, em companhia do compadre Ramiro, já tinha virado uma vez – parou como a recordar. – os jagunços estavam de atalaia, prontos para descer. Os meus e os de outros amigos. Para acabar com a eleição – olhou com seu ôlho são para o exportador, sorriu. – Havia um cabra, bom na pontaria, meu conhecido velho, determinado para o senhor. (Amado 422)

> ["I was prepared to turn Ilhéus upsidedown. It wouldn't have been the first time." He paused in recollection. "My men were alerted and ready to come to town. My men and my friends' men. To break up the elections." He looked at the exporter with his good eye and smiled. "An expert trigger man, a fellow I've known for years, was assigned to get you." (Amado 396)]

To which Mundinho responds:

> —Nós também estávamos com nossos jagunços preparados. Não sei quem iria botar Ilhéus pelo direito depois de o têrmos pôsto pelo avêsso. Também havia um homem designado para o senhor. Não era meu conhecido velho mas era de um amigo meu. Agora, tudo isso acabou para mim também. (Amado 424)

> ["We, too, had our men ready –and one of them was assigned to take care of you, sir. I didn't know your prospective assassin as well as you knew mine, but he was an old and trusted associate of one of my friends. Now, like you, I'm through with all that". (Amado 397)]

Realizing that the violence has ended, Mundinho then graciously offers to let Amâncio handpick the new federal congressman, or to take the position for himself which the colonel politely refuses. Yet, what this exchange demonstrates is that underlying so much progress is the same form of political maneuvering that has always existed. At the novel's end, Mundinho is unmasked as being remarkably similar to the model of antiquated politics and poor government that he has criticized throughout the novel. Just as he has emulated Ramiro's model of trafficking in political influence, he here claims that he was ready to eschew progressive politics and play by the same rules as his opponents, should the need have arisen. Though the reader may doubt if indeed Mundinho had his trigger men waiting in the wings as he claims, the cinematographic adaptation of Amado's novel, *Gabriela* (1983), to which we will later return, succinctly wraps up the situation in a conversation between Nacib Aschar Saad and his friend, João Fulgêncio. Witnessing Amâncio and Mundinho's reconciliation, Nacib comments, "parece que as coisas não vão mudar muito. Vai ficar tudo igual que antes" ["it looks like things are not going to change much. Everything will be the same as before"], to which João responds "igual mas diferente" ["the same, but different"] (my transcription and translation). The exchange would serve to confirm Alceu Amoroso Lima's comment that, in Amado's novel, "assistimos à passagem de uma cidade, do domínio dos coronéis ao domínio dos engenheiros" (162) ["we observe the city's passage from the control of the colonels to the control of the engineers" (my translation)], thus demonstrating that social power, still entirely derived from the cacao economy, keeps any sort of definitive social change to a minimum. Indeed, in terms of a radical social transformation, *Gabriela* gives us few indications of a new social order. The changes that do occur, while important, are best measured in gradients and not in vast paradigm shifts. In this case, the equivalent of a Brazilian "wild west," Mundinho Falcão has simply inserted himself as the new sheriff in town without questioning the legitimacy of the sheriff's authority.

Inasmuch as Mundinho is just as guilty of dirty political tactics as Ramiro, the novel demonstrates a reformulation of the apparent, classically-polarized, melodramatic battle that we see develop in the text. In accordance with the melodramatic structure that the reader is encouraged to follow, the political conflict of the text reaches a resolution, and the happy ending of the novel ensues. Yet, because of the limited difference between the would-be diametrically opposed political chiefs, the resolution of conflict is, in a sense, a return to more of the same. Though the title of political boss has changed hands, the cacao trade continues to control Ilhéan society. A new phase of capitalism has come to reign in Ilhéus, but that economic change is super-structural, altering neither the basic configuration of the community, nor the means of gaining and retaining power. Roberto Reis clearly notes this paradox of Amado's novel and comments that, in *Gabriela*, along with similarly socially-oriented works produced by the Brazilian intellectual elite of the 1930s and beyond, the represented world offers movement only for those in the upper stratum of the social pyramid (20). But, in Amado's case, this seems to be exactly the point of criticism.

By portraying forces that, in a final analysis, are not entirely at odds, Amado underlines the problematically limited scope of social movement in the historical Brazil represented in the text and the contemporary one from which he writes. I would argue that this is not an evasion of the social dynamics that define Amado's work, but rather a subtle –if not perhaps cynical– take on the corrosive marriage of politics in business. Joanna Courteau comments that, in *Gabriela*, Amado, "through a complex parodic structure manages to reconcile polar opposites, to *dar um jeitinho* (to fix something or a situation somehow) where no conciliation seems possible…" (44). But, perhaps the *jeitinho* of the text is more productively read, following the ultimate melodramatic resolution of the novel, as an agreement between two different, but not irreconcilable, business models.[9] This is Amado's great challenge to, and adaptation of the melodramatic mode: the polarized model of conflict is utilized to ultimately demonstrate the vacuity of that very confrontation. In a sense, melodrama is perhaps obliquely satirized in that it is shown to present a dichotomic conflict when one is not truly present.[10] Nevertheless, it is difficult not to note an essential melodramatic relationality operative in *Gabriela*.

---

9 In this sense, it is possible to draw a parallel between *Gabriela* and Amado's more politically radical works. Contrasting Ángel Rama's comments about the conservative nature of the Latin American "social novel" discussed in chapter two, Letícia Malard states, "o romance proletário de Amado é simultaneamente regionalista e modernizador [...]. O romancista não propõe reformas, mas transformações sociais. Portanto, modernização é sinônimo de luta de classes, de ações e reações que a propiciam ou a facilitam" (26) ["Amado's proletarian novels are simultaneously regionalist and modernizing (…). The author does not propose reform, but social transformation. In this sense, modernization is synonymous with class struggle, with actions and reactions that potentiate or facilitate that struggle" (my translation)]. The modernization in *Gabriela* may be read as an implicit presence of political transformation, which the melodramatic structure of the novel evidences as being flawed and grounded in antiquated social modes.

10 Though we may observe a certain questioning of melodrama in *Gabriela*, it is not parodied to the extent that it is in Amado's *Tieta do Agreste* (1977), for example, where the narrator's voice frequently intervenes in the text to auto-reflexively

In spite of the problematization of the confrontational basis of the plot, *Gabriela* continues to draw us in via its melodramatic episodic structure, which has undoubtedly made the text attractive for film and television adaptation. And, the novel's format, which plays upon the design of serialized literature, works relationally to include the reader in the production of the tale. Roberto da Matta views this narrative format embedded in Amado's latter works as a product of the heterogeneous makeup of Brazilian society, the "racial democracy" celebrated by Gilberto Freyre in *Casa Grande e Senzala* (1933), for example. Da Matta argues that the complexity of Brazilian society complicates the possibility of dualistic understanding, instead requiring a comprehension of social norms based in "*relacionar, misturar, juntar, confundir, conciliar*" (12) ["*relating, mixing, joining, confusing, reconciling*" (my translation)]. Applying this socio-historical interpretive model of Brazil to analysis of Amado's works, da Matta sees, from *Gabriela* onward, this same form of social comprehension operative in Amado's novels as his characters are increasingly less models of a determined social ethic and more figures marking the fluidity of communal interaction. For da Matta, the mutability inherent to Amado's characters also projects beyond the confines of the text, as "não se trata somente de contar a história de um herói, mas de encontrar e entrar *com* ele na história. Assim [...] Amado e seus amigos participam da história como contadores-autores e como personagens" (14) ["it is not only a question of telling the story of a hero, but of finding and entering into the story *with* him. In this way (...) Amado and his friends participate in the tale as storyteller-authors and as characters" (my translation)]. Da Matta sees this development and confusion of roles among author, character, and public operating in Amado's works as parallel to that which occurs in popular narrative formats, such as radio, television, and film.

It is not happenstance, then, that these confusions of narrative roles common to mass media are traceable in Amado's works, which is particularly pertinent in *Gabriela*, given that the text has been adapted multiple times for television and film. Indeed, the relationality among narratives that typifies *Gabriela* parallels what Jesús Martín-Barbero perceives as functioning in the melodramatic *telenovela*, in which the practices of watching the story move beyond the realm of simply viewing the tale. For Martín-Barbero, the *telenovela* pro-

---

comment on the plot. In this analytic mode, Eduardo Portella has commented on Amado's parody of melodrama in *Os Velhos Marineiros ou o Capitão de Longo Curso* (1961), noting Amado's employment of kitsch aesthetics (10-11). I would maintain, however, that melodrama is not parodied in *Gabriela* so much as it is expanded, and it is still utilized to underline a social critique.

duces an "Intercambio que es confusión entre relato y vida, que conecta en tal modo al espectador con la trama que éste acaba alimentándola con su propia vida. [...] De ahí que en los sectores populares la telenovela se disfrute mucho más contándola que viéndola, porque es en lo que se cuenta que se produce la confusión entre relato y vida" (*Laberintos* 450) [Exchange that confuses story with real life, connecting the spectator with the plot in such a way that he or she begins to contribute to it with his or her own experiences. (...) For this reason, the *telenovela* is enjoyed much more by popular sectors in its re-telling than in its viewing because it is in what is being told that the confusion between story and life is produced" (my translation)]. To bear witness to a story offers the possibility to enter into the tale vicariously, especially when recounting what transpired in a given episode and how it relates to the rest of the narrative. This re-articulation of the *telenovela* fosters identification with the plot's characters, which is a direct effect of the spectator's emotional investment in that plot. And, that emotional identification between character and spectator/reader is essential to melodrama, which quite intentionally tugs upon its audience's heartstrings to provoke fear, pity, desire, and satisfaction. In the case of Amado's *Gabriela*, that melodramatic emotional involvement most readily passes through the lens of romance.

Yet, melodramatic affect is not employed in *Gabriela* to frivolous ends. The emotion elicited from the representation of romance between Nacib Aschar Saad and Gabriela is ostensibly meant to convey social commentary, so complementing the political drama played out between Colonel Ramiro Bastos and Mundinho Falcão. The centrality of passion in the novel thus illustrates a common melodramatic motif, privileging amorous content to manifest what Hermann Herlinghaus terms "socialidades 'performativas' en que el amor y la felicidad son vividas como problemas de justicia" (*Imaginación* 470-71) ["performative socialities in which love and happiness are lived as problems of justice" (my translation)]. This is precisely the case in *Gabriela*, in which Nacib and Gabriela's romance, an example of true love conveyed in a sensual and emotionally heightened lexicon, challenges social norms but, in so doing, offers a paradigmatic model of social advance.

Following the melodramatic axiom, true love conquers all in *Gabriela*. Yet, in this case, Gabriela and Nacib are forced to take a nontraditional route in order for that true love to prevail. The couple attempts to play by the rules, observing the established protocol for courtship in Ilhéus, but, when that does not work out, they find a new path to happiness. In this way, *Gabriela* again leads us to a predictably melodramatic happy ending, but in so doing –and in this way paralleling the conflict between Colonel Ramiro Bastos and Mundinho Falcão–, it bends the rules of melodramatic engagement. The melodramatic permutations of the complex story linking love and social convention are on display, beginning with Gabriela's emblematic arrival in Ilhéus.

Nacib initially encounters Gabriela while looking for a cook to work at his bar, Vesúvio, and Gabriela is so covered with dust from her trip from the *sertão* to Ilhéus that her beauty is entirely masked. Yet Gabriela's autochthonous depiction is significant because it symbolically links her with the land. As such, her story takes on the additional dimension of symbolically representing Brazil and its people.[11] After cleaning up and assuming her work at Vesúvio, however, Gabriela's beauty, perfectly seasoned dishes, and voracious sexual appetite quickly entrance Nacib, and the couple's romance blooms. Their brief initial tranquility, however, is almost immediately threatened by a number of suitors, including the local judge and Coronel Manuel das Onças, who attempts to lure Gabriela away from Nacib with promises of money and property, a practice common in Ilhéus, where men of means maintain mistresses throughout the city and their families back home at their farms.

Because of the competition for Gabriela's attention, Nacib feels pressure to formalize the relationship. But, his decision is not an easy one, as he is fully aware that marriage with Gabriela flies in the face of accepted social practice, given that Gabriela is an immigrant from the Brazilian backlands, without education, much less an illustrious lineage. Urged by Colonel Ramiro Bastos's son, notary and local playboy Tonico Bastos, Nacib opts to propose, and Gabriela reluctantly accepts. Marriage, however, marks the onset of discord in Gabriela and Nacib's relationship, and the friction between the two is due in large part to the rules that Nacib attempts to impose upon Gabriela. Though Gabriela tacitly accepts having to wear shoes, among other rules that Nacib heaps upon her, it is evident to the reader that she does so only to please her husband and not out of any desire to act in a "civilized" manner. Because of these restrictions, Nacib unwittingly pushes Gabriela further and further away from him, making her more susceptible to the silver-tongued Tonico Bastos who brings about the ultimate demise of the couple's marriage.

Having encountered Gabriela one night after she had disobeyed Nacib's orders and snuck out of the house to attend a local circus, Tonico takes advantage

---

11 Several critics have commented upon Gabriela as a metaphor of Brazilian culture, and Rosana Ribeiro Patricio notes that Gabriela's presence underlines, though perhaps stereotypically, the positive aspects of Brazilian miscegenation (96).

of the situation to seduce her. Gabriela cedes to Tonio's advances, giving into desires she harbors in her marriage to Nacib when she dreams of other men as she makes love to her husband. She, thus, enters into the affair with Tonico without giving it much thought and enjoys the relationship up until the moment when Nacib discovers them. Comprehensibly, Nacib is crushed when he finds the two lovers, but he does not enforce the time-honored local tradition of murdering the two adulterers.[12] Because of his refusal to kill those who deceived him, Nacib believes he will have to abandon Ilhéus in shame. However, Nacib's friend, João Fulgêncio, thinks up an ingenious plot to restore Nacib's honor. João argues that, if Nacib had married under false pretenses (which he knowingly did as Tonico had to fabricate Gabriela's papers), then the marriage was never legitimate and Gabriela had never truly been his wife. In his capacity as notary, Tonico quickly cedes to Nacib's demand to have the couple's union annulled after both parties agree to sign a document to that effect.

Though saddened by the events, Nacib eventually develops a business venture with Mundinho Falcão, planning to open a restaurant to provide an alternative to the food served in local hotels. When Nacib's cook disappears the day before the restaurant's opening (he is actually kidnapped, an act in which Gabriela is indirectly involved), Nacib is persuaded by João to hire Gabriela as the restaurant's cook. From this point onward, the couple gradually resumes the relationship they maintained before their marriage. Gabriela reassumes her role as cook and mistress, and Nacib is able to once again recapture the serenity of life in Ilhéus that was so radically interrupted by his marriage to Gabriela. Order is restored in the lives of Gabriela and Nacib, and the text gives every indication that they will live happily ever after.

Throughout the recounting of Nacib and Gabriela's romance, Amado's novel offers the emotional highs and lows that we may commonly expect of melodrama. Via an intricate plot in which the reader is cued in to secrets that

---

12 Nacib's exercise of self-control is contrasted with the acts of Jesuino Mendonça, who does violently react to his wife's affair (the double homicide with which the novel begins) and is found guilty of the murder of his spouse and her lover at the end of the novel, thus paving the way for a new period of justice in Ilhéus. Another sign of the times in the text is that Coronel Coriolano Ribeiro does not murder his concubine, the much-desired Gloria, when he discovers that she has been seeing the local school teacher, Josué. One after the other, each case that refuses to enforce capital punishment for adultery gradually breaks the bond with one of Ilhéus's infamous traditions. But, although the punishment, or lack thereof, is altered, the actual tradition of maintaining mistresses is not.

the principal character might not know, such as Gabriela's trepidation regarding marriage or her affair with Tonico, we live out the story vicariously, hoping for the best but knowing that certain conflicts will inevitably surface. This key melodramatic interaction between reader and text exemplifies da Matta's view of relationality in Amado's novel, which is only possible given our emotional investment in the tale. And, that affective link between text and reader is equally forged as we witness Nacib's early confusion about whether to marry Gabriela and his latter sadness at her infidelity. Yet, we are also along for the ride when Nacib is finally reunited with Gabriela, offering us a happy ending by neatly tying up one of the novel's principal conflicts when it seemed that all might be lost.

In that denouement, following a standard reading of the melodramatic structure of the novel, *Gabriela*'s seemingly simplistic resolution of conflict initially may be taken as a quite conservative perspective on social evolution. If we start from Peter Brooks's assertion that plot development in melodrama depends on the character's ability to restore stability in a "frightening new world in which the traditional patterns of moral order no longer provide the necessary social glue," we may note an uncomfortable return to more of the same (*Imagination* 20). That is, happiness and tranquility are discovered in a return to normalcy in which any sort of alteration of standing social hierarchy is looked down upon. For example, when the efforts to elevate Gabriela to a new social standing fail, a move that would have necessarily implied a changing view on the socially-acceptable comport of a married woman, her regression to the role of mistress provides the answer to the novel's conflict. Nacib then opts for stability via the reinstatement of his previous circumstances, an action applauded by his peers. And, this development may be read as most unsettling in the sense that it presents a situation in which rules governing social class may potentially be challenged, as Gabriela's social ascent would defy a constraining social order. However, these rules are ultimately upheld when the sensual mulatta returns to her social standing as a cook and a kept woman.

And yet, paradoxical as it might seem, the return to the status quo in *Gabriela* actually does represent an advance, which also may be read in terms of the novel's re-working of the melodramatic aesthetic. While it is true that Gabriela and Nacib's marriage is ended on Nacib's accord, that outcome is a direct result of Gabriela's personal agency. After all, it is she who opts to have an affair with Tonico, thus eschewing the marital norms of the patriarchal society in which she lives. As Gabriela rejects the rules that society would attempt to impose upon her as a married woman, she shows that she prefers to be a mistress as opposed to a wife, just as she prefers trips to the circus as opposed to feigned interest in stuffy literary recitals, options that reject what would be the easy route to ascending in Ilhéan society.[13] As such, Gabriela's return to the status quo in again taking up as Nacib's kept woman is a status quo now marked by the caveat that it is Gabriela who has opted to retain her former status. And, in Gabriela's outright rejection of what would be her recognized "proper" place, the novel transforms our expectations of the melodramatic happy ending.

To be sure, *Gabriela* provides us with that romantic happy ending for which we had hoped. Yet that happy ending is the ultimate result of Nacib and Gabriela's transgression of the melodramatic rule. The final positive outcome of the novel is an effect of the couple's rejection of the social norm, not their adherence to it, so running contrary to a generally accepted perception of melodrama as a conservative mode of narration. When Gabriela and Nacib do not abide by social convention, when a socially-sanctioned marriage ceases to be an option, the novel becomes melodramatically successful. This form of representing a positive narrative outcome is, then, a transformation of the melodramatic tale, as it again uses the guidelines of melodrama but provides a twist that calls into question the established melodramatic basis. That is, *Gabriela*'s nontraditional relationship provides the means for happiness, while the orthodox marital union is presented as a stumbling block to progress. In this way, Amado is able to place on display the social conventions that may have been traditionally upheld by melodrama in order to question their validity. Significantly, in the case of *Gabriela*, those social norms brought under scrutiny are those that would impose limits upon feminine social agency.

As noted above, Gabriela's conflicted stance on marriage marks a clear case of feminine affirmation in Amado's novel, but is not the only case of feminine agency in the text. Additionally, other female characters, like Malvina Tavares and Colonel Coriolano Ribeiro's mistress, Gloria, also determine their own fate for the first time. In Malvina's case, the adolescent girl rejects the rules of her father, Colonel Melk Tavares, carrying on an affair with the engineer, Rômulo Vieira, who was brought from Rio de Janeiro to clear Ilhéus's sandbar. Malvina is brutally beaten by her father when he learns of her romance, and she is shipped to a boarding school, but she escapes to live a life of independence in São Paulo, far from the restraints of Ilhéus. For her part, Gloria,

13 Roberto da Matta has commented that Gabriela's rejection of social status is indicative of the novel's eschewal of a purely economic rationality for analyzing social interactions, as was the case in Amado's foregoing works (16-17).

the concubine of Colonel Ribeiro, first maintains a relationship with the local schoolteacher, Josué, purchasing gifts for him with the money provided to her by the Colonel. She later decides to maintain relations with both her suitors after Ribeiro eventually finds her out. As Bobby J. Chamberlain observes, it is not happenstance that the names of these paradigmatic female characters are used to mark the different chapters of the novel (37-49). Along with the chapter title referencing the tragic tale of the colonial maiden Ofenísia Ávila, who died of an unrequited love for Emperor Pedro II, the novel's chapters dedicated to Gloria, Malvina, and Gabriela mark a progressive increase in feminine agency throughout the text.

This is not to say, however, that the novel does not fall into certain stereotypes of feminine conduct. Critics have rightly noted that female characters in Amado's novel are highly sensualized and oftentimes confined to a limited gamut of social possibilities, and thus only making a partial comment on feminine advance.[14] For example, both Gloria and Gabriela's option to continue as mistresses, though representing an affirmation of personal preference and the advance of feminine agency, does nothing to change the actual social structure of Bahian society. Such a decision fails to radically alter feminine gender roles in Ilhéus, as women are still left with the limited options of being wives, prostitutes, or mistresses. As such, the novel demonstrates that change is possible but only up to the point where it does not drastically challenge the existing order. This ultimately limited range of social mobility serves to connect *Gabriela*'s two principal plot lines and to illustrate Amado's social critique couched in melodramatic aesthetics.

In both the romance between Gabriela and Nacib and the political conflict between Mundinho and Ramiro, *Gabriela* would seemingly manifest that the quickest route to resolving discord resides in maintaining the status quo through super-structural social change. When politics come to a fevered pitch in Ilhéus, tranquility is achieved when power is vested in a new strongman who can unilaterally impose his new view of how the city should function, again offering only a slight alteration of the previous social order. Similarly, when Gabriela returns to a previous stage of her relationship with Nacib, she demonstrates that Ilhéus, though not an entirely static environment, offers only

---

[14] On this point, Chamberlain notes that, "the gradual lessening of the seclusion of *ilhense* women must be viewed in the proper context as early, though significant, steps in the movement toward female equality. Only then can we begin to appreciate the novel, for all its restrictions, as an important precursor of the later feminist works of modern Brazilian and Latin American literature" (48-49).

limited space for feminine agency. The melodramatic structure of the novel, highlighted by this problematic happy ending, puts these facts in evidence by leaving Ilhéus, in many respects, the same as we found it at the beginning of the text. Yet, this paradoxical calm at *Gabriela*'s end works to reveal precisely the social critique voiced through melodrama and manifested in the novel.

In *Gabriela*, melodrama functions as a tool that allows Amado to show, from a historical distance, that the more things change the more they stay the same. The lack of impulse toward radical social change in the novel, a common feature of Amado's earlier works, is couched in a melodramatic model that at once presents polarized figures who are ultimately uncannily similar and triumphant lovers who get lost in nostalgia. We are presented, then, with a paradoxical melodramatic tale in which there are no clear-cut winners or losers. In this way, *Gabriela* problematizes these basic features of melodrama to question the linkage among politics, economics, and conservative social norms in Brazilian society. Given that the power structures represented in the novel remain largely intact, maintained by characters who offer similar social views, *Gabriela* thus questions the viability of social change. In so doing, Amado's novel also adapts the melodramatic model by problematizing the very idea of heroics and the social modes that have historically served to normalize social relations. By maintaining a questionable economic leader in power and by returning Gabriela to her unceremonious rank at the novel's end, *Gabriela* complicates the viability of the melodramatic happy ending, thus pushing the limits of melodramatic plot structure. This same obfuscation is on display, perhaps with more modest goals, in Bruno Barreto's 1983 film adaptation of Amado's novel, simply titled *Gabriela*.

Like Amado's novel, Barreto's film relies on a basic melodramatic relationality to entrance the spectator by leading us through an intertwined series of intrigues that evokes our desire to know just what will happen next. As mentioned above, the very scale of the story provides fodder for such relationality, which speaks directly to the episodic format of the *telenovela* in which *Gabriela* has been reprised on several occasions, the latest adaptation being that of the Brazilian Rede Globo television network in 2012. Yet, in Barreto's adaptation, it is not only the relational episodic structure that seduces the spectator, but also the almost exclusive concentration of the plot on the tale of Gabriela, and more specifically, on the sensuality of Brazilian actress Sônia Braga, which ensnares the audience.[15] In fact, the focus upon Gabriela is so intense that it runs

15 In her excellent article "Os Caminhos de *Gabriela, Cravo e Canela*," Renata Nascimento notes that while criticism contemporary to the publication of Amado's novel

the risk of completely overshadowing the political content that is paramount to the tale told in Amado's novel. To this end, John Martin and Donna L. Van Bodegraven note that "Barreto's film reduces the complex political and economic conflicts so prominent in the novel to rapidly, even sketchily presented subplots, often difficult to follow if one is unfamiliar with the book" (180).

Nevertheless, with regard to the general contours of Amado's novel, the film stays true to the text, even in its suppression of the political tale. As is the case in Amado's novel, Gabriela appears in Ilhéus following a trek from the *sertão*, Gabriela and Nacib fall in love and marry, a (condensed) political battle plays out between Ramiro and Mundinho and a failed assassination almost plunges the population into violence, Gabriela and Nacib separate after Gabriela's affair with Tonico, and ultimately all issues are resolved at the end of the film when Mundinho wins political favor and Gabriela returns to Nacib's side. And so, while the political content of the novel perhaps is not entirely abandoned, it is worth noting that Gabriela and Nacib's romance and tribulations are doubtlessly more prominently represented than Ilhéus's politics throughout the film. We may then ask how an intensely social and historical novel may become whitewashed through film. Why does Barreto's *Gabriela* so insistently fixate on romance and sensuality at the risk of losing sight of the social content of the text? If indeed both the novel and the film share a melodramatic substratum, what is it, then, about melodramatic film that tends more exclusively toward the sentimental, at the cost of the overtly ideological?

We may begin to answer these questions by noting that the greater project of melodramatic film is always geared toward a mass audience. Where Amado's novels –certainly engineered with consideration for the popular masses with whom he consistently expressed his solidarity– must necessarily be consumed by a public with at least the cursory education needed to complete a reading of the text, a filmic version equalizes the literacy requirement. That is, film is available not only to avid readers of extensive novels, but also to a larger public, who may or may not have access to socially sanctioned modes of education. There would, of course, be other stumbling blocks to gaining access to film spectatorship, among which economic means would be a chief hindrance. And even in this broader public setting, for a mass audience composed of varying

focused on the political content of *Gabriela*, that criticism quickly gave way to an increased fixation on the feminine protagonist of the novel, particularly following Sônia Braga's 1975 role in the *telenovela*. The various studies by Sônia Regina Caldas, including "Os Contratos e as Capas de Gabriela," evidence a fascination with the character that became a totalizing force for the text.

sectors of a given society to witness the spectacle of the film, there must be some unifying element that brings spectators together. In other words, popular film as a medium, or certainly the melodramatic film, must serve the purpose of *entertaining* the public. Melodramatic film's audience members gather not necessarily in order to be indoctrinated (which is not to say that melodramatic and other forms of film do not serve a purpose of indoctrination), but rather to enjoy a public spectacle, to bear witness to a good story, ideally in which the good will win out and the wicked will receive their just deserts. Social messages, historical lessons, and economic models may certainly be present. Indeed, it would be impossible for them not to be, but what the melodramatic spectator comes to the theater to see is a tale filled with romance, intrigue, and whatever may conjure the thrills of escaping the everyday.

It is this same public that clamors to see Barreto's *Gabriela*, and it gets what it wants inasmuch as the tale focuses on sensuality, yearning for contentment, and, perhaps most importantly, a happy ending that conveys the idea that all will work out in the end. Gabriela, played by Braga, is the cipher through which all of these desires are realized, and, as such, Gabriela's character may be read as embodying what Amado once envisioned as her function within his tale. Amado comments:

> Quando as mudanças de estrutura, resultantes da passagem de uma economia atrasada para outra mis avançada, forçaram a mudança do poder político e a transformação dos costumes, a mulata cozinheira foi um símbolo do povo na plenitude da fôrça e da sabedoria, foi o instrumento para que todos entendessem a significação dos novos tempos. Gabriela sobrepõe-se à realidade ambiente, sua presença vem dar uma nota lírica á pequena luta política de quando em vez rompida por um tiro ainda disparado pelos coronéis em derrota. (*Carta* 31)
>
> [When changes in structure, resulting from the movement from a backward economy to another more advanced one, force a change in political power and a transformation of customs, the mulatta cook was a symbol of the people in the plenitude of strength and knowledge, she was an instrument so that all could understand the meaning of this new period. Gabriela imposes herself upon this reality and her presence comes to give a lyrical note to the political squabble, once and for all broken by a shot fired by the defeated Colonels. (my translation)]

It is, then, perhaps fitting that Amado's novel is now virtually impossible to separate from its cinematographic and *telenovela* adaptations so intensely focused on romance and the female protagonist for which the text is named. As expressed here, Gabriela was, in the author's mind, a symbol of the times and a means through which social change may have been made easily comprehensible to the public. A similar process may be at work in Barreto's film adaptation of the novel.

Even when the historical and political content of the film appears to be entirely naturalized, Gabriela may be perceived as an agent of subtle but important alterations of the social fabric of Ilhéus. Her carefree temperament works to first seduce and later relax stringent social customs in the town. Gabriela serves, thus, as a cipher of changing social norms, making the shifting sands of a historical period, distant to the film's contemporary audience, accessible and comprehensible. In this way, she very closely mirrors the Gabriela of Amado's novel who, within the most innocent of melodramatic structures, would serve to represent the problematics of the Brazilian social and political environment in the early twentieth century.

Indeed, Amado's novel –and Barreto's film to a lesser extent– uses melodrama to gild the pill so as to make the social content of the text more palatable to the public. As such, Gabriela's apparent simplicity may be seen in a new light as she becomes more than merely a romantic lead. As a trendsetting character, she is identified in the positive melodramatic balance, fostering both the novel's and the film's capacities to convey the desirability for social advance. As seen above, Gabriela's progress is not entirely without its pitfalls, as in both the novel and film her ultimate return to Nacib may be read as a problematic recourse to more of the same. Nonetheless, while functioning within the seemingly innocuous structure of melodrama, Gabriela's actions place her in dialogue with Ilhéus's economic expansion, a change of the political guard and an evolution of social norms. Melodrama in all the incarnations of *Gabriela*, then, is much more than a means of arriving at the happy ending of an appeasing tale, as it places audiences in contact with the fluidity of social structures under the regimen of the cacao economy in Bahia. That melodramatic approach to defining history is equally apparent in the approach to the Mexican Revolution, viewed in the next chapter.

Episodes of Passion and Remorse: The Excesses of *La muerte de Artemio Cruz*

In her now-canonical critical work, *Foundational Fictions: The National Romances of Latin America* (1991), Doris Sommer remarks upon the manner in which the authors of the so-called Boom assumed an oppositional stance toward literary works published throughout Latin America prior to the 1960s (1). Sommer notes that, in substantially developing narrative complexity, the Boom's authors were to some extent successful in shedding the yoke of the historic national romances of the nineteenth century, even if their rejection of linear narrative may have evidenced a begrudged obsession with their object of criticism.[1] Carlos Fuentes (1928-2012), one of those artists most closely associated with the Boom, quickly became a foremost advocate of the polymorphic narrative styles emerging at a pivotal moment in Latin American history.[2] Fuentes fully embraced the stylistic achievements of the Boom, and, in his essay, *La nueva novela hispanoamericana* (1969), he explained the Boom's artistic advance and critiqued what he viewed as the antiquated narrative techniques

---

1 Sommer comments that, "the more romance must be resisted, the more it seems irresistible" (3), noting Mario Vargas Llosa's *La tía Julia y el escribidor* (1977) as one of those post-Boom works that, in a highly stylized format, seeks to destroy "realist" romance within the confines of a "modern" romantic tale. For his part, Aníbal González's *Love and Politics in the Contemporary Spanish American Novel* notes a return to the theme of romance and love in the post-Boom era as a response to a contentious political environment following the 1960s. Nevertheless, as will become evident in this chapter, I would tend to disagree with González on the point that, "the Boom clearly sidelined the exploration and portrayal of human feelings in favor of a vast novelistic project some critics have characterized as the creation of a totalizing metaphor of Spanish America" (2). On the contrary, I argue that the representation of emotion continues to be one of the central projects of *La muerte de Artemio Cruz*.

2 Literary critics commonly draw a connection between the Boom and its historic proximity to the Cuban Revolution as a collective moment of social and artistic renewal in Latin America. This relationship is all the more explicit in the case of Fuentes's *La muerte*, which was partially penned in Havana. Additionally, as Maarten van Delden notes in *Carlos Fuentes, Mexico, and Modernity* (1998), Fuentes vociferously defended the aims of the Revolution in the face of what he saw as fascist aggression from the United States in the 1960s (41-50).

employed by his precursors. Fuentes's treatise argued that the contemporary Spanish American novelist was in search of a new language and universal forms of representation, which inevitably caused a break from the "tendencia documental y naturalista" (*Novela* 11) ["documentary and naturalist tendency" (my translation)] of previous literature so closely linked to portraying the physical environment of its main characters.

Fuentes's *La muerte de Artemio Cruz* (1962), Mario Vargas Llosa's *La ciudad y los perros* (1962), Julio Cortázar's *Rayuela* (1963), Guillermo Cabrera Infante's *Tres tristes tigres* (1967), and Gabriel García Márquez's *Cien años de soledad* (1967), all classics associated with the heterogeneous Boom, confronted the reader with new aesthetic forms that had the clear intention of demonstrating a distance between themselves and their more straightforward, realist precursors. However, as Sommer argues, it is precisely the desire to underline a generational difference that paradoxically demonstrates the Boom's dependence on its literary forerunners. In the sense that the authors of the 1960s were attempting to distance themselves from the literary masters of yesteryear by rejecting previous narrative forms, they continuously (though not always intentionally) acknowledged the indissoluble relationship between the contemporary artist and his predecessor, so manifesting a form of what Harold Bloom has defined as "anxiety of influence."[3] Among the canonical works of the Boom, it is perhaps in Fuentes's *La muerte de Artemio Cruz* (*La muerte*) that this anxiety of influence is most readily apparent.

Literary critics rightly concur in noting *La muerte*'s indebtedness to High Modernist stylings, particularly in its similarity to the works of William Faulkner.[4] Without doubt, the play on narrative time, chronological order, and

---

[3] Though rooted in poetry, Bloom's concept is equally applicable to fictional narrative. For Bloom "poetic influence –when it involves two strong authentic poets– always proceeds by a misreading of the prior poet, an act of creative correction that is actually and necessarily a misinterpretation" (*Anxiety* 30). This misreading thus initiates a productive dialogue as one artist interpellates another, making for aesthetic advance. Bloom does not see this to be the case in Fuentes's novel, and he even states that Fuentes succumbs to his influences, noting that *La muerte* "is excessively derivative: Faulkner's *As I Lay Dying* and *Absalom, Absalom!* are relied on throughout, as are the major fictions of the Cuban novelist, Alejo Carpentier. Orson Welles's *Citizen Kane* is also an obtrusive presence. It is not as though Faulkner, Carpentier, and Welles are transmuted into something rich and strange that is Fuentes's own. The echoes are disturbing because they betray an anxiety of influence that Fuentes lacks the strength to surmount" (*Introduction* 2).

[4] See, for example, Ortega (203) and R. L. Williams (141).

stream of consciousness narrative are all fundamentally questioned and significantly developed in High Modernist prose, and they essentially inform Fuentes's novel. But, another and presumably more contemptible line of influence for Fuentes may be detected in *La muerte*'s perhaps unintentional approximation to previously produced Spanish American works like José Eustasio Rivera's *La vorágine* (1924), Ricardo Güiraldes's *Don Segundo Sombra* (1926), and Rómulo Gallegos's *Doña Bárbara*. Indeed, traces of Rivera's romantic adventurer, Güiraldes's nostalgia for an unrecoverable past, and Gallegos's attempts to grapple with the ramifications of an economically convenient matrimony and its symbolic social and historical significance influence *La muerte* to a greater degree than may be initially perceived in the spiraling structure of the novel.

Similarly, the underlying impulses of melodramatic narrative in *La muerte* –in the form of emotional anguish, romantic encounters, hidden identities, and moralistic definitions of good and evil– are forcefully contained within the ornately crafted artifice that is Fuentes's narrative.[5] In fact, those same melodramatic elements of the novel that Fuentes would seemingly attempt to repress through his narrative technique serve to demonstrate a continuity in representative forms between this classic Boom narrative and the works by those Spanish American predecessors from which Fuentes ostensibly attempted to distance himself.[6] In this sense, the latent melodramatic content of *La muerte* constitutes a culminating point for this study as it puts into play a series of mechanisms essential to the framing of each of the works here analyzed, albeit in a highly stylized fashion. In retaking the themes of prohibitive love expressed in *Doña Bárbara*, the suffering in *El tungsteno*, the personal crises in *El amor brujo*, and the grudging acceptance in *Gabriela, Cravo e Canela*, *La muerte* shows itself to be not so much a definitive breaking point,

5 Joseph Sommers insightfully noted this when he observed that, "there are individual scenes which, in their conception, border dangerously on romantic melodrama: the early love of the protagonist for Regina, a poor peasant girl, and some of the later emotional interchanges with his wife" (163).

6 On this point, John Beverley's comments regarding the confluence of Boom and regionalist ideological positions are particularly illuminating. Beverley notes that, instead of surpassing the ideological framework of the regionalist narratives that they ostensibly wrote against, works of the Boom era were, like their predecessors, articulated within the discourse of liberal romanticism, even though they did signal a crisis of that ideology (*Lazarillo* 117).

but a continuation –if not the very culmination– of the project of melodramatically framing national social strife in Latin American narrative.

Surely, the mere consideration of what often has been considered Fuentes's masterwork in the light of melodrama may appear as nothing short of scandalous to many readers, particularly for a novel that has been so thoroughly celebrated for its aesthetic achievement. We must, however, bear in mind that, at this early stage of Fuentes's literary career, he was not experimenting with ironic historic narrative –as is the case in *Terra Nostra* (1975), for example– or with adaptations of popular genres, as is evident in the use of the "thriller" in *La cabeza de la hidra* (1978). In *La muerte*, melodramatic tropes may be read as being utilized in a manner that does not reflect a postmodern sensibility, but rather they act as tools to depict a world in which moral boundaries, though presented in a decadent state, are still perceived as coherent and definite. As such, *La muerte* –and Fuentes's other early novels along with it, including *La región más transparente* (1958), *Las buenas conciencias* (1959), and *Zona sagrada* (1967)– functions within a High Modernist mode, aspiring to a totalizing representation capable of rationalizing the complexities of Mexican society. As was the case in *La región más transparente*, the desire for national representation is key to *La muerte*, but it is done on a much grander scale. In breaking beyond *La región*'s confines of Mexico City, *La muerte* attempts to encapsulate and critique the entirety of the history of the Mexican Revolution, including the failures of the post-revolutionary presidential administrations. In so doing, *La muerte* demonstrates a literary affiliation beyond the Boom to the body of works constituting the novel of the Mexican Revolution , the dominant literary trend in Mexico from roughly 1915 to well into the 1930s and beyond.

La muerte, however, is generally perceived as surpassing prior narratives connected to the Revolution, seemingly attempting to put an end to the cycle of the novel of the Mexican Revolution itself by presenting Artemio Cruz as the allegorical representative of a most crucial event in the course of modern Mexican history. Yet, in spite of its innovative, elaborate arrangement, *La muerte* comes up short in its attempt to surpass its precursors, as it offers a singular perspective on the Revolution that fails to admit, or generally condones, the subaltern perspective on national upheaval and its ramifications. Accordingly, the reader may come to question if Fuentes's novel truly represents a social perspective capable of incorporating the complex subaltern politics represented in Nellie Campobello's *Cartucho* (1931), for example, or if it is indeed more akin to other more conservative works of the Revolution like Agustín

Vera's *La revancha* (1930), in which a scorned lover exacts justice on a revolutionary soldier who comes to form part of the post-revolutionary government.

Fuentes's novel clearly was conceived as being much more than a romance novel set in the Revolution at the end of which a moral lesson may be taught. However, when we peel back the considerable levels of artifice that encase the nucleus of this story, we discover that the basis for this emotionally charged tale essentially relies upon a series of familial and romantic intrigues that act as morally didactic moments in the life of our flawed protagonist, Artemio Cruz. The reader is presented with the rise and fall of a self-made man, a rags-to-riches tale of the Mexican Revolution, peppered with several trappings of melodramatic narrative that have the clear intention of criticizing the path of national history. Indeed, Fuentes might not have been entirely unaware of his novel's melodramatic leanings, as he had to admit in regard to Vargas Llosa's *La casa verde*, the necessity of "la aceptación del melodrama como uno de los ejes de la convivencia latinoamericana. [...] Cuando se carece de conciencia trágica, de razón histórica o de afirmación personal, el melodrama las suple: es un sustituto, una imitación, una ilusión de ser" (*Novela* 47) ["accepting melodrama as one of the poles of Latin American coexistence. [...] When one lacks a conscience of tragedy, historical reasoning, or personal affirmation, melodrama stands in as a substitute, an imitation, an illusion of being" (my translation)]. The strategies that produce the figure of Artemio Cruz and the select public for which his story is told are the keys to understanding the underlying presence of melodrama in Fuentes's novel.

The first of those strategies and doubtlessly the most initially attention-grabbing element of the novel is the tripartite representation of Artemio through the *yo*, *tú*, and él voices.[7] Narrated from these multiple positions, the story of Artemio Cruz attains its full gravity, as the reader is granted various points of access to the consciousness of this archetypal protagonist. But, equally important to the manifold perspectives from which the tale is told is the moment in which the reader encounters Artemio Cruz. The intermittently conscious Cruz, who will ultimately fall victim to mesenteric infarction, is presented to the reader in an already dilapidated state. Unable to control his bodily functions, much less his immediate future, the *yo* voice of Cruz is trapped, only able to ponder an undesirable present and to remember a past filled with

---

7 This particular aspect of the novel has generated an extensive critical bibliography. Among those works that most coherently address the topic is Carol Clark D'Lugo's *The Fragmented Novel in Mexico: The Politics of Form* (1997).

regret. Similarly, the exterior *tú* voice –a doubling of Cruz that looks in and judges his very being– is unable to have any immediate effect on Artemio's predicament, proclaiming the inevitability of death while laying bare Artemio's self-righteous musings. Finally, the *él* persona appears, and it is through this voice that the reader learns of Artemio Cruz's dealings that have led him to this terminal moment. It is through the *él* sequences that the majority of the dramatic action in the novel is recounted, but it is important to recognize that these third-person sections only attain their full semiotic capacity insofar as they are linked to the *yo* and *tú* voices and, therefore, to the mortality of Artemio Cruz.

It is significant that the meeting point of the three voices is anchored in a moment of physical anguish as that corporal state is key to establishing the tone of the novel.[8] Artemio Cruz's physical pain runs parallel to an emotional torment that is projected onto each of the narrative voices, establishing an emotional continuum in *La muerte* based on grief and remorse regarding the protagonist's present, future, and past. In this way, each of the *yo*, *tú*, and *él* narrative voices in the novel comes to utilize an elevated emotional register variably based in pain, conceit, and regret to frame the narrative action. The multiform story told in Fuentes's novel, thus, fundamentally depends upon the representation of emotion and the construction of particular affective environments, so as to tell the tale at hand. The elaboration of hyperbolic emotional states is a central characteristic of melodramatic narrative, and one could argue that there is perhaps no more affectively charged scene than that of a man's passing from this earth surrounded by his family and friends, even if in *La muerte* this scene is the continuation of a family feud. This is not to suggest that every scene of death is necessarily melodramatic, but the extreme emotional content of such an event lends itself to melodramatic encoding. Certainly, any reader would be acquainted with the familiar notion of one's life passing before his or her eyes in the moment of one's death and the range of emotions that this scene of mortality can potentially conjure for the audience. To convey the affective impact of that scene and to attach a particular social appraisal to it is exactly what Fuentes sets out to do in *La muerte*.

Indeed, as Cruz faces his demise, the reader observes his feelings of guilt and shame, which give way to a process of moralistic personal introspection and judgment that comes to define the entirety of the novel. In this way, the affect-

---

[8] I am indebted to conversations with Peter Elmore for the consideration of anguish as the constant linking various narrative voices of *La muerte*.

ed portrayal of Cruz's death serves as a starting point for reflection upon the ruthlessness with which he –and by inference, so many other revolutionary leaders like him– acts, so intending to produce in the reader a negative perception of a would-be national icon. In his agony, Cruz's actions and perspectives are explicitly connected to that which has transpired within the actual historical parameters of the novel, and we are thus led to emotionally react to this terminal moment, while disapprovingly reflecting by extension upon the numerous *caudillos* who so greedily wrestled for personal power while leaving behind the social aims of the Revolution expressed in the Constitution of 1917.

This affective aspect of *La muerte* showcases the means by which socio-political perspectives are introduced into the framing of the melodramatic tale. That affective component of melodrama –frequently referenced as a shoddy, lowbrow component of the aesthetic– is crucial to the extent that it is through the provocation of emotion that ideology and social critique are communicated. Emotional strife and private experience are perceived in melodrama as coherent means of interpreting social crisis. As Carlos Monsiváis comments, in melodrama:

> Sin cesar, los hechos históricos reales devienen episodios donde lo ocurrido se reelabora en función del juego de sorpresas del melodrama. Los ciudadanos, los patriotas, los nacionalistas, los simples estudiantes de la primaria y la secundaria, se convencen de lo siguiente (con otras palabras): la Historia es la serie interminable cuyos resultados se captan más adecuadamente a través de la emoción. Y a los grandes acontecimientos los suele fijar la óptica melodramática. Si en las revueltas y las revoluciones los seres humanos son "hojas en la tormenta", la visión más difundida de las naciones alterna las mitologías del impulso con los sacudimientos graves. Y el determinismo se desplaza de lo público a lo íntimo. "Si a mi país le ha ido como le ha ido, ¿por qué a mí no?" (*No te vayas* 109)
>
> [Without fail, actual historical events are converted into episodes where that which has occurred is re-elaborated following the game of surprises of melodrama. Citizens, patriots, nationalists, and schoolchildren become convinced of the following (with other words): History is the interminable series of events whose results are best captured through emotion. And the melodramatic optic tends to frame those great events. If in uprisings and revolutions human beings are mere "leaves in the storm," the most widely diffused perception of nations alternates mythologies of impulse with grave convulsions. Determinism is displaced from the public to the intimate. "If it has gone for my country as it has, why should it not for me?" (my translation)]

As is the case in *La muerte*, history provides fodder for a melodramatic explanation of the course of the nation, equating personal and national experience by consistently relying on emotion (both the character's and the reader's) as a means of explaining and interpreting historical events. It is, after all, through the private context of Artemio Cruz's emotional experience that the reader is encouraged to cipher the entirety of the experience of the Mexican Revolution. *La muerte*, then, would seem to indicate that only through the affective guideposts of personal experience may the reader attain a true understanding of Mexican existence.

As such, it is difficult to overestimate the importance of the reader's emotional reaction to *La muerte*. In Fuentes's novel the successful portrayal of affective states and the social commentary that it is meant to posit depend largely, if not entirely, on the reader's appraisal of, and reaction to the representation of emotion. As the novel utilizes an elevated, albeit highly-intellectualized, emotional content to create a bond between the reader and the text, we are meant to feel the experience of Cruz's pain and to participate in his passing. In so doing, Fuentes seduces the reader into falling for the melodramatic plot, enticing us in spite of the novel's extravagant structure into reading a tale whose finale is already evident. After all, it is abundantly clear from the novel's title that Artemio Cruz will die. In spite of this fact, Fuentes is able to play with the sense of anticipation that drives the plot forward. It is in this way that the true melodramatic interplay between author and reader is brought to the fore. The reader follows the story told in *La muerte* not only for pure aesthetic enjoyment, but because he or she wants the answer to the cliffhanger question of *why* Cruz is dying, as well as to find out *how it feels* to arrive at that experience. Through a personal reaction to *La muerte*, be it disgust, remorse, rage, or perhaps sympathy, the reader is invited to become emotionally-invested in that process that is the death of Artemio Cruz.

And so, though it may seem paradoxical given the ornate structure of the text, the underlying emotional appeal of *La muerte* would place the text squarely in the conflictive position which Fuentes viewed as an essential characteristic of "new" Spanish American narrative.[9] *La muerte* offers the reader a reflection upon what Fuentes defined in *La nueva novela hispanoamericana*

---

[9] This apparent contradiction of the "new" novel, however, may be explainable. As René Jara C. has commented, "La nueva novela hispanoamericana surge más del área afectiva que de la racional, da una visión sintética y no analítica de la vida, su coherencia depende de la intuición más que de mecanismos lógicos" (155) ["the new Spanish American novel emerges more from the affective than from the rational, offering a synthetic, non-analytic vision of life, and its coherence depends more on intuition than logical mechanisms" (my translation)].

as that permanent dialectic between renovation and tradition that he considered essential to works of the Boom (35). In a departure from what Fuentes viewed in the late 1960s as "traditional" narrative, *La muerte* seeks a substantial aesthetic renovation, eschewing (or at least attempting to avoid) the trappings of both more straightforward realist and typically melodramatic fiction composed before the Boom. Yet, in *La muerte*, because the protagonist's emotional states are continually emphasized, the distanced and calculating aesthetic nature of the text is compromised. The melding of the ambitious narrative project with one of the most discernable traditions of the Latin American canon –that of romance– is also apparent in the various passages of *La muerte* that deal with Artemio Cruz's amorous encounters.

To be sure, romance functions as one of the chief narrative mechanisms through which Artemio Cruz's trajectory comes to be defined. Cruz is who he is because of his romances, or at least it is through romance that much of his character is presented to the reader. Over the course of four pivotal romantic relationships recounted in the él passages of the text, the reader is presented with an increasingly complete view of the general disregard that Artemio displays toward others, especially women. These female characters in *La muerte* play a critical role in propping up the story detailing Artemio's route to success and corruption.[10] Yet, the romantic relationships that Artemio Cruz maintains with several female characters throughout the novel are curious in the sense that, as Doris Sommer observes, they betray the utopian impulse of presenting romance as a sort of national panacea for social ills present in Latin American literature of the nineteenth and early twentieth centuries. Sommer comments that in *La muerte*, "the foundational love affairs of romance are revealed as rapes, or as power plays that traffic in women" and that Fuentes, thus, "arouses and makes us confront the habits of romantic longing we have learned from national romance" (29). While it would be difficult to argue with Sommer's assertion that romance takes on a negative, violent slant in Fuentes's novel, the reader must observe that Cruz's affairs, flawed as they may be, continue to play a crucial role in the formulation of *La muerte* and in the dystopian national imaginary that it attempts to represent.[11]

---

10 Such has been duly noted by Alberto Díaz-Lastra (352) and Gerald Martin (*Journeys* 209).

11 Here I concur with Maarten van Delden, who comments, "I think that Sommer overstates the extent to which Fuentes in *Artemio Cruz* departs from his precursors, for the story of Lorenzo reveals how Fuentes continues to rely on romance as a way of imagining a political community" (59). I would also argue that Artemio's

In spite of the negative effects of romance in *La muerte*, we find ourselves once again presented with one of the most commonly repeated figures of melodramatic narrative in a manner that is not entirely different from those more schematic works produced decades, or even a century, earlier. As is the case in these foregoing works, *La muerte* demonstrates that the romance functioning within the melodramatic structure need not arrive at what we might term a "happy ending." While we tend to think that melodrama generally ends with justice and the definitive triumph of good over evil, frequently symbolized by a (heterosexual) couple who has overcome the odds to be together, such is not always the case. The hero and heroine do not *have* to ride off happily into the sunset. As long as the work in question can provide for a morally authoritative tale, conveyed through an elevated emotional lexicon, the text does not depend on a positive romantic outcome. In effect, in *La muerte* we are presented with a variation of what Heilman terms a "drama of disaster" or what James L. Smith calls a "melodrama of defeat," in which the audience could be said to feel pity for the suffering protagonists. Yet, in Fuentes's novel, our reaction tends to be something different, a form of melodramatic vindictiveness.

The negative culmination of melodramatic narrative can be just as morally illustrative as a happy ending, showing how those who lose, those who end up lonely and unhappy, were meant to be that way. In flouting the rules of the cosmic balance of good and evil, those guilty characters receive their just deserts when they are excluded from the work's happy ending, and this ultimate poetic justice serves as a corroboration of the reader's moral outlook. A hallmark of melodrama, ethical validation allows for the spectator to feel that he or she is on the right moral path and that those who falter will be punished in due course. Thus when the reader sees the once-powerful and now grief-stricken Artemio in his moments of agony, we may feel ethically vindicated in seeing the reign of a corrupt power broker coming to a necessary end. Doubtlessly, to be excluded from a successful romance is one of the clearest ways in which melodrama manifests its moral assessment, and Artemio Cruz's romantic shortcomings and the social moments that they reference in *La muerte* cohesively illustrate this revengeful melodramatic impulse. Time and time again, the third person narrative of Cruz's failed affairs is used to reprove the protagonist's lack of social consciousness, thus explaining his ultimate solitude. This

---

romances, frustrated as they are, function as indicators of the path of both national development and dysfunction, not only in the case of Lorenzo, Cruz's son, but throughout the entire novel.

form of representation is twofold: it first relies upon narrating the story via a repertoire of recognizable elements of romantic melodramatic discourse and second, symbolically projects those narrative figures onto specific moments within the historical parameters of the tale being told.

In examining the first stage of this process, it is worthwhile to return briefly to Roland Barthes's *A Lover's Discourse*, discussed in the introduction to this study, in which the author proposes elements of what may be termed a romantic vocabulary. This vocabulary does not specifically equate to melodrama, but, as we have seen, the "figures" that Barthes comments upon are closely related to melodramatic, unimpeded, affective communication and appear repeatedly in melodramatic narrative. For Barthes, the figures of the lover's discourse are to be understood as histrionic moments of expression, captured as the lover expounds him/herself before a mute audience. Accordingly, moments of affirmation, anxiety, compassion, declaration, embarrassment, jealousy, solitude, and union constitute for Barthes a framework upon which a story may be structured. But, in that tale, the reader shares in the duty of constructing the meaning of each figure, as in the story itself "he who utters this discourse and shapes its episodes does not know that a book is to be made of them... all he knows is that what passes through his mind at a certain moment is *marked*, like the printout of a code... each of us can fill in this code according to his own history" (Barthes 4-5). The components of this romantic vocabulary, then, are intended to be filled in with meaning, projecting beyond the character's experience so as to connect with the reader's lived experience.

A similar process of connecting the character's reality with that of the reader occurs in *La muerte*, but Fuentes does not leave it entirely to the reader to construct that experience. Fuentes instead situates Cruz's romantic endeavors in moments of particular historical import, so as to imbue that which occurs in Cruz's affairs with an air of social and political significance. For example, it does not appear to be coincidental that the tale of Artemio's first love, Regina, occurs in 1913, a crucial year in the Mexican Revolution, during which Francisco Madero, "the Apostle of Democracy," was betrayed and murdered (T. Benjamin 3). In 1919, the year marking the first meeting of Artemio and his future wife, Catalina Bernal, was that of the death of Emiliano Zapata. The one woman who challenges Cruz and who is both Catalina's friend and Artemio's lover, Laura Rivière, makes her appearance in 1934, the first year of the Lázaro Cárdenas administration during which Mexico saw the first sustained attempts at the reform promised by the revolutionary movement. Finally, the first mention of Lilia, a prostitute who later becomes Artemio's kept woman, is situated in 1947 in Acapulco, high on the tide of president Miguel Alemán's industrial expansion and continued concentration of wealth in the Mexican upper class.

It is important to note, however, that the romantic events recorded at these historical moments in the text are not strictly meant to be allegorical references to the Revolution. Artemio's deception of the Bernal family in 1919, for example, is hardly an act capable of allegorically representing the murder of Mexico's greatest agrarian revolutionary. However, it appears to be more than happenstance that each romance is initiated, or at least referenced, in a moment of particular significance in the Mexican revolutionary process. In this way, Artemio Cruz's romantic endeavors serve to mold the protagonist's personal history, as well as to sequentially mark important moments in the course of the revolutionary movement in Mexico.[12]

Chronologically, Artemio Cruz's first relationship is with Regina. The reader finds the couple in the village of Río Hondo, where the rebel soldiers enjoy a brief respite from their battles with federal soldiers in the wake of Francisco Madero's murder. Our initial introduction to the couple finds them vigorously making love and then –presented in an indirect dialogue that does not specify a timeframe for the conversation– remembering their idyllic first encounter on a beach in Sinaloa when the fatigued revolutionary Artemio crossed paths with the young Regina. The couple's nostalgic evocation details the way in which Regina saw Artemio's reflection in the seawater and how the two fell in love immediately afterward. The recollection of these tender memories is interrupted when the remnants of a federal contingent of Victoriano Huerta supporters initiate an attack on territory already liberated by the rebels, and when Lieutenant Cruz is thrust into the melee. In the battle itself, Artemio demonstrates his cowardice by essentially abandoning his troops when the fighting breaks out, refusing to help a fallen comrade while his thoughts drift back to Regina. However, in the confusion of the fight, Artemio is taken to be a hero, and he is received as such by the townspeople and his fellow soldiers upon returning to the barracks at Río Hondo. Because of his cowardly actions, we read that Artemio "por primera vez en su vida sentía

---

12 As María Stoopen notes, the chronological framing of the text serves as both a historical marker and a means of establishing order in the fragmentation of the novel (109). This symbolic aspect of Artemio's character has clearly not gone unnoticed and, as Robin Fiddian comments, Cruz functions as "the personification of the Revolution, an emblem of its origins, course and results. Several commentators have documented coincidences between the fictional life of Cruz and the process of the Revolution, positing a common progression from an initial stage of idealism, through corruption and betrayal to an institutionalised atrophy" (126).

vergüenza" (Fuentes, *La muerte* 182) ["for the first time in his life felt ashamed" (Fuentes, *The Death* 73)], but that shame would quickly change to sorrow.[13]

Upon his arrival at Río Hondo, Cruz sees that Regina and several other townspeople have been hanged by the federal combatants, and, in bearing witness to his lover's lifeless body, Artemio breaks into tears. But, the delusional protagonist hopes that Regina's death was all a dream and that she will be waiting for him in a nearby village according to the pact they made in case they were separated. Seemingly realizing the futility of his fantasy, Artemio trades his sorrow for rage and vengeance and questions a barracks guard, "¿Para dónde jalaron esos hijoeputa?" (Fuentes, *La muerte* 187) ["where'd the sons of bitches go to?" (Fuentes, *The Death* 77)]. After attaining a general description of the federal soldiers' location, Artemio grabs the reins of the nearest horse and gallops off to brazenly avenge Regina's death.

> Una fogata, también, iluminaba la entrada al puente. Los kepís de los pelones reverberaban con palidez rojiza. Pero los cascos del caballo negro arrastraban toda la fuerza de la tierra, iban recogiendo hierba y polvo y espina, iban dejando una estela de chispas derramadas por la tea empuñada por el hombre que se lanzó sobre el puesto del puente, saltó por encima de la fogata, disparó la pistola contra los ojos azorados, contra las nucas oscuras, sobre los cuerpos que no entendían, que hacían retroceder los cañones, que no sabían distinguir en la noche la soledad del jinete que debe llegar al sur, al siguiente pueblo, donde lo esperan...
>
> —¡Abran paso, pelones jijos de su repelona! —gritan las mil voces de ese hombre.
>
> La voz del dolor y del deseo, la voz de la pistola, el brazo que arrima la tea a las cajas de pólvora y hace estallar los cañones y pone en fuga a los caballos sin jinete, en medio del caos de relinchos y llamaradas y estallidos que ahora tienen un eco lejano en las voces perdidas del pueblo, en la campana que comienza a repicar en la torre rojiza de la iglesia... (Fuente, *La muerte* 187-88)

> [A bonfire burned at the end of the bridge. The bastards' kepis shone pale. His black horse drove forward, hooves pounding grass and dust and thorns, and sparks streamed back from the torch as he rode straight at the fire and leaped it, emptying his pistol at their stunned eyes, their dark backs, the spinning figures who did not know and could not understand what was happening. They dragged the cannon hastily back, unaware that the attack was a single horseman who had to head south, get to the next town, where she waited.
>
> "Out of my way, you bastard sons of bitches!"
>
> Voice of pain and desire, voice of the pistol, voice of the torch flung at the limber ammunition cases. Then the powder was exploding and their teams were stamped-

13 Unless otherwise noted, the remainder of the quotations in this chapter come, like this one, from Sam Hileman's 1966 translation.

ing, a chaos of shouts and whinnies and crashes that now found echo sounds from the pueblo, where the bells in the flame-lit pink tower were clanging. (Fuentes, *The Death* 78)]

The totality of this passage is significant because it clearly demonstrates the elevated dramatic representation of Artemio Cruz's actions. In this patently melodramatic sequence that carefully details Cruz's emotional transitions, the ultimate product is action based on a primal response to the protagonist's emotional state. Through this cinematographically framed scene that smacks of a western showdown, the reader feels Artemio's pain and rage via melodramatic framing, delighting in anticipation as Cruz inquires about his enemies' whereabouts and so building expectation of what promises to be a dangerous face-off.

Moreover, this segment of the novel demonstrates a confusion of Cruz's revolutionary activity and his romantic motives. In fact, Artemio is plainly conscious that he has acted cowardly as a revolutionary soldier but becomes worthy of the nationalistic praise heaped upon him through his attempts to avenge Regina's death. That is, he fights the federal troops, not for the Revolution, but to exact revenge for his lost love, embodying the role of the offended lover so typical of melodrama. This confusion of the terms of battle reveals the importance of romance as Artemio's hyperbolic melodramatic gesturing, and his personal amorous motives clearly supplant any sort of explicit political ideology supporting the Revolution. But, not even Cruz's ultimate revenge is capable of covering up the fact that this now offended lover is hardly an ideal mate.

Before Artemio runs headlong into the federal stronghold, the reader discovers that the romantic story of Cruz and Regina's initial encounter on the beach is nothing more than a fabrication accepted by the couple so as to hide the secret that Artemio raped Regina. In his desperate moments following Regina's death, it is this foundational lie that Artemio wants to believe:

> Él debía creer en esa hermosa mentira, siempre, hasta el fin. No era cierto: él no había entrado a ese pueblo sinaloense como a tantos otros, buscando a la primera mujer que pasara, incauta, por la calle. No era verdad que aquella muchacha de dieciocho años había sido montada a la fuerza en su caballo y violada en silencio en el dormitorio común de los oficiales, lejos del mar, dando la cara a la sierra espinosa y seca. No era cierto que él había sido perdonado en silencio por la honradez de Regina: cuando la resistencia cedió al placer y los brazos que jamás habían tocado un hombre lo tocaron por primera vez con alegría y la boca húmeda, abierta, sólo repetía, como anoche, que sí, que sí, que le había gustado, que con él le había gustado, que quería más, que le había tenido miedo a esa felicidad. (Fuentes, *La muerte* 186).

[He ought to believe her pretty lie forever, until the end. It had no trace of truth. Neither did the truth: it was not true that he had gone into that Sinaloan pueblo just as he had gone into so many others, ready to grab the first woman who incautiously ventured outside. It was not true that a girl of eighteen had been thrown helplessly across his horse and carried back to the officers' dormitory to be violated in silence. It was not true that her honesty had silently forgiven him: her resistence (sic.) melted into pleasure and arms that had never touched a man before him with joy, and her moist mouth had repeated, as last night, that yes, yes, she had liked it, with him she had enjoyed and loved it, she wanted more, she had been afraid of such happiness. (Fuentes, *The Death* 76)]

Regina's rape demonstrates that what could have been a paradigmatic example of revolutionary passion is founded in sexual violence, so problematizing the chivalry that Artemio would personify. Because Artemio and Regina's relationship is born out of rape, it evokes heterosexual relations, not as a productive union, but as an embodiment of violence in a moment of national chaos, so supporting Doris Sommer's reading of the text mentioned above. For the reader, this violent sexual possession clearly appears as criticism of Artemio, the archetypical participant in the revolutionary history of contemporary Mexico.

Moreover, the representation of Regina and Artemio's encounters offers feminine subjugation and acceptance in an emotionally charged lexicon that borders on soft-core pornography. In fact, the initial description of Artemio and Regina's love making at the beginning of the segment is equally provocative as we read that, overcome by emotion, "Regina se pierde y se deja vencer y contesta con el aliento grueso, frunciendo el ceño y con los labios sonrientes que sí, que sí, que le gusta, que sí, que no la deje, que siga, que sí, que no se acabe, que sí..." (Fuentes, *La muerte* 172) ["Regina lost herself and answered with thick breath (...) with her lips smiling yes, yes, she liked it, yes, she was ready, don't stop, yes, go on, go on, let it never end, yes" (Fuentes, *The Death* 63)]. These passages in which Fuentes leaves little to the imagination serve to problematize the verisimilitude of the tale, as such a radical change in Regina's character, from a timid, violated young woman to a passionate and willing lover, is at minimum, problematic. How has Regina come to passionately desire the man who victimizes her? Has she suffered some form of psychological break? Though such a sequence of events is not entirely implausible, it is not psychologically developed in the novel, a curious fact in a novel so geared toward intense psychological examination.

Regina's sudden change of heart, however, may reasonably be explained through its melodramatic presentation. The immediate transformation of her personality –reflecting a cinematographic sensibility of the text, as her character is portrayed only in brief flashes of experience– is presented as being coherent in the novel as melodrama searches to present characters as whole entities. Regina must love or hate Artemio, but she cannot relate ambiguously to him. That same whole melodramatic characterization plays into the entirety of the negative portrayal of Artemio Cruz, emphasizing his flawed character at multiple junctures.[14] The type of wholeness seen in Artemio, however, is more complicated in the representation of his wife, Catalina Bernal, whose apparent contradiction and the emotional crisis that it causes her are directly informed by the melodramatic aesthetic that guides *La muerte*.

Artemio seeks out and marries Catalina, not because of his love for her, but rather because, while jailed in 1915, Artemio shared a cell with Catalina's idealist brother, Gonzalo. Gonzalo professed a profound devotion to revolutionary agrarian reform, in spite of his pertaining to the landholding social class. Artemio takes advantage of his encounter with Gonzalo, learning of the Bernal family riches in the moments preceding Gonzalo's death by firing squad. Artemio would have likely encountered the same fate were it not for his calculated tactics in dealing with the *Villista* General Zagal and the attack on the jail by General Álvaro Obregón's federal military, which saves him (melodramatically) in the nick of time. The liberated Artemio then takes roughly four years to formulate a plan to take over the Bernal family's land and wealth. Cruz searches out Gonzalo and Catalina's father, Gamaliel, and pitches him a plan to ruthlessly collect on his rented lands. Gamaliel is aware that Artemio's offer is ultimately a losing proposition for the family, but he nonetheless hands over the reins to the family's properties, aware that he himself participated in similar land-grabbing methods following Benito Juárez's accent to power in the mid 1800s. Gamaliel then arranges for his daughter's marriage to the revolutionary drifter.

---

14 I am aware that this may be a contentious point with some readers, as certain critics and even the author himself view Cruz as a psychologically dense character with many emotional levels. Luis Harss and Barbara Dohmann note that, "To a considerable extent Fuentes has achieved the complexity of characterization needed to give Artemio specific weight and gravity. He has avoided the dangers of caricature. Artemio Cruz, the prototype of the Mexican caudillo, is a type of personality, he says, that 'given our tendency in Mexico to see things in black and white, is easily classifiable as black. My intention, which became increasingly evident to me as the character developed, was to show there's no such thing as black and white. Artemio Cruz is at once the book's hero and antihero'" (300). The argument I develop in this chapter is that Cruz's apparent complexity is betrayed as it only serves to represent a one-sided, self-chastising viewpoint.

Catalina is unhappy in the marriage because Artemio has run off her boyfriend and, more importantly, because she believes Artemio to be responsible for Gonzalo's death. Catalina seeks to avenge her brother's death "abrazando a este hombre, abrazándolo pero negando la ternura que él quisiera encontrar en ella. Matándolo en vida, destilando la amargura hasta envenenarlo" (Fuentes, *La muerte* 158) ["by embracing this stranger, embracing him but denying him the tenderness he would like to find in her. She would murder him living, distilling bitterness until he would be poisoned" (Fuentes, *The Death* 48)]. In spite of this fact, the reader discovers that Catalina must do everything in her power to control herself when she is confronted by Artemio's irresistible sensuality. She is ultimately unsuccessful and resorts to hating her husband by day but giving into his sexual advances by night. In Catalina's interior dialogue, we read, "Yo pidiendo perdón por haber olvidado en el gusto las razones de mi rencor… Dios mío, ¿cómo puedo responder a esta fuerza, al brillo de estos ojos verdes? ¿Cuál puede ser mi propia fuerza, una vez que ese cuerpo feroz, tierno, me toma entre sus brazos y no me pide permiso, ni perdón por lo que yo pudiera echarle en cara…" (Fuentes, *La muerte* 205) ["I beg forgiveness for having forgotten in my pleasure the reason for my hatred. Dear God, how can I help but respond to such strength, to the force in those green eyes? What can my own strength be once that ferocity and tenderness turn upon me without asking whether I welcome them, without asking pardon for the guilt I could throw in his face?" (Fuentes, *The Death* 96)].

In this way, the novel takes up the theme of Artemio's irrepressible attractiveness as an essential factor of his character. In true melodramatic fashion, Artemio's physical stature is presented as a key element of power. Artemio's green eyes, referenced in various instances in the novel, "reveal inherent force, liveliness, charisma, and sensuality" (Faris 51). Yet, it is important to note that Artemio's physical attractiveness serves not to define him as a positive character, but as a dangerous one. Similar to Doña Bárbara's attempted seduction of Santos Luzardo discussed in the first chapter of this study, Artemio's allure is threatening to Catalina because it infringes upon familial order and the social standing of the Bernal family on the whole. All the same, the attraction that Catalina feels for Artemio –a love or hate situation similar to Regina's cast that is problematic for the reader given the circumstances of the relationship– produces a sense of shame that connects with the feeling of regret that Artemio frequently experiences in the *yo* and *tú* narratives. When Catalina lays bare her innermost feelings, she replicates that sensation of emotional desperation that Artemio feels on his deathbed. So much so is the case that we hardly notice that we have been granted access to a conscience other than Artemio's, which is ultimately an incongruence of the novel as we are only to be privy to Artemio's thoughts.[15] Even so, Catalina's emotionally charged crisis once again illustrates the centrality of melodramatic desperation in communicating Artemio's tale, even if the couple never arrives at the desired melodramatic happy ending.

The one relationship that does present –albeit briefly– the potential for happiness is that between Artemio and Laura Rivière. Artemio and Luara share a chance meeting at the opera that turns into something more. The two become lovers who share an affinity for the finer things in life: music, painting, travel, and sumptuous décor. Their relationship is based on materialistic consumption, which, curiously enough, is presented in *La muerte* as the one possibility for an equitable relationship, as it is here that neither of the participants is forced into the relationship, nor subdued into continuing it.

The reader encounters the couple in Laura's new apartment, presumably somewhere in Mexico City, where she has chosen to relocate after having separated from her husband. Artemio plays records, and the two enjoy scotch whiskey as Laura finishes preparing for their night on the town. Laura's readying is interrupted when her friend, Catalina Bernal, calls her on the telephone. As much as illustrating Laura and Artemio's betrayal of a friend and wife, Catalina's call suspends the lover's idyllic memories of foreign travel, trips to the museum, and dancing in elegant ballrooms. Nostalgia gives way to discord as Laura pushes Artemio to commit to their relationship and leave Catalina. Obeying a sense of self-preservation, Cruz refutes Laura's arguments, stating:

> —No te engañé. No te obligué.
> —No te transformé, que es distinto. No estás dispuesto.
> —Te quiero así, como hemos sido hasta ahora.
> —Como el primer día.
> —Sí, así.
> —Ya no es el primer día. Ahora me conoces. Dime.
> —Date cuenta, Laura, por favor. Esas cosas dañan. Hay que saber cuidar...
> —¿Las apariencias? ¿O el miedo? Si no pasará nada, ten la seguridad de que no pasará nada. (Fuentes, *La muerte* 314)
>
> ["I haven't deceived you. I haven't forced you."
> "And I have not changed you, which is quite different. You aren't ready."

[15] Daniel de Guzmán is among the few critics to have noticed this inconsistency, and he wonders how Catalina's intrusion into the novel "is to be reconciled with the overall point of view of the novel itself" (113). This is an important question for a novel with such a consistently complex structure.

"I want you like this, as we have been until now."

"As we were the first day."

"Yes, like that."

"It's not the first day now, Artemio. You know me now. Tell me."

"Be careful, Laura, please. These things can hurt us both. You have to be careful..."

"Of what? Appearances? Or of fear? If nothing is going to happen, you can be sure that nothing will happen." (Fuentes, *The Death* 211)]

Shortly after this exchange, Artemio exits the apartment, leaving behind the possibility of any reconciliation. Judith Payne has interpreted Cruz's rejection of Laura to be a product of his binary social view "in which each participant in a relationship must occupy a position of either inferiority or superiority with respect to the other" (74). Payne comments that, because Artemio is incapable of considering a mutually equitable relationship, he "remains trapped in his isolation. His plight serves as an example of patriarchal might turned against itself in the intimate life of one of its foremost models" (74). Payne's argument is persuasive because it epitomizes Cruz's need for control, not only in this romantic relationship, but also in his other affairs and business dealings. Lest the reader forget, Artemio struggles to maintain control over his family by toying with them and by not revealing the location of his will and testament. Polarized alternatives of oppressor and oppressed, winners and losers, are key to the structuring of melodrama, but, in this scene, the melodramatic impulse of the text is most readily found in the unrequited desire that inhabits Laura's apartment.

That unfulfilled desire is mutual since neither Artemio nor Laura really gets what he or she wants. We discover in this same passage that, in the years following this breakup, Artemio attempted to return to a café on the Rue Caumartin in Paris, where he and Laura shared a clandestine meeting, but he was unable to locate the spot. This fact demonstrates that, in some measure, the regret over lost love stays with Cruz well past the moment he abandons Laura's apartment, which is seemingly driven home in the only other mentions of Laura that reader finds in the novel. In a decadent party at his Coyoacán estate, partygoers gossip about Artemio's former lover, who has allegedly left Mexico City and remarried. The reader understands that Laura and Artemio have followed quite different trajectories and that, when he left Laura, Artemio cancelled his possibilities of happiness while Laura moved on to bigger and better things.

Significantly, Artemio turns his back on Laura in 1934 (the year of Lázaro Cárdenas's ascent to Mexico's presidency), an act that may perhaps symbolically be read as turning his back on the implementation of revolutionary nationalist policies to follow a path of further corruption embodied in his relationship with Lilia. Indeed, those passages that represent Artemio and Lilia's relationship are among the most decadent of the novel, as the reader first finds the couple in 1947 in Acapulco, an example of the growth and corruption that characterized Miguel Alemán's presidential administration. At this point in time, Artemio's relationship with Lilia consists of him having rented her out to be a weekend companion, unbeknownst to Catalina, to whom Artemio remains married. But, the fact that Lilia is only a lover for hire does not hamper Artemio's desire to keep her, like the other women in his life, under strict control.

On their trip, Lilia and Artemio are scheduled for a yacht ride, and Artemio unsuspectingly discovers that they will share the boat with an attractive young man named Xavier Adame, who had also been promised a ride at that same time. Lilia immediately takes to Adame, and Artemio hears her laugh as he had never heard her laugh before, basking in Adame's attention and the happiness that she does not find with Artemio. Cruz nevertheless believes that that happiness masks the realities Lilia seeks to hide. As the couple waves goodbye to Adame, Cruz is reflective:

> Como durante el almuerzo a la orilla de la rada, bajo el techo de palma, hubiese querido ver lo que no encontró en los ojos castaños de Lilia. Xavier no había preguntado. Lilia no había contado esta triste historia de melodrama que él saboreaba para sus adentros mientras distinguía los sabores mezclados del Vichysoisse. Ese matrimonio de clase media, con el lépero de siempre, el machito, el castigador, el pobre diablo; el divorcio y la putería. Quisiera contárselo – ah, quizás debiera contárselo – a Xavier. Le costaba recordar la historia, sin embargo, porque había huido de los ojos de Lilia, esta tarde, como si durante la mañana el pasado hubiese huido de la vida de la mujer. (Fuentes, *La muerte* 257).

> [The breeze rippled her blouse and in her eyes was nothing of what he would have preferred to see. Xavier had not asked. Lilia had not told him that sad little melodrama. He savored it as he enjoyed, at the edge of the harbor, beneath the palm frond roof, the composite aroma of Vichysoisse: the middleclass marriage, the usual bastard bully, woman-beater, poor devil, the divorce and the whoredom. He wanted to tell it to Xavier, perhaps he ought to. Doubtless it would be difficult to recall the story, because it had gone from Lilia's eyes this afternoon, as though during the morning, the past had left her. (Fuentes, *The Death* 151)]

It appears as though Lilia has found happiness, which is nothing short of disheartening for Artemio. After all, if she forgets her own "sad little melodrama," she may abandon Artemio like Laura had done some thirteen years prior. But, because Lilia is only a girl whom Cruz has paid to be his weekend companion, it would stand to reason that she would not have the same emotional sway that Laura or Regina had had over him. In spite of this fact, Artemio is angered at having to compete with Adame for Lilia, even when nothing is truly on the line.

It is, nevertheless, interesting that Artemio is capable of recognizing traces of melodrama in Lilia's story but not in his own history. As the timeline of his romantic endeavors demonstrates, Artemio's relationships thrive on those same theatrics and tear-jerking moments of sadness and self-doubt for which he criticizes Lilia. The couple will share one final moment of romantic melodramatic excess at Artemio's New Year's party in 1955 in Coyoacán, a scene that marks the end of Artemio's romantic escapades. Years after their fateful trip to Acapulco, Artemio is still with Lilia, maintaining her economically and keeping her under lock and key while he is still married to Catalina. Lilia's contempt at her captivity spills over, embarrassingly for Artemio, when she shouts before the other guests:

> —¡Ya me aburrí de ver programas de tele todo el día… viejito!
>
> A cada paso del viejito, la voz de Lilia se aflautaba más. – Ya me sé todas las historias de vaqueros… pum-pum… el Marshall de Arizona… el campamento piel-roja… pum-pum… ya sueño con las vocecitas esas… viejito… tome Pepsi… nada más… viejito… seguridad con comodidad; pólizas…
>
> La mano artrítica abofeteó el rostro despintado y los bucles teñidos cayeron sobre los ojos de Lilia. Dejó de respirar. Dio la espalda y se fue, despacio, tocándose la mejilla. Él regresó al grupo de los Régules y Jaime Ceballos. (Fuentes, *La muerte* 350)
>
> ["I'm sick of watching TV all day, little old manny-man! I already know all those cowboy stories. Bang-bang-bang! the marshal of Arizona, camp of redskins. Bang-Bang! I dream about their damn voices, old man! Have a Pepsi… and that all, old man. Security with comfort. Policies…"
>
> His arthritic hand struck her and the dyed curls fell over her eyes.
>
> She held her breath. Then she turned and slowly left, a hand to her cheek. He returned to the group of Régules and Jaime Ceballos. (Fuentes, *The Death* 248-49)]

The scene cannot help but remind the reader of Orson Welles's *Citizen Kane* (1941) and the strained relationship between Charles Foster Kane (played by Welles himself) and Susan Alexander (played by Dorothy Comingore), when Kane attempts to keep Susan locked away at his Xanadu estate.[16] Furthermore,

16 For an in-depth analysis of the many similarities between Fuentes's novel and Welles's film, see "*La muerte de Artemio Cruz* and *Citizen Kane*: A Comparative Analysis," by Lanin Gyurko.

the reader will also note the reference to Roberto Régules and Jaime Ceballos, characters from Fuentes's own *La región más transparente*. But, what clearly shines through in this episode are the heightened theatrics that define both Lilia and Artemio's gesturing. Lilia's rather nonsensical rant must be shouted to show the dire nature of her confinement. Clearly, Artemio's violent response speaks even more loudly than Lilia's words, allowing the reader to identify him as cowardly and patently non-chivalric for violently striking his lover. The reader is once again made aware of the elevated emotional nature of the scene, as Lilia and Artemio both reach a boiling point, unable to control themselves and so acting out melodramatically.

As exemplified in this scene, each romantic passage functions via the use of melodramatic aesthetics to portray the generally negative, if not downright villainous, nature of Artemio Cruz. But, melodrama also serves to frame the character's humble beginnings in a way that ultimately displays a negative perception of the role of miscegenation in Mexican national development. It is only in the final *él* passages of the novel that the reader gains access to the story of Cruz's childhood in Veracruz. Here we discover that Artemio is the son of Atanasio Menchaca –from whom he has inherited his piercing green eyes– and Isabel Cruz. Artemio's father's family came to power during the volatile presidencies of General Antonio López de Santa Ana, ultimately amassing the large tobacco plantation on which the family lives. Isabel Cruz, of Afro-Cuban descent, was a servant on the plantation, who, upon being raped by Atanasio and later giving birth to Cruz, is beaten and run off the hacienda. It is said that Atanasio likely would have killed his bastard child were he himself not murdered when he, along with his brother Pedro, attempted to recover their father Ireneo's remains after his death in the defense of Santa Ana.

Artemio's uncle, a mulatto man named Lunero, raises the young Cruz, while at the same time making candles and building canoes so as to support the now decadent Menchaca family who has fallen upon hard times following the liberal reform during Juárez's presidencies, French intervention in Mexico, and the onset of the Porfirio Díaz's stranglehold on Mexican politics. So far has the Menchaca family fallen that only the drunken Pedro (Atanasio's brother and Artemio's uncle) and Ludivinia (Atanasio's mother and Artemio's grandmother) are left to live among the ruins of the once thriving plantation. When a functionary arrives at the family property to enlist Lunero to work at a nearby plantation, Cruz, Lunero, Pedro, and Ludivinia sense that an end to their meager lifestyle is near. The young Artemio is most upset at this prospect, seizing a shotgun from the plantation big house so as to defend Lunero. But, Cruz accidentally kills his uncle Pedro and, at fourteen years of age, is forced to abandon the only life he has ever known. The reader then knows little about what happens between this violent episode in 1903 and Artemio's revolutionary actions in 1913 other than that he comes under the influence of the *maestro* Sebastián, who indoctrinated him into the Revolution and teaches him to "leer, escribir y odiar a los curas" (Fuentes, *La muerte* 174) ["read and write and to hate priests" (Fuentes, *The Death* 65)].

As noted above, Artemio's revolutionary activity is, at a minimum, problematic, and, from the Revolution onward, Artemio grows increasingly corrupt. But, we may ask, what role do Artemio's modest beginnings play in explaining what Artemio Cruz has become? After all, the story of Artemio's birth and childhood are the very culmination of the plot, as if the novel were explained to the reader in reverse. This fact then makes Fuentes's representation of Mexican *mestizaje* key to understanding the novel, especially when viewed through the lens of melodramatic interpretation. Melodrama seeks to flesh out hidden truths, buried in the past so that justice may ultimately be exercised. In the case of Artemio Cruz, that hidden truth is revealed in the protagonist's African-tinged mestizo heritage. How, then, may the reader interpret the symbolic value of Cruz's racial makeup?

Several critics have noted that, because of his family history, Artemio Cruz embodies the very definition of the Mexican archetype of the "hijo de la chingada."[17] Indeed, following Octavio Paz's postulations on the Mexican condition in *El laberinto de la soledad* (1950), such a reading is valid, so underlining the allegorical aspect of Artemio Cruz's story as that of mestizo Mexico. But, beyond this general symbolic portrayal of conflictive miscegenation, Fuentes presents the reader with a unique case of racial hybridity in Mexico. Just how unique is difficult to say, given that Mexico's federal government does not keep census records of racial categories, perhaps embracing José Vasconcelos's revolutionary dream of a "cosmic race" in which racial distinctions cease to exist.[18] Clearly, it would be a mistake to comment that African culture did not play an important part in constructing culture in Mexico, particularly in the Gulf region (Gates 59-68). However, given the specificity of the case of

[17] On this point, see Boldy (70), Faris (67), Meyer-Minnemann (91), and Stoopen (25).

[18] In *Black in Latin America* (2011), Henry Louis Gates Jr. wonders if a Vasconcelian celebration of miscegenation did not have a counter-productive result, commenting that "brown pride only served to marginalize black culture qua black culture and to marginalize black people economically and socially who had not mixed with whites or with indigenous peoples even further" (89).

mestizaje that Fuentes presents to the reader, we are left to wonder why Cruz is cast in such a negative light.

Is Artemio's African heritage responsible for his downfall? Is the text's intent to explain Cruz's corruption via the representation of his racial makeup?[19] Such a reading may be a stretch, but Artemio's African heritage without a doubt marks him as a singular character in the text. Besides Artemio's mother and uncle Lunero, who appear only briefly at the novel's end, there are no other characters of African heritage explicitly mentioned in the novel. It then becomes significant that the sanction Artemio receives from the author far exceeds any criticism levied against other characters in the text, be they *gringo* businessmen, corrupt "revolutionary" politicians, or Artemio's jilted lovers. Indeed, the revelation of Artemio's heritage would serve to show a negative melodramatic recognition: instead of demonstrating why the hero is genetically so heroic in this instance, recognition helps the reader understand the damning poetic justice of Artemio's ultimate fall from grace. This is a truly curious fact given that *La muerte* was partially penned in Havana and published in the aftermath of the Cuban Revolution, a movement that Fuentes supported and which passionately argued the importance of African heritage in the nationalist movement.

Given that Cruz is born of a violent sexual act, one that he will later re-enact with Regina, he is incommensurate to the role of hero within the melodramatic framing that tacitly orients *La muerte*.[20] Seemingly in line with a classical conception of theatrical melodrama in which a hero/heroine must come from a celebrated lineage that may have been masked or unbeknownst to the character, Artemio is imminently doomed to fail because of his ignominious origins, suffering from the internal schism that it causes him. Up until the age of fourteen, he is brought up to live a simple life in union with nature. Later, upon entering into the Revolution, Cruz fights for the rights of the downtrodden,

---

19 Few critics have delved into this crucial aspect of the novel. Among those who have approached the topic, Marco Polo Hernández Cuevas has noted that, "*La muerte* is a text where the modern Mexican nation is still being narrated in accordance to the 'cosmic race' creed; a belief that the 'improvement' of the nation rested on the cleansing, by mixing out, of all black African traces of the population" (188). See also Alberto Ribas, "Una herencia perdida: La identidad afromexicana de Artemio Cruz," for a discussion of the loss of singular racial identity in post-revolutionary mestizo Mexico.

20 I have written elsewhere about a comparable, yet clearly more classically melodramatic tale, in which a similar rule holds true. See bibliography for complete details on "A History of Violence: Melodrama and *Mestizaje* in Enrique López Albújar's *Matalaché*."

at least in appearance. But, in the aftermath of the Revolution, Cruz turns his back entirely on the reminders of his upbringing and what Fuentes tacitly presents as the ideals of the *pueblo mexicano*, giving into political corruption and so repeating the story of his paternal lineage. It is the latter portion of this schism that defines Cruz, a dark side in which trafficking influence and domination over the weak is the norm, presenting him much more as a villain than as a "good" or sympathetic character. In this way, the melodramatic underpinnings of the text again re-appear, as the reader perceives that the wicked will be punished, even if they have made some attempt to make amends for their deeds.

And Cruz does try to make up for his life of misdeeds when he returns with his son, Lorenzo, to the Cocuya, Veracruz estate where Artemio was born. By essentially ignoring his daughter Teresa and gaining her scorn when she witnesses his final agony, Artemio devotes himself to Lorenzo with the hope that he can wash away his own history. Through Lorenzo's return to this paradise lost, Artemio would live vicariously through his son, so giving both father and son the possibility of starting anew. But, that nostalgia for life among the elements in Veracruz goes unrequited for Artemio due in great part to his own missteps. Instead of remaining at Cocuya, Lorenzo leaves to take part in the Spanish Civil War, attempting to emulate what he believes were his father's revolutionary actions. Lorenzo is heroically killed in the war, in this sense shadowing his uncle Gonzalo's actions closer than those of his father. Artemio, thus, loses a son and the possibility of redemption by proxy, again illustrating the vindictive melodramatic principle of *La muerte*. As Gerald Martin notes, Fuentes seems to stack the cards against Cruz, subjecting him:

> To a trial under bourgeois law, in which all the mitigating circumstances of existence – fatality, original sin, biology and the like – including the social determinisms – poverty, illegitimacy, discrimination – are put on one side of the balance, and all Cruz's negative qualities and actions – sacrificing others instead of himself, in refusal of Christian and revolutionary doctrine – are placed on the other. Needless to say, in this frothy concoction of social democratic values masquerading as revolutionary criticism (Fuentes was a 'young Marxian' at this time, with concepts of alienation, reification, use and exchange values, free love), mixed in with a gentle-Jesus revolutionary Christianity, the trial is something of a sham and Cruz is condemned when we are shown that he is subject, 'in spite of everything', to the 'blade of liberty'. Never was a character more explicitly judged, and yet rarely was the evidence more obviously 'fixed'. (*Journeys* 211-12)

Martin's assessment of *La muerte* insightfully notes the vindictive slant of Fuentes's novel and the class-based perspective that the text represents. Indeed,

La muerte was written for a middle class audience, sympathetic to the generalized moral outlook and historical interpretation of the Revolution that Fuentes presents. As M. J. Fenewick has noted:

> Fuentes uses a fine literary technique that involves the reader in the national bourgeois guilt, but he speaks to us and for us with the presumption that all readers are bourgeois and all are guilty. The narrative reproduces a historical collage of the Mexican structure, but it's all from a bourgeois perspective. The narrator claims all the perspectives just as do the bourgeois political and corporate leaders who claim legitimate majority rule, when in fact the bourgeoisie is never a majority. Fuentes strongly suggests that the ruling class crisis was a result of psychological or spiritual disintegration on a national scale, rather than a result of the socio-economic disintegration intrinsic to a class society. (95-96)

As Fenewick's comments indicate, at the core of Fuentes's novel, there appears to be a confusion between a supposedly authoritative social ethic and the actual sociological processes set into action by the Revolution. In structuring *La muerte* to contest the former, Fuentes inherently espouses the dominant view of the Revolution as a singular and definite project that may be held up for critique. This cannot but suggest a paradox: Fuentes evaluates the entirety of the Revolution via the sole figure of Artemio Cruz, so endorsing the myth of the Revolution as a uniform event, which had always been the official version of the Partido Revolucionario Institucional (PRI). That is, both the critic and the defendant make claims to the singularity of the Revolution, so displaying a difference of approach to the issue but not an essential divergence of historical comprehension.

While Fuentes's ostensibly negative perception of Mexico's revolutionary elite without fully questioning the social structure that maintains that paradigm may be viewed as somewhat problematic, the PRI's construction of consensus in framing the Revolution is typical of party operations. As Héctor Aguilar Camín and Lorenzo Meyer note in *In the Shadow of the Mexican Revolution: Contemporary Mexican History 1910-1989* (1993), the PRI held sway in Mexican politics throughout the twentieth century:

> Because it is mainly a pragmatic coalition of interests, the timely incarnation of what some authors call the 'interclassism' of the Mexican Revolution, the possibility to reunite in the same political task the interests of all classes: conservatives and revolutionaries, poor peasants and large landowners, workers and business people, in such a way that in pragmatic negotiation, behind closed doors, everyone may get something, and those who do not at least receive hope. (256)

Nevertheless, modern historiography of the Mexican Revolution has taught us that generalized categorizations of a unified Mexican revolutionary process, like those employed by the PRI, are highly troublesome. As Alan Knight has notes in his meticulous study *The Mexican Revolution* (1986), "in its provincial origins, the Revolution displayed kaleidoscopic variations; often it seemed less a Revolution than a multitude of disparate revolts, some endowed with national aspirations, many purely provincial, but all reflecting local conditions and concerns" (*Vol. 1* 2). As is clear in *La muerte*, Fuentes is less concerned with producing an historic account of the Revolution and its complexities than with chastising the post-revolutionary ruling class; he imposes a stern view of the failings of the Revolution, and there were many, to be sure. However, because of his self-contained, dominant view on the Revolution, Fuentes ignores the viability of grass-roots participation in the Revolution, much less any possible gain from national upheaval. As Gilbert M. Joseph and Daniel Nugent note in their introduction to *Everyday Forms of State Formation: Revolution and Negotiation of Rule in Modern Mexico* (1994), this same disavowal of "popular" participation in the Revolution has plagued a great deal of studies of the event, thus relegating grass-roots revolutionary involvement "to a subordinated, almost inconsequential role" (7). *La muerte* would apparently fall into the same trap of viewing history as a top-down process, only capable of comprehending popular participation via the young idealistic Cruz, converting it into a demonized figurehead of national decay. Fuentes's novel, then, proves incapable of understanding social change aside from that which is devoured by the corruption inherent to big politics.

La muerte, thus, is unable to represent the multiplicity of the Revolution, which is certainly a curious fact for a novel purported to be the culmination of the novel of the Mexican Revolution. This is even more odd, given that Fuentes would later trumpet that same genre as the first Spanish American narrative capable of introducing literary ambiguity since "en la dinámica revolucionaria los héroes pueden ser villanos y los villanos pueden ser héroes" (Fuentes, *Novela* 15) ["in the revolutionary dynamic heroes can be villains and villains can be heroes" (my translation)]. This is very much the case in a number of predecessors to *La muerte*, among which Azuela's *Los de abajo* (1915) and Rafael F. Muñoz's *Vámonos con Pancho Villa* (1931) stand as formidable examples. But, Artemio Cruz, in spite of his multiple levels of consciousness, is less complex than Azuela's Demetrio Macías, who violently charges headlong into a Revolution whose official, nationalist political causes he cannot articulate. The same holds true when comparing Cruz to Muñoz's Tiburcio Maya, who dies defending Pancho Villa, the same man who he has witnessed murder his family. Both Muñoz and Azuela's novels allow for a subversive, un-integrable voice within their narrative (a subaltern conscious if that is indeed possible) that *La muerte* is simply incapable of imagining.

The one-dimensional take on the Revolution is indicative of the melodramatic framing of *La muerte*. Via the employment of melodramatic condemnation, the novel reinforces a top-down perspective on the Revolution, typical of the 1960s Mexican middle class that, with good reason, was growing increasingly exasperated by the rule of the PRI. Indeed, it would be only six short years after the publication of Fuentes's novel that a boiling point would be reached, and the farce of the PRI would be on full display in the Plaza de Tres Culturas in the Tlatelolco Massacre. It is this middle class frustrated by the stagnation of the Revolution that is the intended audience for Fuentes's novel, a middle class that is the target audience for melodrama in general. Through the parable that is the life of Artemio Cruz, a melodramatically-tinged tale lays bare the political perspective encoded in the text: Cruz is of the corrupt revolutionary elite, concerned first and foremost with his own personal benefit, and for that he is villainized.

It is important, however, to underline the fact that Fuentes's novel is not representative of what we may recognize as an everyday melodrama. *La muerte* presents the reader with a style of writing that would be impossible to classify within a "classic" concept of melodrama, and such is not the intention of this chapter. In spite of this fact, we would be remiss if we did not notice that some of the most typical, if not the most conservative, motifs of melodrama are quite clearly integrated into Fuentes's novel, so exposing a paradox of the text: melodrama serves as a formative factor in a novel that overtly rejects the melodramatic narrative mode. In his attempts to write "new" narrative, Fuentes reproduces, perhaps unintentionally, those same melodramatic narrative tropes that may be found in *Doña Bárbara*, that melodramatic classic of which Fuentes was critical in *La nueva novela hispanoamericana*. For example, are Artemio Cruz and Doña Bárbara's hidden origins really so different? Are both characters not born of a symbolic violence that gives form to a dangerous embodiment of miscegenation condemned in both works? Does romance not serve as a narrative figure, through which the social situation of each of these "bad" characters is explained? Clearly, in Gallegos's novel, Bárbara is the evil character who must be eliminated from the story, but is this same narrative strategy not also repeated in Cruz's ultimate demise in *La muerte*? Given these unexpected coincidences between the two texts, perhaps the most productive means of comparing these works would be to read them as the heads and tails of melodrama: *Doña Bárbara* ostensibly works toward good's triumph over evil, and *La muerte* intuits that that triumph is increasingly less plausible but sees no other way out of representing conflict than by the means first employed by its predecessors.

Postscript: And then... Melodrama Beyond the Boom

As has been presented at length in the cases examined in this study, melodrama serves as a structuring tool that attempts to make sense of the social experience. Yet, what becomes clear in Latin American melodrama is that the very aesthetic format frequently is at odds with itself. Latin American melodrama actively engages our emotions, affectively prodding us to hope for the best outcomes only to show us that even in the happiest of endings, the social ground remains unstable. In other words, Latin American melodrama refuses to neatly resolve the conflicts that it puts into motion, and in this sense it distinguishes itself from other melodramatic narratives around the globe. The inconclusive nature of Latin American melodrama is ultimately attributable to the very social heterogeneity that has characterized the region since the era of the Conquest. Indeed, Latin American melodramatic narrative is still in search of just how to plot out the successful union of so many dissimilar elements that constitute the modern Latin American environs. This heterogeneity represents a fundamental basis for the history of the region and essentially confounds Latin American melodrama. We only to need consider disparate instances of race, ethnicity, religion, and social class in the paradigmatic narrative examples from across the region examined in this study to understand the complications that melodrama confronts when attempting to present a coherent social picture in the Latin American context.

Yet, in Latin America, where stark social contrasts continue to dominate the everyday experience, it is not surprising that melodrama continues to find such widespread acceptance. That which is observed in the most basic *telenovela* speaks to the public for the simple fact that many of the dichotomies played out therein are those that the public lives out on a daily basis. Melodramatic emotional exaggeration, then, is not simply a crutch utilized by television actors or by authors lacking subtlety. Rather, melodramatic affectivity is employed in the Latin American context in order to convey to the public that they are not alone, that others also share their predicaments, and that it is acceptable to *feel* the experiences that shape their lives.

The present analysis has led us up to the so-called Boom of Latin American literature, that all-important moment when Latin America –along with the rest of the global reading public– took stock of its literary tradition while radically expanding upon it. Though it still remains difficult to overestimate the importance of the Boom within the context of Latin American literary history, it is plainly evident that Latin American letters were not magically ushered into existence at the beginning of the 1960s. As any student of Latin American literature can discern, the innovative aesthetic legacy of Jorge Luis Borges, Juan Rulfo, and Juan Carlos Onetti, among others, left a strong impression on the authors of the Boom. Yet, as I have argued in my analysis of Fuentes's *La muerte de Artemio Cruz*, the traditions of melodrama, specifically family melodrama, can also be observed in the Boom-era classics. Even in the indisputable exceptionality of works like Julio Cortázar's *Rayuela* (1963) or Gabriel García Márquez's *Cien años de soledad* (1967), is the central focus on familial and/or romantic relationships –even when deliberately fragmented and critiqued– not somehow strangely reminiscent of that which may be found in José Mármol's *Amalia* (1851) or Jorge Isaacs's *María* (1867)? Without question, the Boom works have drastically different aesthetics from their forerunners, but together they share common concerns that serve to unite the two distinct (and arbitrary) literary groupings, no matter how hard the Boom novels work to show their difference.[1]

Even so, Nobel Prize winning Boom author Mario Vargas Llosa attempted to show the outright superiority of the "nueva novela" over its narrative precursors and staged the collapse of the latter in his post-Boom novel *La tía Julia y el escribidor* (1977). Departing from his all-encompassing social analyses in *La ciudad y los perros* (1963), *La casa verde* (1966), and *Conversación en la catedral* (1969), *La tía Julia* ostensibly attempted to show the precarity of authorial voice, playing the largely autobiographical narration of the precocious Varguitas against that of the tales supposedly written by Pedro Camacho, the scriptwriter for highly popular but clichéd and increasingly chaotic melodramatic radio soap operas that populate the text. As Carlos Alonso has shown in his masterful analysis of Vargas Llosa's novel, Camacho's ultimate authorial demise serves to affirm Varguitas's –and, through him, Vargas Llosa's– narrative superiority and so belittles any affront to the absolute linguistic control of the author (*Modernity* 138). In this sense, we may perceive that melodrama is chided in Vargas Llosa's novel as being an illegitimate narrative form, an undesirable holdover from Latin America's narrative history that is suitable only for unsightly popular formats. Nevertheless, even in this unsubtle rejection

1 We again are reminded here of Doris Sommer's affirmation that, within the Boom, "the more national romance must be resisted, the more it seems irresistible" (3).

of melodramatic form, Vargas Llosa's novel cannot but exhibit a grudging acknowledgement of Camacho's melodramatic tales. Following Alonso's reading of Vargas Llosa's novel, we discern that the presence of melodrama, set against Varguitas's supposedly more eloquently narrated romance, allows for the very definition of what Vargas Llosa implicitly deems as legitimate high narrative form. That is to say, high form is revealed as being dependent on the would-be banality of melodrama to affirm its superiority; it needs an implicit "low" other for self-affirmation. Vargas Llosa's depreciative, yet self-implicating approach, however, is not echoed by other authors of the post-Boom era.

Indeed, as is commonly recognized, many works of the post-Boom era actively search for common ground between high and popular formats based in melodrama. To be sure, the Argentine author Manuel Puig's *La traición de Rita Hayworth* (1968) or *El beso de la mujer araña* (1976) show no fear in working to fully integrate melodramatic functionality into the text. From the outset, Puig's works invoke an orality that is ultimately undermined in Vargas Llosa's novel. And, as is clearly implied in the title of *El beso de la mujer araña*, Puig draws the reader into the narrative web, relying upon the all-important affective bond between narrator and reader that is essential to melodrama. In order to so flawlessly merge the distinct narrative voices operative in his novels, Puig embraces the influence of mass media formats like film, radio, and television where melodrama abounds, like many other Latin American authors associated with the post-Boom, a period that denotes a connection to postmodern aesthetics for most readers. The Brazilian author Clarice Lispector's *A hora da estrela* (1977) also shares an affinity for melodramatic popular culture in its representation of radio programming and a final encounter with a fortune teller that serves to mark the trajectory of the poverty-stricken protagonist of the novel. Differing from Puig's works, Lispector's novel would hold up elements of popular culture for critique and offer a distancing of narrator and reader, even when the text itself is narrated in an oblique first person. Lispector's dialogue with melodrama via the elements of popular culture invoked by the novel make the melodramatic mode a necessary point of consideration for the text.

Such experiments with melodrama have more recently been taken to extremes by the Argentine author César Aira. One might say that nothing is sacred for Aira, as his works play upon conventions that move well beyond the realm of melodrama, critiquing historiography and nationalism along with broader issues of avant-garde aesthetics and, in the process, questioning that which is conceivable within the format of the novel itself. Because of this consistent innovative impulse in his works, Sandra Contreras, in her study *Las vueltas de César Aira* (2002), has convincingly presented a connection between Aira's works and those of the Latin American *vanguardias* of the early twentieth century. Clearly, Aira's vast body of work displays much evidence to support this claim. Yet, it is evident that many of Aira's novels also work within a postmodern vein, recycling elements of mass media culture to playfully distort the melodramatic conventions that shape popular narrative formats. To name just a few examples, we could consider Aira's *El congreso de literatura* (1997), *La mendiga* (1998), *Las aventuras de Barbaverde* (2008), or *El error* (2010) as works that respectively draw upon adventure narrative and science fiction, the *telenovela*, comics, and serial novel conventions. Each of the distinct narrative formats that Aira gleefully distorts in these works finds commonalities with the hero and villain dynamics and the happy endings prevalent in melodrama.

Aira's aesthetic experiments, nevertheless, would appear to pertain to a different conceptual field of aesthetics than that of the melodramas analyzed in this study when viewed through the lens of Jorge Volpi's commentary upon the state of affairs of Latin American politics and literature in *El insomnio de Bolívar: Cuatro consideraciones intempestivas sobre América Latina en el siglo XXI* (2009). On the eve of the bicentennial celebrations of the Latin American independence movements, Volpi's essay proposes to take stock of the successes and shortcomings of the modern Latin American nation-states and to evaluate how contemporary Latin American democracy would measure up to Simón Bolívar's emancipatory vision. It would be an understatement to say that Volpi finds little to celebrate in the political arena. He sharply critiques Latin American political leaders, both past and present, for their failures to live up to their own purported democratic standards. Yet, Volpi's political analysis is, at times, contradictory. For example, he seemingly suggests that the term "latinoamericano" no longer holds any meaning, but he consistently employs the same denomination to voice his analysis and finds a multitude of shared points of criticism to underline the commonalities he perceives across the region. Volpi's analysis, I believe, is more at home when discussing Latin American literature. Yet, contradictions still surface as Volpi seeks to distance himself and his contemporaries from the authors of the Boom, but also to affirm that the Boom, similar to the most recent literary generation (his own), was criticized for embracing aesthetic traditions foreign to the Latin American experience. For Volpi, however, the fundamental difference between contemporary Latin American authors and their Boom forefathers is the former's active rejection of any socio-political engagement on the author's part. I cite here a passage that is significant with regards to Volpi's perception of the changing face of Latin American literary and political engagement, which directly relates to my discussion of the political aesthetic of Latin American melodrama. Volpi writes that:

> Los escritores nacidos a partir de 1960 no necesitan consolidar una tradición –como hicieron Fuentes, Vargas Llosa o García Márquez–, no poseen su anhelo bolivariano y no aspiran a convertirse en voceros de América Latina: su apuesta, más modesta pero también más natural, consiste en afrontar los problemas e historias de sus respectivos países, e incluso los de toda la región, con toda naturalidad, sin el tono salvífico o politizado de algunos de sus predecesores. Más que descubrir un continente, colocar en el mapa una región antes olvidada, convertirse en sus portavoces o posicionarse a la vanguardia de sus élites, los nuevos narradores hablan de sus países sin resabios de romanticismo o de compromiso político, sin esperanzas ni planes de futuro, acaso sólo con el orgulloso desencanto de quien reconoce los límites de su responsabilidad frente a la historia. En vez de presentarse como inventores de América Latina, contribuyen a descifrarla y desarmarla. Sus libros no pretenden sumarse a las piedras con que los novelistas del XIX hasta el *Boom* levantaron la catedral de literatura latinoamericana, sino ser fragmentos dispersos que condensan, en sí mismos, toda la información posible sobre los desafíos que hoy enfrenta América Latina. El paradigma ya no consiste en edificar una nueva torre o una nueva cúpula, sino en trazar un *holograma*: novelas que sólo de manera oblicua y confusa, fractural, desentrañan el misterio de América Latina. (170-71)
>
> [Authors born after 1960 do not need to consolidate a tradition –as did Fuentes, Vargas Llosa, or García Márquez–, they do not possess the Bolivarian desire, nor do they aspire to become the voice of Latin America: their project, at once more modest and more natural, consists of confronting the problems and histories of their respective countries, if not the whole region, with naturalness and without the redemptive and politicized tone of some of their predecessors. More than discovering a continent, putting a forgotten region on the map, becoming the spokespersons, or positioning themselves in the forefront of the elites, the new narrators speak of their countries without remnants of romanticism or of political engagement, without hopes or plans for the future, and perhaps only with the proud disenchantment of he who recognizes the limits of his responsibilities before history. Instead of presenting themselves as the inventors of Latin America, the new narrators contribute to its decipherment and undoing. Their books do not aim to be incorporated among those edifying blocks with which novelists of the nineteenth century up to the *Boom* constructed the cathedral of Latin American literature, but rather to be disperse fragments that condense in themselves all of the possible information on the challenges that confront Latin America today. The paradigm no longer consists of constructing a new tower or new cupola, but to trace a *hologram*: novels that only obliquely and confusedly, fragmentedly, decipher the mystery of Latin America. (my translation)]

Volpi's gloomy vision of the present state of Latin American politics and its potential for literary representation reveals a considerable paradigm shift with regards to the very concept of fictional narrative in Latin America. Though Volpi is quick to criticize his own country's political past in the treachery of the Mexican Partido Revolucionario Institucional and the contemporary political programs of Hugo Chávez, Cristina Fernández, or Evo Morales with a similar contempt, his perception is that Latin American writers now respond to politics with a "proud disenchantment."

With regard to Volpi's view, I would offer two brief responses. The first is to note the paradox of the author who purports to have nothing to say about Latin American politics but who has written an extensive essay to explain his views on the (imaginary) region he critiques. Indeed, Volpi's essay is not politics represented in novelistic form, but it is far from the political indifference that the author intimates. And, secondly, I would remark that, where Volpi perceives an absence of political engagement and where, in many cases, he persuasively argues his cause, the political unconscious of Latin American literature may be found to manifest itself in even the most seemingly apolitical texts.[2] The literary object –Latin American or otherwise– simply cannot be read independently of its national political environs. And so, when the contemporary authors to which Volpi refers write, for instance, about Russia or China or the United Kingdom, the reader is not wrong to consider the author's national and class affiliations and the general social milieu that facilitates the construction of such a text. That is to say, any given text is not produced in a vacuum and is a product of a given set of historical and social conditions that the author must negotiate. I concur with Volpi in that contemporary Latin American authors should not be unreflexively criticized for the selection of such subject matter, but I do not feel that they can be socially or politically divorced from the historical processes that have given form to their national environs. The same holds true with regards to non-Latin American authors –Volpi at times refers to United States authors as a counterpoint– whose ideological formation inherently influences the perspectives voiced in their works.

Accordingly, Volpi's commentary is curious in its discussion of Fernando Vallejo's *La virgen de los sicarios* (1994) or Alan Pauls's *Historia del llanto* (2007), which notes the former's focus on the particularities of style, speech, and fame as opposed to a macro political analysis or the latter's general political disenchantment. Volpi's approach would propose that such narrative elections could ostensibly offer the possibility to read such works as apolitical. Yet,

---

[2] Clearly, I am drawing from a Fredric Jameson's landmark work *The Political Unconscious: Narrative as a Socially Symbolic Act* (1981).

given the specificity of each of these works' national backdrops and their respective positions with regard, or in opposition to political authority, would it in fact be possible to read them independently of their particular socio-political environs? That is, could we read Vallejo's novel without considering its insertion into the politicized debate on narco-society in Colombia or Pauls's novel entirely divorced from a position within progressive politics in the Southern Cone, specifically in Argentina?

Nevertheless, Volpi's provocative essay does clearly demonstrate that there is a marked difference with regard to representing the political in contemporary Latin American literature. Indeed, when Volpi discusses the absence of any prospect for redress for past crimes committed against the Guatemalan indigenous community in Rodrigo Rey Rosa's *El material humano* (2009), we may note a contrast from the prophetic and politically engaged tone of one of Rey Rosa's national precursors, the Nobel laureate Miguel Ángel Asturias. Whereas Rey Rosa's first person narrative reads like a personal testimony of disillusionment with a trajectory of violence without any hope for the possible prosecution of evil, Asturias wrote in a different era and against a different socio-political backdrop, with purpose and the conviction of an author who fervently believed in the transformative power of social literature. Asturias's principles are abundantly clear in his "trilogía bananera," *Viento fuerte* (1950), *El papa verde* (1954), and *Los ojos de los enterrados* (1960), which charts the dirty dealings, abuses, and eventual downfall of collusion between national politics and United States' corporate farming interests in Guatemala. Collectively these novels rely upon a melodramatic contrast of good and evil in which indigenous and peasant laborers are continually betrayed by the monolithic wickedness of international capitalism. In fact, this unequivocal representation of evil was a narrative deployment that Asturias had also utilized in an earlier and more renowned work, *El Señor Presidente* (1946).

The story told in Asturias's classic work recounts the ubiquity of oppressive dictatorial power in Guatemala at the beginning of the twentieth century. Though Guatemala itself is not explicitly represented in the text, Asturias's personal experience and the fact that he penned his novel over a period spanning from 1922 to 1932 and was unable to publish the text until the arrival of the democratically elected Juan José Arévalo in 1944, lends credence to the general perception that the novel refers to the dictatorship of Manuel Cabrera Estrada (1898-1920) (and is also contextualized by the latter authoritarian regime of Jorge Ubico [1931-1944]). Asturias's novel relates a series of events in which the President –psychologically present in every action in the text, though physically present in just a handful of scenes– manipulates a series of characters to do his biddings and to betray one another in fear of his absolute power. When one of the President's trusted generals is murdered in the opening of the novel, it offers the strongman the opportunity to purge potential political rivals, ostensibly in the name of justice. To carry out this eliminatory process, the President relies upon his closest henchman, Miguel Cara de Ángel.

Cara de Ángel turns out to be surprisingly unreliable as he attempts to dispose of one of the President's perceived rivals, General Canales, only to fall in love with the general's daughter, Camila. Camila's extended family –in fear of falling from grace with the President– denies her shelter after her father's flight from the capital. Through the process of caring for Camila, Cara de Ángel seemingly comes to see the error of his ways while working on the President's behalf, and tacitly comes to reject his all-powerful employer. Gerald Martin, one of Asturias most dedicated and insightful readers, notes that, for Cara de Ángel, "[Camila's] predicament and his growing love gradually begin to distance him, then to alienate him morally from the President, and finally to turn him into an opponent, albeit a passive and unheroic one, of the regime." (*Landmarks* 63). Indeed, Cara de Ángel's complicit inaction within the government will come to cost him, as the President becomes increasingly suspicious of his favorite servant. The President eventually imprisons Cara de Ángel after leading him to believe that he would be sent into foreign service, after which Cara de Ángel had intended to send for the pregnant Camila. Ultimately, Cara de Ángel perishes in prison falsely believing that Camila has betrayed him and is now the President's mistress. This is not the case, and we read that Camila and Cara de Ángel's son lives out some form of an (unhappily) ever after in the countryside.

I will not attempt to take on the prolific critical history or the sacred indigenous and Christian underpinnings of Asturias's landmark novel here. Recurring allusions to the Mayan deity of war, Tohil (the title initially given to Asturias's novel [Himelblau 437]), and the constant references to Cara de Ángel as being "bello y malo como Satán" ["beautiful and evil like Satan"] have provided for a multitude of productive readings. Instead, I would briefly remark upon the insistence in which the specific themes of love and morality –hallmarks of melodrama– re-appear throughout the text. Though it would be greatly reductive to say that the novel only explores in some tawdry way the romance between Miguel Cara de Ángel and Camila Canales and the moral lesson that it offers, it is important to note that this romance serves as a focal point of the novel and a narrative device linking so many characters trapped by the pervasive dread produced by the President.

For example, Fedina Rodas, one of the novel's most grotesquely tragic figures, is a maid in Camila's home and is arrested under suspicion of collaborating in General Canales's escape. Following her arrest, Fedina is imprisoned, tortured, and is left to watch her infant child perish, only to be sold to a brothel and to eventually go insane. Conversely, Major Farfán is saved by Cara de Ángel when the latter informs him of the President's plan to do away with him. Farfán ultimately repays Cara de Ángel's favor by betraying him, serving as the arresting officer when Cara de Ángel is captured while attempting to leave the country at the novel's end. In this way, just as all the novel's characters are somehow bound to the puppet-master President, the characters functioning in the sentimental nucleus of the novel also connect the majority of the active players in the text. In a sense, we are presented with what would be the fodder for a sweeping film in which a multitude of minor and outwardly inconsequential encounters have a dramatic impact on the novel's principal characters and the text's final outcome. Perhaps it is for this reason that Arturo Arias has observed:

> A pesar de la importancia de la significación social ya indicada de su temática y de su contexto, el texto como tal es por encima de todo una melodramática historia de amor: la pasión de Miguel Cara de Ángel con Camila Canales, la hija del general del mismo nombre, en la mira del dictador por su rectitud y honestidad. Todo el juego político del texto gira en torno de la relación intimista, cuyo melodramatismo sentimental es casi un acto performativo en el sentido de ser un gesto semiótico cuya actividad crea lo que describe. (680)
>
> [In spite of the important social significance already noted by the novel's topic and context, the text itself is above all a melodramatic love story: Miguel Cara de Ángel's passion for Camila Canales, the daughter of the general targeted by the dictator because of his integrity and honesty. The entirety of the text's political game revolves around this intimate relationship whose sentimental melodramatism is almost a performative act in the sense that it is a semiotic gesture whose activity creates what it describes. (my translation)]

I coincide entirely with Arias's reading of the novel, which underlines the melodramatic significance of the romantic anecdote that will ultimately work to display the greater political message of the text. This centrality of romance has sometimes been seen as an anachronistic defect of the novel.[3] However, I would argue that, similar to the cases we have seen in the preceding chapters,

3 Both Luis Harss and Emir Rodríguez Monegal (see bibliography) found the melodramatic content of Asturias's novel to be detrimental to the text.

El Señor Presidente again presents us with a situation in which love is a case for social justice, a most melodramatic circumstance.

That connection between the romantic and social elements of Asturias's novel is offered up to the reader in no uncertain terms in the moment of Cara de Ángel's instant moral, and consequentially political, conversion. Through the melodramatic device of immediately transfigured characters, the President's associate finds himself changed when, in a last-ditch effort to cure her ills, he agrees to marry Camila, whom Cara de Ángel has been watching over after her escape from the family home. Significantly, the spiritualist Tícher (so nick-named because of his profession as an English teacher) marries the couple and quotes the Song of Songs at the end of his ceremony, saying, "Make the another self, for love of me!" (Asturias 254). Love, in this instance, has the double effect of indicating devotion and conversion. As Gerald Martin notes, "as love purifies [Cara de Ángel's] soul and the recognition of the President's true significance brings a kind of moral redemption, so light triumphs inside him (successfully uniting goodness and consciousness at the crucial moment in the novel), and the darkness without moves to destroy him. Cara de Ángel is in a sense a static figure, as all the characters are: it is good and evil, and other themes, which are the mobile elements in the novel" (*How to* 231). In the analytical scheme Martin lays out, love is to good, just as the President's malice is to evil. Such a narrative framework exhibits classic characteristics of melodrama, which should not be considered as a slight to Asturias's novel. Melodramatic framing in *El Señor Presidente* offers a most coherent means of conveying the political content of the text. As Arturo Arias notes, the melodramatic reading of Asturias's novel attempts, not to "reconstruir la memoria pública a través de la patente cursilería de los sentimientos privados, sino más bien al revés. De explotar la pequeñez de esta última, y ampliarla, elevándola a un plano metafísico más denso" (693) ["reconstruct public memory through the patent sappiness of private sentiment, but rather the other way around. To expand the littleness of the latter, amplifying it and elevating it to a denser metaphysical plane" (my translation)]. As I have argued throughout this study, this is precisely the task performed in melodrama. Exemplified here in the case of Asturias's novel, melodramatic private sentiment is converted into a political emotion, expanding the private into the public and blurring the boundary separating the personal and the social.

As Arias notes, melodramatic sentimentalism makes it possible for Asturias to communicate with a vast public via these characters, showing their tribulations to be those of *the people*. This is perhaps the only way that we might be able to account for such an indulgent romantic tale at the core of what is widely recognized to be the first great Latin American "dictator novel." In its specific use of romantic intrigue *El Señor Presidente*, is, in fact, quite unique since other dictator novels have taken a drastically different approach to representing the experience of social repression. After all, the amorous intrigue found in Asturias's novel is utterly lacking in the Paraguayan Augusto Roa Bastos's verbal labyrinth, *Yo el supremo* (1974), or in the Argentine Ricardo Piglia's cryptic *Respiración artificial* (1980). Though Piglia's novel does not represent the dictatorial figure in such a direct manner as it is represented in Roa Bastos's novel, both works were published at historical moments when repressive regimes governed the authors' respective countries, and both works take on the experiences of authoritarianism. In any case, both of these latter works circuitously use language to represent the dread induced by authoritarian political power. The novelistic work then becomes a maze in which the reader is submersed, offering a semiotic model for the experience of autocracy and governmental suppression. Unlike Asturias's novel, romantic love is not offered up as a model to escape that rubric or as a possible idyllic paragon to counter an authoritarian logic of social order. Moreover, in the absence of romantic intrigue, Roa Bastos and Piglia's novels are emptied of the affective mechanisms reflected upon throughout this study. Neither *Yo el supremo*, nor *Respiración artificial*, offers a concerted attempt to create an emotional impact in the reader, so as to affectively convey the novel's content. Contrary to the body of works examined in this study, the verbal and rational play of Roa Bastos and Piglia's novels coolly engages the reader's intellect without explicitly asking us to *feel* what is happening throughout the text. Thus, we may think of Roa Bastos and Piglia's novels as conscientiously anti-melodramatic.

As such, it is not difficult to discern that Asturias's novel provides a thoroughly different means of representing the experience of repression by injecting emotion and romance into the political tale. And, in spite of their historical differences and perspectives on the social capacities of literature, we may perhaps find some affective commonalities between *El Señor Presidente* and *El material humano* by Rodrigo Rey Rosa. Though Rey Rosa's novel does not refer as concretely to romantic intrigue as Asturias's novel does, it navigates a series of familial relations while simultaneously reflecting upon internal national conflicts. In this way, the sentimental recollection of family relationships becomes intimately entwined with the archival investigation of national violence that plays out in the novel, imbuing the dual storylines with a similar tense, nervous emotion and confounding the spheres of private and public.

The emotional/national trajectory charted in Rey Rosa's novel ultimately serves to connect it to *El Señor Presidente* and offers an example of a trend prevalent in contemporary Latin American literature. To some extent bearing out Jorge Volpi's assessment of contemporary Latin American literature in its focus on the intimate sphere, many present-day Latin American authors may be seen as retreating inward, from the larger public scene toward the personal. Nevertheless, contrary to Jorge Volpi's commentary discussed in the preceding, I would argue that this move should not necessarily be read as anti-political. Indeed, as played out in Rey Rosa's novel, personal, emotional attachments become intertwined with the national political imagination, making it impossible to definitively separate the two. This model of inward retreat could paradoxically place us face to face with the literary paradigm of the nineteenth century Latin American canon, as argued by Doris Sommer. Perhaps we are now reading what we may see in the future as a new foundational fiction: those narratives that reset the representation of citizenship with regard to Latin American nation-states in light of the bicentennial independence celebrations. In any case, the return to the representation and provocation of emotion is made infinitely more facile through the broad use of melodrama, a narrative mode that currently finds acceptance among a broad reading public and across a wide range of literary styles. In the contemporary setting in which melodrama has increasingly lost the pejorative connotation that it once held among readerly publics, academic and otherwise, intensely emotional narratives aid the public in its decipherment of a respective national past borne out across a host of recent texts.

For example, *Palacio Quemado* (2007), by the Bolivian Edmundo Paz Soldán, follows a path not entirely different from that of Rey Rosa in examining the failings of the contemporary state. Again mixing familial relationships with political intrigues, Paz Soldán combines intimate memories with a critique of bureaucracy in the winds of political change, an affectively charged combination that cannot but suggest to the reader a certain melodramatic inclination. In a similar sense, some works that have emerged from the period of violence shaping Peru's recent history also utilize affective structures to analyze social and political conflict. Alonso Cueto in *La hora azul*, mentioned in the introduction to this study, and Iván Thays in *Un lugar llamado Oreja de Perro* (2008) each employ an emotionally charged lexicon and repertoire of images in order to return to the figure of the family to investigate veiled identities, affective bonds, and the possibilities for individual fulfillment. These elements constitute the hallmarks of melodrama, and, by relying on such emotional guideposts to convey their tales, the authors demonstrate melodrama's intention to make sense of abstract historical processes, which is, nevertheless, complicated by the ambiguous resolutions of Cueto's and Thays's respective novels.

There are also works that, while less straightforwardly political in nature, still utilize melodramatic structures to convey their socially contextualized tales. I refer here to novels sometimes classified under the heading *sicaresca*, those texts that represent the experience of societies touched by the violence of drug trafficking and the cultures it engenders. In the Mexican case, works by Élmer Mendoza and Luis Humberto Crosthwaite offer representative examples. Mendoza's *Un asesino solitario* (1999) recounts in first person the adventures of a hit man with clandestine ties to the federal government, charged with the assassination of a political leader in northern Mexico: a tale intimately related to the assassination of Luis Donaldo Colosio, presidential candidate of the Partido Revolucionario Institucional in 1994. Utilizing a colloquial vernacular, Mendoza's novel narrates this adventure –interspersed with largely unsuccessful attempts at rekindling a romance with the protagonist's best friend's wife– in an emotionally heightened register in which the reader is left wondering about the result of so many close calls and veiled intentions. As such, we could call Mendoza's novel a page-turner, a melodramatically-tinged adventure that keeps building until the very end. Similarly, Crosthwaite's *Tijuana: Crimen y olvido* (2010) also maintains an emotional tension throughout the text to attempt to unravel the disappearance of two romantically involved journalists, who apparently are casualties of the violent drug trafficking trade along the United States and Mexican border. In its experimental structure, Crosthwaite's novel calls for much reader interaction with the text by leading us to conjecture about missing information, while at the same time provoking the anxiety and anticipation inherent to the best hard-boiled detective novel. In this sense, it is not difficult to connect the melodramatic affective current of Crosthwaite's novel with certain characteristics of the Columbian Jorge Franco's *Rosario Tijeras* (1999). Franco's novel revels in narrating the exploits of *narco* culture in Columbia, drawing the reader into an adventure-laden tale. And, like Crosthwaite's novel, romance is a central element of the text. Indeed, the protagonist, Rosario's, sexuality is at the forefront of the entire story, a commonality Franco's novel would share with the classic melodramatic example of Gallegos's *Doña Bárbara*, making the text ripe for both film and *telenovela* adaptations.

Yet, we may also find melodrama in works that do not appear to be socially critical. In the Uruguayan case, Pablo Casacuberta and Dani Umpi offer two strikingly different examples of contemporary melodrama. On the one hand, Casacuberta's *Aquí y ahora* (2002) may best be characterized as an awkward bildungsroman, in which the narrator becomes aware of family secrets, his sexuality, and the obligations of adulthood. The presentation of the tale is melodramatic in the sense that each discovery feels to the reader as if were of desperate importance, and, in this way, Casacuberta brings to life the overwhelmingly-affective adolescent experience without venturing into outright mockery of that episode. Umpi's *Aún soltera* (2003) or *Miss Tacuarembó* (2004) also re-live highly melodramatic experiences, but they do so by consciously toying with the popular cultural elements that define the texts' characters. Umpi's novels portray characters who aspire to look and act like television actors and to win dance contests, not purely to ridicule these elements of massified popular culture, but because these are the events that are central to defining the social environs of the text. Also in the Southern Cone, the Argentine Pablo De Santis's *El enigma de París* (2007) certainly displays aspects of melodrama. Indeed, the detective drama in De Santis's novel essentially relies upon the intrigue provoked by melodrama to activate the melodramatically-affective rationality of reader and text, making the reader surge ahead with the reading to discover just who the mastermind behind the novel's crime is.

This list could surely go on, and I do not pretend here to offer an exhaustive catalog of the contemporary texts in which we may locate melodramatic tendencies. Indeed, in this brief recounting, I have not ventured into discussion of the contemporary cases of *telenovela* or film, in which melodrama continues to be a driving narrative force, in both its most straightforward and nuanced, self-referential examples. Nevertheless, what is striking is that the melodramatic impulse may be so readily located in such drastically different works of Latin American narrative. This may then help us to recognize that melodrama is, has been, and will continue to be a basic paradigm of the Latin American literary and social imagination, though certainly not an inflexible one. As demonstrated above, there is virtually no limit to the differing forms that melodrama is capable of adapting, and it does so with the purpose of making perceptible those social forces that elude the public's grasp legible. It makes sense of the social by legitimizing an affective reading of the present available to all across a wide aesthetic spectrum.

Melodrama, thus, remains an operative narrative format throughout Latin America because it speaks to and shapes a broader social experience. To bear this out, we need only look to the recent example of Brazilian President Dilma Rousseff's postponed plans in October 2012 to attend a rally for elections in the all-important city of São Paulo for fear that her attendance may be overshadowed by the conclusion of *Avenida Brasil*, a *telenovela* that had captivated the national imagination for months on end. In eschewing a visit from the President, the Brazilian public demonstrated that melodrama is the true language of the global socio-historical experience because it allows for comprehension of that which cannot be reasoned through political jargon. Through melodrama, Latin America, along with the rest of globalized society, is allowed to feel its way forward and to embrace the experiences of their favorite fictional characters, alongside the political platforms of charismatic leaders, when social equality seems fleeting. As such, melodrama has shaped a long history of political and social directives and has aided a host of socially concerned narratives, a fact that will no doubt be continued in future episodes.

Bibliography

Aguilar Camín, Héctor and Lorenzo Meyer. *In the Shadow of the Mexican Revolution: Contemporary Mexican History, 1910-1989.* Trans. Luis Alberto Fierro. Austin: U of Texas P, 1993.

Ahmed, Sara. *The Cultural Politics of Emotion.* New York: Routledge, 2004.

Alonso, Carlos. *The Spanish American Regional Novel: Modernity and Autochthony.* Cambridge: Cambridge UP, 2008.

— *The Burden of Modernity: The Rhetoric of Cultural Discourse in Spanish America.* New York: Oxford UP, 1998.

Altamirano, Carlos and Beatriz Sarlo. *Literatura/Sociedad.* Buenos Aires: Librería Hachette, 1983.

Altman, Rick. "Reusable Packaging: Generic Products and the Recycling Process." *Refiguring American Film Genres: History and Theory.* Nick Browne, editor. Berkeley: U of California P, 1998. 1-41

Alves, Ívia. "A Difícil Relação da Crítica Literária e a Ficção de Jorge Amado." *Leituras Amadianas.* Ívia Alves, Alvanita Almeida, Carla Patrícia Santana and Nancy Vieira, editors. Salvador: Quarteto/Casa de Jorge Amado, 2007. 113-35.

— "As mudanças de posição e a produção de Jorge Amado." *Em torno de Gabriela e Dona Flor: Ensaios.* Ívia Alves, editor. Salvador: Fundação Casa de Jorge Amado, 2004. 9-34.

Amado, Jorge. *Gabriela, Clove and Cinnamon.* Trans. James L. Taylor and William L. Grossman. New York: Vintage Books, 2006.

— "Carta a uma Leitora sôbre Romance e Personagens." *Jorge Amado: Povo e Terra.* São Paulo: Livraria Martins Editora, 1972. 23-36.

— *Gabriela, Cravo e Canela (Crônica de uma Cidade do Interior).* São Paulo: Livraria Martins Editora, 1960.

Amar Sánchez, Ana María. *Juegos de seducción y traición: Literatura y cultura de masas.* Rosario, Argentina: Beatriz Viterbo Editora, 2000.

Amícola, José. *Astrología y fascismo en la obra de Arlt.* Buenos Aires: Weimar, 1981.

Amoroso Lima, Alceu (Tristão de Athayde). "Gabriela ou o Crepúsculo dos Coronéis." *Jorge Amado: Povo e Terra.* São Paulo: Livraria Martins Editora, 1972. 159-63.

Arditi, Benjamin. *Politics on the Edges of Liberalism: Difference, Populism, Revolution, Agitation.* Edinburgh: Edinburgh UP, 2007.

Arias, Arturo. "*El Señor Presidente*: Amor y sentimentalidad, problemático tropo de la unidad frente a la dictadura." *El Señor Presidente: Edición Crítica*. Miguel Ángel Asturias and Gerald Martin. Nanterre: ALLCA XX, Université Paris X, 2000. 679-94.

Arlt, Roberto. *El amor brujo*. Buenos Aires: Losada, 2002.

Arlt, Roberto and David Viñas. *Obras. Tomo I, Novelas*. Buenos Aires: Losada, 2008.

Asturias, Miguel Ángel and Gerald Martin. *El Señor Presidente: Edición Crítica*. Nanterre: ALLCA XX, Université Paris X, 2000.

Austin, J. L. *How to Do Things with Words*. Cambridge, Massachusetts: Harvard UP, 1962.

Barthes, Roland. *A Lover's Discourse: Fragments*. Trans. Richard Howard. New York: Hill and Wang, 1979.

Benavides, O. Hugo. *Drugs, Thugs and Divas: Telenovelas and Narco-Dramas in Latin America*. Austin: U of Texas P, 2008.

Benjamin, Thomas. *La Revolución: Mexico's Great Revolution as Memory, Myth, and History*. Austin: U of Texas P, 2000.

Benjamin, Walter and Peter Demetz. "The Author as Producer." *Reflections: Essays, Aphorisms, Autobiographical Writings*. New York: Schocken Books, 1986. 220-38.

Benjamin, Walter and Hannah Arendt. "The Work of Art in the Age of Mechanical Reproduction." *Illuminations: Essays and Reflections*. New York: Schocken Books, 1969. 217-51.

Bentley, Eric. *The Life of Drama*. New York: Atheneum, 1964.

Berlant, Lauren. *The Female Complaint: The Unfinished Business of Sentimentality in American Culture*. Durham: Duke UP, 2008.

Beverley, John. "*El tungsteno* de Vallejo: Hacia una revindicación de la 'Novela social'." *Revista de Crítica Literaria Latinoamericana* 15.29 (1989): 167-77.

— *Del Lazarillo al Sandinismo: Estudios sobre la función ideológica de la literatura española e hispanoamericana*. Minneapolis: The Prisma Institute, 1987.

Bloom, Harold. "Introduction." *Carlos Fuentes' The Death of Artemio Cruz*. Harold Bloom, editor. New York: Chelsea House Publishers, 2006. 1-3.

— *The Anxiety of Influence: A Theory of Poetry*. New York: Oxford UP, 1997.

Boldy, Steven. "Fathers and Sons in Fuentes' *La muerte de Artemio Cruz*." *Carlos Fuentes' The Death of Artemio Cruz*. Harold Bloom, editor. New York: Chelsea House Publishers, 2006. 67-80.

Booth, Michael R. *English Melodrama*. London: Herbert Jenkins, 1965.

Brecht, Bertolt and John Willett. "A Short Organum for the Theatre." *Brecht on Theatre: The Development of an Aesthetic.* New York: Hill and Wang, 1964. 179-205.

Brooks, Peter. *The Melodramatic Imagination: Balzac, Henry James, Melodrama, and the Mode of Excess.* New Haven: Yale UP, 1995.

— "Melodrama, Body, Revolution." *Melodrama: Stage, Picture, Screen.* Jacky Bratton, Jim Cook and Christine Gledhill, editors. London: British Film Institute, 1994. 11-24.

Buckley, Matthew S. "Refugee Theatre: Melodrama and Modernity's Loss." *Theatre Journal* 61 (2009): 175–190.

Burga, Manuel y Alberto Flores Galindo. *Apogeo y crisis de la República Aristocrática.* (1980) *Obras completas II* [of Alberto Flores Galindo]. Lima: Fundación Andina/Sur Casa de Estudios del Socialismo, 1994.

Burns, E. Bradford. *A History of Brazil.* New York: Columbia UP, 1980.

Bush, Matthew. "Un asunto familiar: Entre afecto y violencia política en *La hora azul* de Alonso Cueto y *Un lugar llamado Oreja de Perro* de Iván Thays." *Revista Iberoamericana* (Forthcoming).

— "A History of Violence: Melodrama and *Mestizaje* in Enrique López Albújar's *Matalaché.*" *Chasqui: Revista de literatura latinoamericana* 41.1 (2012): 3-17.

— "Cohesión y contradicción: Los excesos narrativos de *Todas las sangres.*" *Revista de Crítica Literaria Latinoamericana* 72 (2010): 277-98.

Cabrujas, José Ignacio. *Y Latinoamérica inventó la telenovela.* Caracas: Alfadil, 2002.

Caldas, Sônia Regina. "Os Contratos e as Capas de Gabriela." *Leituras Amadianas.* Ívia Alves, Alvanita Almeida, Carla Patrícia Santana and Nancy Vieira, editors. Salvador: Quarteto/Casa de Jorge Amado, 2007. 15-34.

Cândido, Antônio. "Literatura e Subdesenvolvimento." *A Educação pela Noite e Outros Ensaios.* São Paulo: Ática, 1987. 140-62.

— and Howard S. Becker. "Literature and Underdevelopment." *On Literature and Society.* Princeton, N.J.: Princeton UP, 1995. 119-41.

Carpentier, Alejo. "La novela latinoamericana en vísperas de un nuevo siglo." *Historia y ficción en la narrativa hispanoamericana: coloquio de Yale.* Roberto González Echevarría, editor. Caracas, Venezuela: Monte Avila, 1984. 19-48.

Castro-Klarén, Sara. *The Narrow Pass of Our Nerves: Writing, Coloniality and Postcolonial Theory.* Madrid/Frankfurt: Iberoamericana/Vervuert, 2011.

CERQUEIRA, Nelson. *A política do partido comunista e a questão do realismo em Jorge Amado*. Salvador: Fundação Casa de Jorge Amado, 1988.

CHAMBERLAIN, Bobby J. *Jorge Amado*. Boston: Twayne Publishers, 1990.

CHAMBI JIMÉNEZ, Martín. *Víctor Mendívil y El Gigante de Paruro*. 1925. Photograph (Selenium toned silver gelatin print). Lehigh University Art Galleries Permanent Art Collection, Bethlehem, PA.

CLAYTON, Michelle. *Poetry in Pieces: César Vallejo and Lyric Modernity*. Berkeley: U of California P, 2011.

CORNEJO POLAR, Antonio. *Literatura y sociedad en el Perú: La novela indigenista. Obras completas de Antonio Cornejo Polar Volumen II*. Lima/Berkeley: Centro de Estudios Literarios "Antonio Cornejo Polar", Latinoamericana, 2005. 9-74.

CORONADO, Jorge. *The Andes Imagined: Indigenismo, Society, and Modernity*. Pittsburgh, PA: U of Pittsburgh P, 2009.

CORONIL, Fernando. *The Magical State: Nature, Money, and Modernity in Venezuela*. Chicago: The U of Chicago P, 1997.

COURTEAU, Joanna. "Gabriela, Clove and Cinnamon: Rewriting the Discourse of the Native." *Jorge Amado: New Critical Essays*. Keith H. Brower, Earl E. Fitz and Enrique Martínez-Vidal, editors. New York: Routledge, 2001. 43-56.

CVETKOVICH, Ann. *An Archive of Feelings: Trauma, Sexuality, and Lesbian Public Cultures*. Durham: Duke UP, 2003.

DA MATTA, Roberto. "*Dona Flor e Seus Dois Maridos*: Um Romance Relacional." *Tempo Brasileiro* 74 (1983): 3-33.

DABOVE, Juan Pablo. *Nightmares of the Lettered City: Banditry and Literature in Latin America 1816-1829*. Pittsburgh, PA: U of Pittsburgh P, 2007.

DELEUZE, Gilles and Félix GUATTARI. *Kafka: Toward a Minor Literature*. Trans. Dana Polan. Minneapolis: U of Minnesota P, 1986.

DERRIDA, Jacques. "Signature Event Context." *Limited Inc*. Evanston, IL: Northwestern UP, 1988. 1-23.

— *The Truth in Painting*. Trans. Geoff Bennington and Ian McLeod. Chicago: U of Chicago P, 1987.

— "The Law of Genre." *On Narrative*. W. J. T. Mitchell, editor. Chicago: The U of Chicago P, 1981. 51-77.

DÍAZ, Lisiak-Land. "Jerarquía social y económica en *El tungsteno* de César Vallejo". *Inti* 36 (1992): 59-71.

DÍAZ-LASTRA, Alberto. "Carlos Fuentes y la revolución traicionada." *Homenaje a Carlos Fuentes: Variaciones interpretativas en torno a su obra*. Helmy F. Giacoman, editor. New York: Las Americas, 1971. 345-54.

Díaz Seijas, Pedro. "Aproximación semiótica al universo narrativo de *Doña Bárbara.*" *Rómulo Gallegos ante la crítica*. Pedro Díaz Seijas, editor. Caracas: Monte Ávila, 1980. 182-235.

D'Lugo, Carol Clark. *The Fragmented Novel in Mexico: The Politics of Form*. Austin: U Texas P, 1997.

Eagleton, Terry. *Marxism and Literary Criticism*. London: Routledge, 2002.

Eliot, T. S. "Wilkie Collins and Dickens." *Selected Essays*. New York: Harcourt, Brace and Company, 1950. 409-18.

Elsaesser, Thomas. "Tales of Sound and Fury: Observations on the Family Melodrama." *Home Is Where the Heart Is: Studies in Melodrama and the Woman's Film*. Christine Gledhill, editor. London: British Film Institute, 1987. 43-69.

Faris, Wendy B. *Carlos Fuentes*. New York: Frederick Ungar, 1983.

Fenewick, M. J. "A Re-reading of *La muerte de Artemio Cruz*: Critique of the Liberal Perspective from the 60's." *Interpretaciones a la obra de Carlos Fuentes: Un gigante de las letras hispanoamericanas*. Ana Ma. Hernández de López, editor. Madrid: Beramar, 1990. 89-97.

Fiddian, Robin. "Carlos Fuentes: *La muerte de Artemio Cruz*." *Landmarks in Modern Latin American Fiction*. Philip Swanson, editor. London: Routledge, 1990. 96-117.

Flatley, Jonathan. *Affective Mapping: Melancholia and the Politics of Modernism*. Cambridge: Harvard UP, 2008.

Flint, Jack M. *The Prose Works of Roberto Arlt: A Thematic Approach*. Durham: U of Durham, 1985.

Flores Galindo, Alberto. *Los mineros de la Cerro de Pasco, 1900-1930: Un intento de caracterización social*. (1974) *Obras completas I*. Lima: Fundación Andina/Sur Casa de Estudios del Socialismo, 1993. 1-229.

Foster, David William. *Currents in the Contemporary Argentine Novel: Arlt, Mallea, Sabato, and Cortázar*. Columbia: U of Missouri P, 1975.

Foucault, Michel. "What Is an Author?" *The Foucault Reader*. Paul Rabinow, editor. New York: Pantheon Books, 1984. 101-20.

Franco, Jean. *César Vallejo: The Dialectics of Poetry and Silence*. Cambridge: Cambridge UP, 1976.

Fuentes, Carlos. *La muerte de Artemio Cruz*. Madrid: Cátedra, 1998.

— *La nueva novela hispanoamericana*. México: Joaquín Mortiz, 1969.

— *The Death of Artemio Cruz*. Trans. Sam Hileman. New York: Noonday Press, 1966.

GALDO, Juan Carlos. "'Tempestad en los Andes': Alegoría y revolución en *El tungsteno*, de César Vallejo." *Revista Iberoamericana* 73.218-219 (2007): 175-92.

GALLEGOS, Rómulo. *Doña Bárbara*. Madrid: Cátedra, 2007.

— *Doña Bárbara*. Trans. Robert Malloy. New York: Peter Smith, 1948.

GARCÍA CANCLINI, Néstor. *Hybrid Cultures: Strategies for Entering and Leaving Modernity*. Minneapolis: U of Minnesota P, 1995.

GATES, Henry Louis. *Black in Latin America*. New York: New York UP, 2011.

GAWELTI, John G. "The Evolution of Social Melodrama." *Imitations of Life: A Reader on Film and Television Melodrama*. Marcia Landy, editor. Detroit: Wayne State UP, 1991. 33-49.

GERASSI-NAVARRO, Nina. *Pirate Novels: Fictions of Nation Building in Spanish America*. Durham: Duke UP, 1999.

GEROULD, Daniel. "Melodrama and Revolution." *Melodrama: Stage, Picture, Screen*. Jacky Bratton, Jim Cook and Christine Gledhill, editors. London: British Film Institute, 1994. 185-98.

— "Russian Formalist Theories of Melodrama." *Imitations of Life: A Reader on Film and Television Melodrama*. Marcia Landy, editor. Detroit: Wayne State UP, 1991. 118-34.

GLEDHILL, Christine. "Rethinking Genre." *Reinventing Film Studies*. Christine Gledhill and Linda Williams, editors. London: Hodder Arnold, 2007. 221-43.

— "Melodrama and Cultural Disorder." *The Aesthetics of Popular Art*. Jostein Gripsrud, editor. Bergen: Program for kulturstudier Norges forskningsråd, 2001. 63-76.

— "The Melodramatic Field: An Investigation." *Home Is Where the Heart Is: Studies in Melodrama and Women's Film*. Christine Gledhill, editor. London: British Film Institute, 1987. 5-39.

GNUTZMANN, Rita. "La relación hombre – ciudad en *El amor brujo* de Roberto Arlt." *Roberto Arlt: Una modernidad argentina*. José Morales Saravia and Barbara Schuchard, editors. Madrid/Frankfurt: Iberoamericana/Vervuert, 2001. 77-92.

GONZÁLEZ, Aníbal. *Love and Politics in the Contemporary Spanish American Novel*. Austin: U of Texas P, 2010.

GONZÁLEZ ECHEVARRÍA, Roberto. *The Voice of the Masters: Writing and Authority in Modern Latin American Literature*. Austin: U of Texas P, 1985.

GRAMSCI, Antonio and David FORGACS. *The Gramsci Reader: Selected Writings, 1916-1935*. New York: New York UP, 2000.

GRIMSTED, David. *Melodrama Unveiled: American Theater & Culture 1800-1850*. Berkeley: U of California P, 1987.

GUERRERO, Diana. *Roberto Arlt: El habitante solitario*. Buenos Aires: Granica, 1972.

GUTIÉRREZ GIRARDOT, Rafael. *César Vallejo y la muerte de dios*. Santafé de Bogotá: Panamericana, 2000.

GUZMÁN, Daniel de. *Carlos Fuentes*. New York: Twayne Publishers, 1972.

GYURKO, Lanin A. "*La muerte de Artemio Cruz* and *Citizen Kane*: A Comparative Analysis." *Carlos Fuentes, A Critical View*. Robert Brody and Charles Rossman, editors. Austin: U of Texas P, 1982. 64-94.

HARSS, Luis. "Miguel Ángel Asturias o la tierra florida." *El Señor Presidente: Edición Crítica*. Miguel Ángel Asturias and Gerald Martin. Nanterre: ALLCA XX, Université Paris X, 2000. 799-805.

HARSS, Luis and Barbara DOHMANN. *Into the Mainstream: Conversations with Latin-American Writers*. New York: Harper & Row, 1967.

HAYES, Aden W. *Roberto Arlt: La estrategia de su ficción*. London: Tamesis, 1981.

HAYS, Michael and Anastasia NIKOLOPOULOU, Editors. *Melodrama: The Cultural Emergence of a Genre*. New York: St. Martin's P, 1996.

HEILMAN, Robert Bechtold. *Tragedy and Melodrama: Versions of Experience*. Seattle: U of Washington P, 1968.

HERLINGHAUS, Hermann. "Imaginación melodramática, narración anacrónica e identidades diferentes: aporías y nuevas expectativas del debate cultural latinoamericano." *Heterotropías: Narrativas de identidad y alteridad latinoamericana*. Carlos A. Jáuregui and Juan Pablo Dabove, editors. Pittsburgh, PA: Instituto Internacional de Literatura Iberoamericana, Universidad de Pittsburgh, 2003. 461-76.

— "La imaginación melodramática. Rasgos intermediales y heterogéneos de una categoría precaria." *Narraciones anacrónicas de la modernidad: Melodrama e imtermedialidad en América Latina*. Hermann Herlinghaus, editor. Santiago, Chile: Cuarto Propio, 2002. 21-59.

HERNÁNDEZ CUEVAS, Marco Polo. "Modern National Discourse and *La muerte de Artemio Cruz*: The Illusory 'Death' of African Mexican Lineage." *Carlos Fuentes' The Death of Artemio Cruz*. Harold Bloom, editor. New York: Chelsea House, 2006. 179-90.

HIMELBLAU, Jack. "Tohil and the President: The Hunters and the Hunted in the Popol Vuh and *El Señor Presidente*." *Romance Quarterly* 31.4 (1984): 437-50.

HOPKINSON, Amanda and Martín CHAMBI. *Martín Chambi*. London: Phaidon, 2001.

HTUN, Mala. *Sex and the State: Abortion, Divorce, and the Family Under Latin American Dictatorships and Democracies*. New York: Cambridge UP, 2003.

ISER, Wolfgang. *The Act of Reading: A Theory of Aesthetic Response*. Baltimore: The Johns Hopkins UP, 1980.

JARA C., René. "El mito y la nueva novela hispanoamericana. A propósito de '*La muerte de Artemio Cruz*'." *Homenaje a Carlos Fuentes: Variaciones interpretativas en torno a su obra*. Helmy F. Giacoman, editor. New York: Las Americas, 1971. 147-208.

JARKOWSKI, Aníbal. "*El amor brujo*: La novela 'mala' de Roberto Arlt." *Yrigoyen, entre Borges y Arlt. (1916-1930). Historia social de la literatura argentina, t. 7.* Graciela R. Montaldo, editor. Buenos Aires: Contrapunto, 1989. 109-28.

JENKINS, Henry. *The Wow Climax: Tracing the Emotional Impact of Popular Culture*. New York: New York UP, 2007.

JOHN, Juliet. *Dickens's Villains: Melodrama, Character, Popular Culture*. Oxford: Oxford UP, 2001.

JOSEPH, Gilbert M. and Daniel NUGENT. "Popular Culture and State Formation in Revolutionary Mexico." *Everyday Forms of State Formation: Revolution and Negotiation of Rule in Modern Mexico*. Gilbert M. Joseph and Daniel Nugent, editors. Durham: Duke UP, 1994. 3-23.

KELLETER, Frank and Ruth MAYER. "The Melodramatic Mode Revisited." *Melodrama! The Mode of Excess from Early America to Hollywood*. Frank Kelleter, Barbara Krah and Ruth Mayer, editors. Heidelberg: Universitätsverlag Winter, 2007. 7-17.

KNIGHT, Alan. *The Mexican Revolution (2 Volumes)*. Lincoln: U of Nebraska P, 1986.

LACLAU, Ernesto. *Emancipation(s)*. London: Verso, 1996.

LACLAU, Ernesto and Chantal MOUFFE. *Hegemony and Socialist Strategy: Towards a Radical Democratic Politics*. London: Verso, 2001.

LARRA, Raúl. *Roberto Arlt, el torturado*. Buenos Aires: Alpe, 1956.

LARSEN, Neil. *Determinations: Essays on Theory, Narrative and Nation in the Americas*. London: Verso, 2001.

LASARTE VALCÁRCEL, Javier. "Mestizaje y populismo en *Doña Bárbara*: de Sarmiento a Martí." *Iberoamericana* 24.2/3, 78/79 (2000): 164-86.

LAVRIN, Asunción. *Women, Feminism, and Social Change in Argentina, Chile, and Uruguay, 1890-1940*. Lincoln: U of Nebraska P, 1995.

LEGRÁS, Horacio. *Literature and Subjection: The Economy of Writing and Marginality in Latin America*. Pittsburgh, PA: U of Pittsburgh P, 2008.

LELAND, Christopher Towne. *The Last Happy Men: The Generation of 1922, Fiction, and the Argentine Reality*. Syracuse: Syracuse UP, 1986.

LIMA DUARTE, Constância. "As relações sociais de gênero em *Gabriela, cravo e canela*, de Jorge Amado." *Jorge Amado: Leituras e diálogos em torno de uma obra*. Rita Olivieri-Godet and Jacqueline Penjon, editors. Salvador: Fundação Casa de Jorge Amado, 2004. 165-74.

LISCANO, Juan. *Rómulo Gallegos y su tiempo*. Caracas: Monte Avila Editores, 1969.

LÓPEZ, Ana. "Tears and Desire: Women and Melodrama in the 'Old' Mexican Cinema". *The Latin American Cultural Studies Reader*. Ana Del Sarto, Alicia Ríos and Abril Trigo, editors. Durham: Duke UP, 2004. 441-58.

LÓPEZ PARADA, Esperanza. "El milagro de Martín Chambi: Una exposición recupera en la Fundación Telefónica de Madrid la memoria del fotógrafo peruano." *ELPAIS.com*. El País, 2 de octubre 2006. Web. 1 August 2011.

MAHONY, Mary Ann. "The Local and the Global: Internal and External Factors in the Development of Bahia's Cacao Sector." *From Silver to Cocaine: Latin American Commodity Chains and the Building of the World Economy, 1500-2000*. Steven Topik, Carlos Marichal and Zephyr Frank, editors. Durham: Duke UP, 2006. 174-203.

MALARD, Letícia. *Literatura e Dissidência Política*. Belo Horizonte: Editora Universidade Federal de Minas Gerais, 2006.

MARCOUX, J. Paul. *Guilbert de Pixerécourt: French Melodrama in the Early Nineteenth Century*. New York: Peter Lang, 1992.

MARTIN, Gerald. "Miguel Ángel Asturias: *El Señor Presidente*." *Landmarks in Latin American Fiction*. Philip Swanson, editor. New York: Routledge, 1990. 50-73.

— *Journeys through the Labyrinth: Latin American Fiction in the Twentieth Century*. London: Verso, 1989.

— "*El Señor Presidente* and How to Read It." *Bulletin of Hispanic Studies* 47.3 (1970): 223-43.

MARTIN, John and Donna L. VAN BODEGRAVEN. "Mythical Patterns in Jorge Amado's Novel *Gabriela – Clove and Cinnamon* and Bruno Barreto's Film *Gabriela*." *Film and Literature: A Comparative Approach to Adaptation*. Wendell Aycock and Michael Schoenecke, editors. Lubbock: Texas Tech UP, 1988. 179-88.

MARTÍN, Annabel. *La gramática de la felicidad: Relecturas franquistas y posmodernas del melodrama*. Madrid: Libertarias, 2005.

MARTÍN-BARBERO, Jesús. "Laberintos narrativos de la contemporaneidad." *Heterotropías: Narrativas de identidad y alteridad latinoamericana*. Carlos A. Jáuregui and Juan Pablo Dabove, editors. Pittsburgh, PA: Instituto Internacional de Literatura Iberoamericana, Universidad de Pittsburgh, 2003. 447-59.

— *De los medios a las mediaciones: Comunicación, cultura y hegemonía*. México: G. Gili, 2001.

— *Communication, Culture and Hegemony: From the Media to Mediations*. Trans. Elizabeth Fox and Robert A. White. London: Sage, 1993.

MARTÍN-BARBERO, Jesús and Sonia MUÑOZ. "Introducción." *Televisión y melodrama: Géneros y lecturas de la telenovela en Colombia*. Bogotá: Tercer Mundo, 1992. 11-17.

MASOTTA, Oscar. *Sexo y traición en Roberto Arlt*. Buenos Aires: Jorge Álvarez Editor, 1965.

MEYER-MINNEMANN, Klaus. "*La muerte de Artemio Cruz*: Tiempo cíclico e historia del México moderno." *Simposio Carlos Fuentes: Actas*. Isaac Jack Lévy and Juan Loveluck, editors. Columbia: U of South Carolina, 1978. 87-98.

MONSIVÁIS, Carlos. "Entrevista con Carlos Monsiváis." *El Hablador* 15. Web. 25 July 2011.

— "El melodrama: 'No te vayas, mi amor, que es inmoral llorar a solas." *Narraciones anacrónicas de la modernidad: Melodrama e intermedialidad en América Latina*. Hermann Herlinghaus, editor. Santiago, Chile: Cuarto Propio, 2002. 105-23.

— "Se sufre, pero se aprende: El melodrama y las reglas de la falta de límites." *A través del espejo: El cine mexicano y su público*. Carlos Monsiváis and Carlos Bonfil, editors. México: El Milagro – Instituto Mexicano de Cinematografía, 1994. 99-224.

NASCIMENTO, Renata. "Os Caminhos de *Gabriela, Crave e Canela*." *Leituras Amadianas*. Ívia Alves, Alvanita Almeida, Carla Patrícia Santana and Nancy Vieira, editors. Salvador: Quarteto/Casa de Jorge Amado, 2007. 63-85.

NOWELL-SMITH, Geoffrey. "Minnelli and Melodrama." *Imitations of Life: A Reader on Film and Television Melodrama*. Marcia Landy, editor. Detroit: Wayne State UP, 1991. 268-74.

NÚÑEZ, Ángel. *La obra narrativa de Roberto Arlt*. Buenos Aires: Minor Nova, 1968.

ORTEGA, Julio. "*La muerte de Artemio Cruz* y el relato de la des-fundación nacional." *Hispania*. 85.2 (2002): 198-208.

Osorio, Nelson. "*Doña Bárbara* y el fantasma de Sarmiento." *Casa de las Américas* 152 (1985): 64-74.

Oviedo, José Miguel. *Historia de la literatura hispanoamericana. Vol. 3 Postmodernismo, Vanguardia, Regionalismo*. Madrid: Alianza, 2001.

Paes, José Paulo. *De "Cacau" a "Gabriela": Um Percurso Pastoral.* Salvador: Fundação Casa Jorge Amado, 1991.

Paoli, Roberto. "Observaciones sobre el indigenismo de César Vallejo." *Revista Iberoamericana* 36.71 (1970): 341-44.

Pastor, Beatriz. *Roberto Arlt y la rebelión alienada.* Gaithersburg, MD: Hispamérica, 1980.

Pauls, Alan. "Arlt: La máquina literaria." *Yrigoyen, Entre Borges y Arlt. (1916-1930). Historia social de la literatura argentina, t. 7.* Graciela R. Montaldo, editor. Buenos Aires: Contrapunto, 1989. 307-22.

Payne, Judith. "Laura's Artemio: Failed Sexual Politics in *La Muerte de Artemio Cruz.*" *Hispanófila* 112 (1994 Sept): 65-76.

Peluffo, Ana. *Lágrimas andinas: Sentimentalismo, género y virtud republicana en Clorinda Matto de Turner.* Pittsburgh, PA: Instituto Internacional de Literatura Iberoamericana, 2005.

Perus, Françoise. *Historia y crítica literaria: El realismo social y la crisis de la dominación oligárquica*. La Habana, Cuba: Casa de las Américas, 1982.

Piglia, Ricardo. "Roberto Arlt, una crítica de la economía literaria." *Ficciones argentinas: Antología de lecturas críticas*. Adriana Mancini, editor. Buenos Aires: Norma, 2004. 55-71.

— *Crítica y ficción*. Barcelona: Anagrama, 2001.

Podestá, Guido. *César Vallejo: Su estética teatral.* Minneapolis/Valencia/Lima: Institute for the Study of Ideologies & Literature, Instituto de Cine y Radio-Televisión, Universidad Nacional Mayor de San Marcos, 1985.

Poole, Ralph J. and Ilka Saal. "Passionate Politics: An Introduction." *Passionate Politics: The Cultural Work of American Melodrama from the Early Republic to the Present*. Ralph J. Poole and Ilka Saal, editors. Cambridge: Cambridge Scholars Publishing, 2008. 1-25.

Portella, Eduardo. "Jorge Amado: A Descontração Poética no País do Carnaval." *Revista Brasileira de Lingua e Literatura* 1.2 (1979): 8-12.

Postlewait, Thomas. "From Melodrama to Realism: The Suspect History of American Drama." *Melodrama: The Cultural Emergence of a Genre*. Michael Hays and Anastasia Nikolopoulou, editors. New York: St. Martin's P, 1996. 39-60.

RAHILL, Frank. *The World of Melodrama*. University Park: The Pennsylvania State UP, 1967.

RAMA, Ángel. *Transculturación narrativa en América Latina*. Buenos Aires: El Andariego, 2008.

RANCIÈRE, Jacques. *Dissensus: On Politics and Aesthetics*. Trans. Steven Corcoran. London: Continuum, 2010.

— *The Politics of Aesthetics*. Trans. Gabriel Rockhill. London: Continuum, 2009.

REIS, Roberto. "Espelho Retrovisor: Considerações Sobre a Transição Brasileira." *Travessia* 27 (1993): 12-23.

REISING, Russell. *Loose Ends: Closure and Crisis in the American Social Text*. Durham, Duke UP, 1996.

RIBAS, Alberto. "Una herencia perdida: La identidad afromexicana de Artemio Cruz." *Afro-Hispanic Review* 28.1 (2009): 99-116.

RIBEIRO PATRICIO, Rosana. *Imagens de mulher em Gabriela de Jorge Amado*. Salvador: Fundação Casa de Jorge Amado, 1999.

ROCHE, Jean. *Jorge bem/mal Amado*. Trans. Liliane Barthod. São Paulo: Editora Cultrix, 1987.

RODRÍGUEZ MONEGAL, Emir. "Los dos Asturias." *El Señor Presidente: Edición Crítica*. Miguel Ángel Asturias and Gerald Martin. Nanterre: ALLCA XX, Université Paris X, 2000. 839-42.

— "*Doña Bárbara*: texto y contextos." *Relectura de Rómulo Gallegos*. Caracas: Ediciones del Centro de Estudios Latinoamericanos Rómulo Gallegos, 1980. 211-20.

ROMERO, Simon. "Building a New History by Exhuming Bolívar." *New York Times* 3 August 2010. Web. 28 Feb. 2011.

ROSENBERG, Fernando J. *The Avant-Garde and Geopolitics in Latin America*. Pittsburgh: U of Pittsburgh P, 2006.

RUFFINELLI, Jorge. *La escritura invisible: Arlt, Borges, García Márquez, Roa Bastos, Rulfo, Cortázar, Fuentes, Vargas Llosa*. Xalapa, Ver.: Universidad Veracruzana, 1986.

SAÍTTA, Sylvia. *El escritor en el bosque de ladrillos: Una biografía de Roberto Arlt*. Buenos Aires: Debolsillo, 2008.

SALAÜN, Serge. "La novela vallejiana o la conquista conflictiva de la madurez (1927-38)." *César Vallejo: La escritura y lo real*. Nadine Ly, editor. Madrid: Ediciones de la Torre, 1988. 71-86.

SAMUELS, Shirley. "Introduction." *The Culture of Sentiment: Race, Gender, and Sentimentality in Nineteenth-Century America*. Shirley Samuels, editor. New York: Oxford UP, 1992. 3-8.

SARLO, Beatriz. *El imperio de los sentimientos*. Buenos Aires: Norma, 2004.

— *Una modernidad periférica: Buenos Aires 1920 y 1930*. Buenos Aires: Nueva Visión, 2003.

SHARP, William. "Structure of Melodrama." *Melodrama*. James Redmond, editor. Cambridge: Cambridge UP, 1992. 269-80.

SHAW, D. L. *Gallegos: Doña Bárbara*. London: Grant & Cutler, 1972.

SINGER, Ben. *Melodrama and Modernity: Early Sensational Cinema and Its Contexts*. New York: Columbia UP, 2001.

SKIDMORE, Thomas E. and Peter H. SMITH. *Modern Latin America*. New York: Oxford UP, 2005.

SMITH, James L. *Melodrama*. London: Methuen & Co., 1973.

SOMMER, Doris. *Foundational Fictions: The National Romances of Latin America*. Berkeley: U of California P, 1991.

SOMMERS, Joseph. *After the Storm: Landmarks of the Modern Mexican Novel*. Albuquerque: U of New Mexico P, 1968.

SPECK, Paula Kathleen. *Roberto Arlt and the Conspiracies of Fiction*. Diss. Yale U, 1978. Ann Arbor, UMI, 1978.

STOOPEN, María. *La muerte de Artemio Cruz: Una novela de denuncia y traición*. México: Universidad Nacional Autónoma de México, 1982.

TÁTI, Miécio. *Jorge Amado: Vida e Obra*. Belo Horizonte: Editora Itatiaia Limitada, 1961.

VALLEJO, César. *Tungsten*. Trans. Robert Mezey. Syracuse: Syracuse UP, 1988.

VALLEJO, César and Enrique BALLÓN AGUIRRE. *Colacho hermanos o Presidentes de América. Teatro completo. Tomo II*. Lima: Pontificia Universidad Católica del Perú, 1979. 9-143.

VALLEJO, César and Manuel Miguel DE PRIEGO. *Ensayos y reportajes completos*. Lima: Pontificia Universidad Católica del Perú, 2002.

VALLEJO, César and Ricardo GONZÁLEZ VIGIL. *César Vallejo: Novelas y cuentos completos*. Lima: Petroperú, Ediciones Copé, 1998.

VAN DELDEN, Maarten. *Carlos Fuentes, Mexico, and Modernity*. Nashville: Vanderbilt UP, 1998.

VELÁSQUEZ CASTRO, Marcel. "Imaginación y melodrama." *El Dominical* (Suplemento de Actualidad Cultural de *El Comercio* [Lima, Perú]). 27 de mayo 2007: 8-9.

VOLPI, Jorge. *El insomnio de Bolívar: Cuatro consideraciones intempestivas sobre América Latina en el siglo XXI*. Buenos Aires: Debate, 2009.

WALLACH, Jeremy, Harris M. BERGER and Paul D. GREENE. "Affective Overdrive, Scene Dynamics, and Identity in the Global Metal Scene." *Metal Ru-*

les the Globe: Heavy Metal Music Around the World. Jeremy Wallach, Harris M. Berger and Paul D. Greene, editors. Durham: Duke UP, 2011. 3-33.

WILLIAMS, Linda. *Playing the Race Card: Melodramas of Black and White from Uncle Tom to O. J. Simpson*. Princeton: Princeton UP, 2001.

WILLIAMS, Raymond. *Marxism and Literature*. Oxford: Oxford UP, 1977.

WILLIAMS, Raymond Leslie. *The Writings of Carlos Fuentes*. Austin: U of Texas P, 1996.

Index

A

B

L

M

N

O

P

R

S

T